Reimagining the Judiciary

COMPARATIVE POLITICS

Comparative Politics is a series for researchers, teachers, and students of political science that deals with contemporary government and politics. Global in scope, books in the series are characterized by a stress on comparative analysis and strong methodological rigor. The series is published in association with the European Consortium for Political Research. For more information visit

www.ecprnet.eu

The series is edited by Susan Scarrow, John and Rebecca Moores Professor of Political Science, University of Houston, and Jonathan Slapin, Professor of Political Institutions and European Politics, University of Zurich.

OTHER TITLES IN THIS SERIES

The New Kremlinology
Understanding Regime Personalization in Russia
Alexander Baturo and Johan A. Elkink

Party System Closure
Party Alliances, Government Alternatives, and Democracy in Europe
Fernando Casal Bértoa and Zsolt Enyedi

The New Party Challenge
Changing Cycles of Party Birth and Death in Central Europe and Beyond
Tim Haughton and Kevin Deegan-Krause

Multi-Level Democracy
Integration and Independence Among Party Systems, Parties, and Voters in Seven Federal Systems
Lori Thorlakson

Citizen Support for Democratic and Autocratic Regimes
Marlene Mauk

Democratic Stability in an Age of Crisis
Agnes Cornell, Jørgen Møller, Svend-Erik Skaaning

Coalition Governance in Central Eastern Europe
Edited by Torbjörn Bergman, Gabriella Ilonszki, and Wolfgang C. Müller

The Reshaping of West European Party Politics
Agenda-Setting and Party Competition in Comparative Perspective
Christoffer Green-Pedersen

Parliaments in Time
The Evolution of Legislative Democracy in Western Europe, 1866–2015
Michael Koß

Inequality After the Transition
Political Parties, Party Systems, and Social Policy in Southern and Postcommunist Europe
Ekrem Karakoç

Democracy and the Cartelization of Political Parties
Richard S. Katz and Peter Mair

Reimagining the Judiciary

Women's Representation on High Courts Worldwide

MARIA C. ESCOBAR-LEMMON,
VALERIE J. HOEKSTRA, ALICE J. KANG,
AND MIKI CAUL KITTILSON

ecpr

OXFORD
UNIVERSITY PRESS

OXFORD
UNIVERSITY PRESS

Great Clarendon Street, Oxford, OX2 6DP,
United Kingdom

Oxford University Press is a department of the University of Oxford.
It furthers the University's objective of excellence in research, scholarship,
and education by publishing worldwide. Oxford is a registered trade mark of
Oxford University Press in the UK and in certain other countries

First Edition published in 2021

Impression: 2

Published in the United States of America by Oxford University Press
198 Madison Avenue, New York, NY 10016, United States of America

British Library Cataloguing in Publication Data
Data available

Library of Congress Control Number: 2021936253

ISBN 978–0–19–886157–7

DOI: 10.1093/oso/9780198861577.001.0001

Printed and bound by
CPI Group (UK) Ltd, Croydon, CR0 4YY

For Mary, and Pedro Escobar, never forgotten
For Mike Caul, never forgotten
For Michael, Sam, and Max
For Dai, Justin, and Rosa

Table of Contents

Acknowledgments

In 2012, with Michelle Taylor-Robinson, Maria invited Miki and Alice to a conference at Texas A&M University on "Identity, Gender, and Representation: Empirical Analysis of Representation of Women's Interests." The paper that Miki presented, a co-authored project with Elizabeth Andrews Bond and Valerie, ultimately became a chapter "Gender, High Courts, and Ideas about Representation in Western Europe" in the resulting edited volume *Representation: The Case of Women.* Maria had previously attempted a project on women on high courts. Alice mentioned the lack of global data. This led Miki to suggest that the four of us write a grant proposal to collect this data globally. At the time, none of us realized that the decision to say yes would mean we would spend the next nine years talking or emailing almost every week about women on high courts. Over the years, we incurred many debts of gratitude.

The research and data collection for this project were supported by National Science Foundation Grants #SES-1323949, 1323968, and 1324181, "Collaborative Research: Policy Diffusion: International Influences on Appointments to High Courts." We thank the Center for the Study of Religion and Conflict at Arizona State University for their support—both substantive and administrative—for facilitating this grant and research. We are indebted to Carolyn Forbes and Laurie Perko. At the University of Nebraska-Lincoln, Alice received a faculty development leave and support through a Carl J. Schneider Research Grant, Senning Summer Fellowship, Layman Seed Award, and Research Council Award. Maria received a faculty development leave from Texas A&M University which provided time to complete fieldwork in Colombia. Valerie and Miki thank the Institute for Social Science Research at Arizona State University which provided a seed grant to study the feasibility of such an ambitious project. Miki and Valerie were both awarded a sabbatical from the School of Politics and Global Studies at ASU to conduct fieldwork in Canada and Ireland.

Building a cross-national and over-time database on women on high courts was an ambitious undertaking, even more than we realized when we proposed the project to NSF. We greatly appreciate the ministers of justice, justices, court presidents, legal librarians, and court registrars from around the world who replied to our requests for additional information. Our undergraduate and graduate student research assistants helped scour secondary sources; call, fax, and email government and court officials; and organize and maintain datasets. The team at ASU included Alexis Baick, Elizabeth Andrews Bond, Ivan Babanovski, Jill Carle, Jose Gomez, Jessica Jenner, Jennifer Kahn, Jennifer Kartner, Fatima Rodriguez,

Jon Stinogel, Jonathon Ross, Patrick Shields, and Justin Sprague. Further, we would like to thank our Junior Fellows: Athar Al-Mansoub, Joshua Barro, Leila Fleming, Emma Galligan, Grace Lira, Brigette Maggio, Janae Stevenson, and RaNiya Taylor. At Texas A&M, we acknowledge the graduate and undergraduate students who worked on the project: Jennifer Baldwin, Justin Bramlett, Kristen Carrol, Kendall Funk, Abhisekh Ghosh Moulick, Liana Gonzalez, MacKenzie Hammond, Soren Jordan, Thiago Nascimiento da Silva, E. Sidonia Mitchell, Morgan Polk, and Thiago Talzzia, Debra Cardona and Claudia Avellaneda for stimulating her interest in women on comparative high courts. At UNL, we were ably assisted by Rula Jabbour, Alex Kroeger, and Abdulameer Waly along with Margo Berends, Ruth Boettner, Radim Brach, James Garza, Jr., Sophia Loveless, and Cheick Ouedraogo. Kia Brodersen provided stellar assistance in compiling the references.

We thank the lawyers, judges, government officials, law professors, and civil society actors we interviewed for the case studies. Some we do not identify by name because we promised anonymity. Even though we cannot or do not name you here, we are truly, deeply grateful for your assistance. In Canada, we thank the Hon. Kim Campbell, Hon. Patricia Hennessy, Barbara Kincaid, Carissima Mathen, Hon. Anne McLellan, and Senator Nancy Ruth for their insights. In Colombia, we are deeply grateful to the Magistrados/as and the Magistrados/as Auxiliares of the Corte Constitucional, the Consejo de Estado, and the Corte Suprema de Justicia, and those from NGOs whose insights and experience were fundamental in our understanding of the process. Thank you for picking up your cell phones or sending emails to open doors and make this project possible. For our research in Ireland, we thank Jerry Carroll, Justice Frank Clarke, Jennifer Caroll MacNeill, Adam McAuley, and Gary Murphy. In addition, we appreciate the assistance, time, and gracious meetings over tea with members of the Law Society and Bar Associations of Ireland. Kevin T. McGuire, at University of North Carolina was instrumental in helping Valerie with contacts in Ireland, and provided valuable feedback on draft chapters. She credits the wealth of information from Kevin to a bit of the luck of the Irish (on her part). In South Africa, we thank members of the Judicial Service Commission, judges, lawyers, professors, and women's activists who spoke with us and also extend our gratitude to Dawne Curry and archivists Gabriele Mohale and Zofia Sulej of the Historical Papers Archive at the University of Witwatersrand for their time and help. While not everything you told us made it into the book, it shaped and informed our thinking about all four countries and for that we are grateful.

We are grateful to colleagues, professors, judges, and friends who gave feedback, provided invaluable information, and answered questions during the course of the project, although any errors or omissions in this book are our own. In particular, we appreciate Cathi Albertyn, Nancy Arrington, Sylvia Bashevkin, Nathan Brown, Jennie Burnet, Ruth Cowan, J. Jarpa Dawuni, Antonio De Lauri, Mamadou Dramé, Shirin Ebadi, Rachel Ellett, Melinda Gann Hall, Shireen

Hassim, Lori Hausseger, Magda Hinojosa, Isabel Cristina Jaramillo Sierra, Patrick Kenney, Jonathan Klaaren, Monika Lindbekk, Stefanie Lindquist, Hon. Eusebia Munuo, Sara Kimble, Peace Medie, Tabeth Masengu, Ziba Mir-Hosseini, Tamir Moustafa, Ghulam Farooq Mujaddidi, Marie Provine, Juan Carlos Rodríguez Raga, Christine Rothmayr Allison, Liliana Sánchez Mejía, Mary Szto, Michelle Taylor-Robinson, Camelia Toader, Hon. Ekaterina Trendafilova, Aili Mari Tripp, Keren Weinshall, Olajumoke Yacob-Haliso, and Karolina Zaczek for sharing their time and expertise. Sally Kenney has been a major source of inspiration through her scholarship and gave us critically constructive comments that helped improve this book. We also want to warmly thank Anne Goldstein of the International Association of Women Judges for her constant encouragement and critical feedback on our project.

Earlier versions of our work were presented at meetings of the American Political Science Association, Midwest Political Science Association, a Thyssen Foundation Conference organized by Amy Alexander, Farida Jalalzai, and Catherine Bolzendahl, and the European Conference on Politics and Gender. We thank the discussants and attendees for their generative questions and suggestions, including Soledad Artiz Prillaman, Louise Chappell, Susan Franceschet, Melanie Hughes, Diana Z. O'Brien, Malliga Och, Zoe Oxley, Jennifer Piscopo, Jessica Preece, Cameron Thies, and Margaret Williams. We also received helpful feedback presenting this research at Georgia State University, the International Association of Women Judges in Washington, DC, University of California-Berkeley's African Studies Center, University of Missouri-Kansas-City, UNL's IR/CP Brownbag, and TAMU's comparative politics speaker series.

A partial version of chapter 2 appears in *The Journal of Politics* as "Breaking the Glass Ceiling: The Appointment of Women to High Courts Worldwide." We are grateful to the anonymous reviewers for their helpful and critical comments that helped refine the paper. After the article was accepted, we were able to update the dataset slightly. Chapter 2 however, goes beyond the article with additional description and discussion not previously published, whereas the article includes some analysis not included in the book. Data for this chapter are archived at ICPSR as the Women on High Courts Database. Additionally, the first woman data are part of the Global Governance Forum's Gender Equality in Governance Index. We extend our thanks to Amanda Ellis and Augusto Lopez-Claros for inviting us to contribute to the Governance Index. We thank the Constitutional Court Trust in South Africa for permission to reproduce excerpts of the Oral History Project in this book.

At Oxford University Press, we are exceedingly fortunate to have had Dominic Byatt as our editor. He has patiently and graciously responded to all our inquiries and helped shepherd the project to completion. We are also incredibly grateful to the Oxford University Press Comparative Politics Series editors Susan Scarrow and Jon Slapin for encouraging our work. We received excellent comments from three anonymous readers that showed us how to strengthen our book. We also thank Angela Chnapko at Oxford for her early advice on the book. We are grateful to Dolarine Sonia Fonceca, Jennifer Laing, and Olivia Wells as well as everyone else involved in the copyediting, typesetting, and production of our book. Literally, we could not have done it without you.

Finally, we have our families to thank. Miki would like to thank Greg, Michael, and Nikolas for their support and patience. In addition, Miki would like to thank her co-authors for both their brilliance and friendship. Alice thanks Daizaburo Shizuka for being a wonderful partner and for his assistance in making the maps. Her sister Jackie Kang Bousquin cleaned up some of our figures and is a terrific aunt to Justin and Rosa. Alice appreciates her mother, Sung Sook Shin, for being a source of encouragement and looking after her grandchildren at key moments. Valerie would like to thank her amazing spouse, Michael Nickelsburg, for always being a sounding board, general IT support, and for raising our sons, Samuel and Maxwell, to support all forms of gender equality. As Ruth Bader Ginsburg has said, "Women will only have true equality when men share with them the responsibility of bringing up the next generation." She also thanks Sam and Max for being patient when she was busy on Zoom and for their curiosity after overhearing so many Skype and Zoom meetings. Valerie is so grateful to her co-authors for guiding her through the world of comparative and gender politics. Maria is profoundly grateful to Mark for supporting research trips, field work, writing, and her generally. Phoebe and Zachary serve as a constant reminder that girls and boys both need women role models. Alice and Maria also thank their co-authors for kindnesses large and small and for their hard work in taking this from idea to reality.

In the time since we began this project our personal and professional lives have changed dramatically. But so have high courts around the world. Women now occupy more seats on high courts than ever before and yet, gender parity remains an elusive goal. Additionally, while we have worked on this book the world has seen the passing of the US feminist icon Ruth Bader Ginsburg, and one of the founders of the International Association of Women Judges, Argentinian Supreme Court Justice Carmen Argibay. As we mourn their passing, we also hope that our work—and that of women who sit on courts everywhere—inspires the next generation of women judges and pays homage to their perseverance. One high court justice interviewed in Colombia commented that it is hard for a woman to earn a seat on the court, but it is even harder to *be* a woman on the court. We are grateful for the sacrifices made by women around the world to serve as high court justices and acknowledge the important role they have played as way pavers and role models inspiring future women judges. Without them, there would have been nothing to write about.

List of Illustrations

1

Women's Representation on High Courts

Concomitant with the rise in the number of democracies after World War II is the increasing recognition that women's rights are human rights. Women's rights have important consequences for all of society—not just for women. A wealth of research finds that women's rights and gender equity improve economic growth, health outcomes, and global peace and security (Hudson, Bowen, and Nielsen 2020; McKinsey Global Institute 2015). Despite advances toward equality and in the fair treatment of women, UN Women (2019) reports that more than 2.5 billion women are affected by laws that discriminate based on gender, "whether it's for applying for a passport or in the choice of employment, receiving inheritance and deciding when and whom to marry." At the same time, leaders ratify international accords to respect women's rights, and legislatures pass laws addressing gender discrimination. In many places, it is domestic high courts that adjudicate on and determine how laws and treaties are enforced.

Supporters of women's rights and gender equality wage fierce battles to combat discrimination through new legislation. Yet, the long and painstaking process of building legislative support for anti-discrimination laws can unravel if those laws are struck down as unconstitutional. Pressuring presidents or prime ministers to sign international women's rights accords may not impact the lives of women if courts do not hold those provisions enforceable. Consequently, peak courts, which in this book encompass supreme courts in countries with a single peak court and separate constitutional and final appellate courts in countries with multiple peak benches, play an indispensable role in safeguarding women's rights and protecting rights gained in other venues (Escobar-Lemmon and Taylor-Robinson 2014). As high courts have grown increasingly powerful and visible in democracies and non-democracies (Tate and Vallinder 1995; Ginsburg 2003; Moustafa 2007; Ginsburg and Moustafa 2008), the importance of having women on these courts is vital for equality.

Women's full participation on the highest courts helps fulfill the integrity of the process of adjudication on matters of human rights, and to maintaining the rule of law. As Kaufman and Lindquist (1995) write, "legal rights do not stand alone; they are embedded in the dominant social and cultural milieu" and interpreting rights is conditioned by a "socially constructed world, where women's experience is seldom recognized" (115–116). Excluding women in their full diversity deprives the judicial process of integral perspectives, backgrounds, and experiences. In 2019, the UN Commission on the Status of Women launched a new initiative,

Reimagining the Judiciary: Women's Representation on High Courts Worldwide. Maria C. Escobar-Lemmon, Valerie J. Hoekstra, Alice J. Kang, and Miki Caul Kittilson, Oxford University Press. © Maria C. Escobar-Lemmon, Valerie J. Hoekstra, Alice J. Kang, and Miki Caul Kittilson 2021. DOI: 10.1093/oso/9780198861577.003.0001

"Equality in Law for Women and Girls by 2030: A Multistakeholder Strategy for Accelerated Action" as part of the 2030 Agenda for Sustainable Development. At the launch event, Vanessa Ruiz, then president of the International Association of Women Judges (IAWJ) commented, "Women judges with their lived experience as women . . . bring their perspectives to bear so that court decisions are fully informed and avoid discriminatory impact or interpretations" (UN Women 2019).

Although women have entered the legal profession and judiciary in increasingly larger numbers since the 1970s, women's gains in education, legal education, and as lawyers and judges have not automatically translated into seats on high courts. In a worldwide study of the legal profession, Abel, Hammerslev, Sommerlad, and Schultz (2020) find that women and other marginalized groups are disproportionately limited to "lower level professional strata" (26). It has only been in recent decades that gains in women's representation on high courts have been made. In the 1970s, women's representation on high courts was extremely low, and all-men courts were the norm. By 2013, it became commonplace for high courts to have at least one woman justice, and women on a number of peak benches made up at least a third of the justices.

This book examines the factors that facilitate the inclusion of women on peak courts, while recognizing that many courts have a long way to go before reaching gender parity. Why has women's representation advanced on high courts worldwide? As a first step toward addressing this, we ask: When and why did women break the judicial glass ceiling for the first time? We then go on to ask: Where and why have women made the most significant strides? Our book addresses these questions with a cross-national and over-time data set. We then turn to a set of case studies to examine how gains in women's representation are made, and what disrupts entrenched patterns that had long sustained men-only courts.

Monocausal explanations are insufficient. The appointment of judges are complex processes with multiple sources of influence. This book provides an analytic framework to explain the gains women have made on high courts. We focus on three sets of explanations: pipelines to high courts, domestic institutions including selection mechanisms, and international influences. All play an important role in leading toward gender equality on the bench, and none alone is sufficient to explain women's inclusion. Our combination of cross-national quantitative time-serial analyses and detailed country studies allow us to examine these influences across a variety of structures, institutions, and regional contexts.

Pipelines of eligible nominees prove important, but not sufficient. Entrenched institutions and practices act as filters in the pipeline. Established practices that perpetuate women's exclusion must be altered to promote women's appointments. Where there are institutional incentives for selecting women, these can be leveraged by political actors to select women. Women's representation on high courts has advanced when traditional ideas about who can and should be a judge are transformed, and this transformation is often facilitated by regional and international influences. Underlying this transformation are domestic women's advocacy organizations that create, link, and disseminate new ideas and norms about the composition of the judiciary and women's equality in national-level decision-making.

1.1 Why the Inclusion of Women in the Judiciary Matters

One important indicator of diversity in the judiciary is women's participation as judges at all levels, including at the very top in apex courts. A wealth of research demonstrates how the presence of women matters in decision-making bodies such as legislatures and cabinets (e.g., Atchison and Down 2009; Atchison 2015; Carroll 2001; Childs 2008; Clayton and Zetterberg 2018; Clayton, O'Brien, and Piscopo 2019; Reingold 2003; Swers 2002; Thomas 1991). The courts are no exception. Kenney (2012: 163) has cogently argued that "a jury or judiciary drawn from the full range of citizen identities and experiences is more conducive to the production of justice, will yield better deliberations, and will command more support than a judiciary drawn from a narrow cross-section of the public."

A diverse and inclusive judiciary has both intrinsic and extrinsic value. Women's participation on the highest bench, as one dimension of diversity, is an intrinsic good. Fundamentally, it is a human right to participate in decisions that affect oneself. The interpretation of the constitution affects everyone in a country. Excluding half the population denies them a chance to participate in the decisions that will ultimately affect their lives. Women's inclusion as judges on courts is a question of equal opportunity. All citizens should have the same chances to be included in the political process, in governance, and in the adjudication of law. It would strike many as inconceivable to purposefully exclude men from serving as judges: the same must be held for women.

Diverse and inclusive judiciaries also have extrinsic or instrumental value, benefitting both the judicial system and society through (1) enhanced collective decision-making, (2) strengthened public confidence in the judiciary and judicial decisions, (3) representation, and (4) broader access to the judicial process.

First, having women on the bench can enhance deliberations, providing better outcomes. As Justice Thurgood Marshall observed regarding whether a White man could challenge the exclusion of Black jurors in the United States, "When any large and identifiable segment of the community is excluded from jury service, the effect is to remove from the jury room qualities of human nature and varieties of human experience, the range of which is unknown and unknowable" (Peters v. Kiff 1972). Judicial decision-making processes are enriched when they include a variety of perspectives and lived experiences, especially of those who experience multiple and intersecting forms of marginalization (Means, Eslich, and Prado

2019). Greater diversity of views brings more perspectives to bear in deliberations. Diverse views rooted in different backgrounds and experiences strengthen group decision making (Mansbridge 1999; Bonilla-Silva 2017). While some research suggests that decision making in diverse groups may heighten conflict (Mannix and Neale 2005), diversity in the composition of a group increases the preparedness of members and encourages more accurate decisions and innovative approaches (see Phillips 2014).

A tradition of scholarship (e.g., Songer and Crews-Meyer 2000; Palmer 2001a; Palmer 2001b; Boyd, Epstein, and Martin 2010; Boyd 2016) has examined the decisions in legal cases asking whether women decide differently from men. While acknowledging the impact of that work, we focus on the transformative effect upon judicial systems as a whole rather than on individual case outcomes. More recently, scholars examine judicial decision-making by the panel as a whole, rather than at the level of individual judges (e.g. Harris and Sen 2019). That literature reaches important conclusions including showing that panels that included at least one woman judge were more likely to support the plaintiffs' claims regarding sex discrimination (Boyd, Epstein, and Martin 2010; Farhang and Wawro 2004; see Gryski, Main, and Dixon 1986 for state high courts and Peresie 2005 for federal panels) and to adopt a hostile work environment standard (Moyer and Tankersley 2012).

Second, diverse and inclusive high courts contribute to public confidence in the judiciary and the legitimacy of judicial decisions. Institutions of governance, including courts, benefit when citizens perceive them to be legitimate. Courts in particular rely on their legitimacy to maintain the rule of law and encourage citizen acceptance of their decisions (Gibson et al. 1998). Courts can gain or lose legitimacy for many reasons, and one critical factor can be the degree to which judges on a court reflect the populations they serve. Empirical studies point to the importance of diverse perspectives in the judiciary for perceptions of legitimacy. Scherer and Curry (2010) find the presence of Black judges bolsters support for the courts among African-American citizens in the United States. Walker (2008) concludes that women in Costa Rica, Nicaragua, and El Salvador saw the judicial system as more unequal than did men, attributing that difference to beliefs in unequal access to justice for the poor. Arrington's (2020: 2) survey experiments reveal that "respondents were more likely to indicate that the selection process was fair when the outcome included both male and female judges." Perceptions of an unfair selection process or unequal access to justice can undermine confidence in the judiciary.

Processes of representation in governing bodies are not limited to the legislature. Other institutions such as the judiciary are integral as well (Dovi and Luna 2020; Kenney 2012). Of course, representation can have different meanings in different contexts. In most countries around the world, with the exception of some states in the United States and Bolivia, judges are appointed and therefore are not representatives in the same way as elected officials. Yet, one can still speak of a judiciary as being unrepresentative. Drawing on Pitkin's (1967) theory of symbolic representation, Kenney (2012) argues that judges "stand for" a group and points out that in many countries, appointers already select justices to represent people on the basis of geography and language. In Canada, it is commonplace for leaders and citizens to think about justices as representing linguistic minorities and regions. Importantly, valuing judges as representatives of groups need not depend on essentialist thinking. It is not correct to assume that all French-speaking judges decide the same, and that they are necessarily different from all English-speaking ones. When decisions are being made—particularly in democracies where political equality is a fundamental ideal—who sits at the table matters in terms of who gets to see themselves represented.

Finally, a diverse and inclusive bench can transform the judiciary by broadening access to justice. In some cases, women have used their position as judges to influence the ways in which women interact with and are treated by the judicial system as a whole. This work can help transform the distribution of justice in more equitable ways and contribute to the legitimacy of the judicial system. Chief Justice Georgina Wood of Ghana created a Family Justice Center to address issues of gender violence in the judicial process and provide support to survivors. Similarly, in Argentina, Vice President of the Supreme Court, Justice Elena Inés Highton de Nolasco, helped create an office within the court that specializes in providing support to survivors of domestic violence. Initiatives addressing issues of domestic violence can play an important role in reinforcing the legitimacy of the system and help ensure that women who have been victimized are not subsequently taken advantage of by the judicial system.

The appointment of women to high courts can empower women in the legal profession building a pipeline of future women judges. Ginsburg and Brill (1995: 281) write that the first women "way pavers" in the United States federal judiciary made it "realistic for legions of women in the future to aspire to—and achieve—a full life in the law." When Dawuni (2016: 426) asked a woman judge of the High Court of Ghana why she wanted to join the bench, the judge replied, "I joined the bench because of Justice Mrs. Sawyer-Williams who gave a talk and the confidence she portrayed made me have personal ambition to become a judge based on her as a role model." In Colombia, when the Constitutional Court became one-third women it was noted that this was sign for the future. Carolina Vegel, professor of law at the Universidad Externado, argued, "That there are three women on the Constitutional Court has an important symbolic effect. Boys have as referents symbolic figures: the helmeted astronaut, the uniformed policeman, and the lawyer with a tie. They grow up thinking of these figures and dream of being like them. Girls now have a referent. They will grow up seeing them as judges. And maybe they will become students of law inspired by these three women, convinced that it is possible to sit on the Constitutional Court" (Medellín Cano 2017).

1.2 Women's Representation on High Courts

One of the great transformations affecting the judicial branch in recent decades has been the appointment of women judges to high courts. Figure 1.1 displays the percentage of women on high courts based on available data at three points in time: 1970, 1990, and 2010. If a country has two high courts and we have

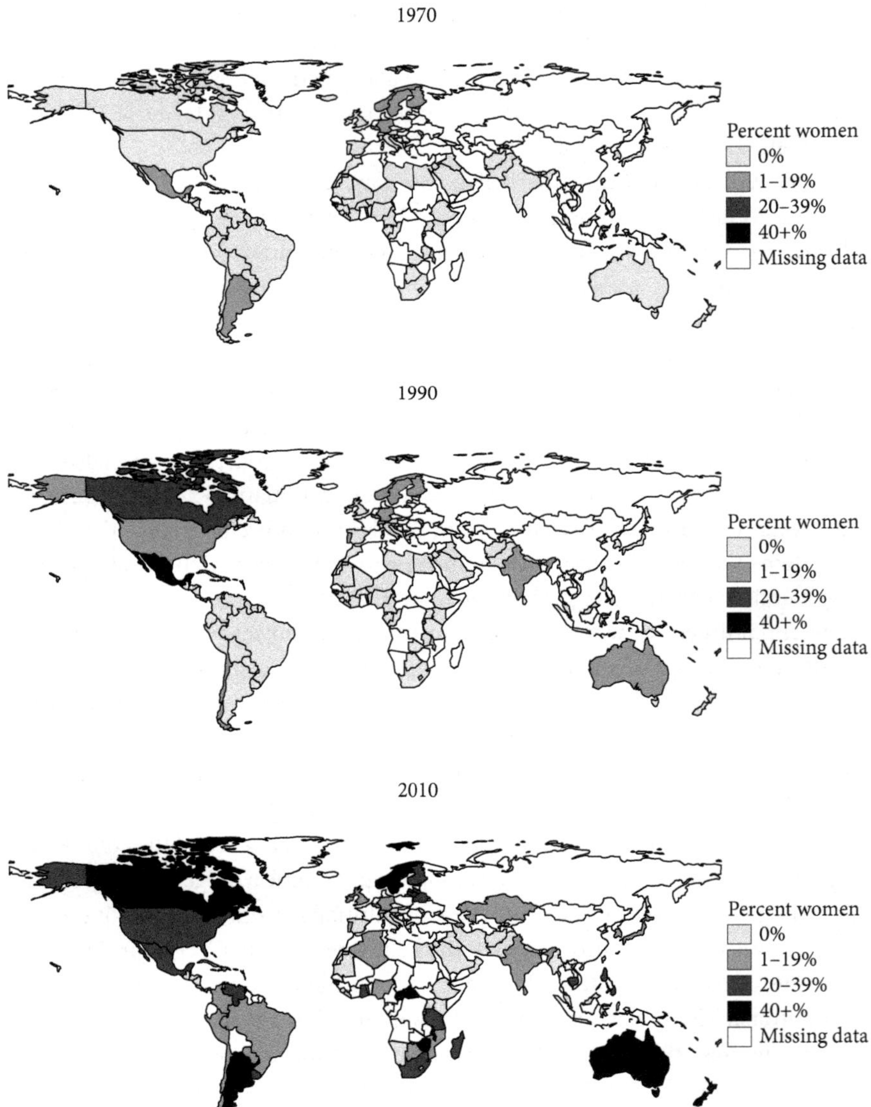

Figure 1.1 The Percentage of Women on High Courts
Source: The Women on High Courts Database.

information on each of them, we report the average percentage of women across both entities. For countries where there is one high court, they are in white if we have missing data on the peak court. For countries with multiple high courts, if we lack information on one or both high courts, they are recorded as having missing data and are in white. This gives us information on women's high court representation in eighty-four countries in 1970, ninety-one countries in 1990, and ninety-three countries in 2010.

In 1970, women comprised 0.6 percent of justices in 84 countries, and it was common for high courts in all the major world regions to have no women justices. By 1990, the presence of women was more than five times higher yet remained extremely low, constituting 3.1 percent of justices on 91 high courts. Twenty years later, in 2010, the average percentage of women in countries for which we have data was 19.3 percent. This reflects a dramatic increase, but it also indicates that women are still underrepresented at the apex of the judiciary.

Figure 1.1 demonstrates that gains toward gender equality have been made in places that would be unexpected for readers who assume that progress is made first in the Global North. The early inclusion of women to high courts is not limited to countries in Scandinavia or other wealthy democracies. For instance, in 1970, Argentina and Mexico had a larger percentage of women on high courts than did the United States and much of Western Europe outside of Scandinavia. By 2010, of the world regions Scandinavia had the highest levels of women's representation, but countries in Africa such as Rwanda had made major gains in diversifying their judiciaries. Yet, as Figure 1.1 also shows, gains are not automatic, nor irreversible, as some countries had lower levels of women's representation in 1990 than in 1970 (e.g., Argentina).

Figure 1.1 illustrates that the gender transformation of high courts has been uneven among countries in the same region that might otherwise seem comparable. In 2013, three of the nine judges on the Supreme Court of Canada were women (33.3 percent), whereas in the United Kingdom, only one of 12 judges on the highest court was a woman (8.3 percent). Sixty percent of the judges of the Constitutional Court of Guatemala were women compared to 20 percent in Chile's Constitutional Court and zero percent in Costa Rica's Constitutional Chamber. All four sitting judges on Burundi's Constitutional Court in 2002 were women, while no women were on Niger's Constitutional Court at that time.

Although women's ascendance to power has been well-studied in the legislative and executive branches (e.g., Escobar-Lemmon and Taylor-Robinson 2016; Annesely, Beckwith and Franceschet 2019; Jalalzai 2013; Krook and O'Brien 2012; Norris and Lovenduski 1995; Paxton, Hughes, and Green 2006; Tripp and Kang 2008), we know less about when, where, and why women are appointed to high courts. Of the comparative research conducted thus far on gender equality in the judiciary, nearly all focuses on a cross-section of countries at a single point in time or on one country or region of the world, and existing studies largely focus on domestic structural influences (e.g., Arana Araya, Hughes, and Pérez-Liñán 2021; Bauer and Dawuni 2016; Dawuni and Kang 2015; Hoekstra, Kittilson, and Bond 2014; Schultz and Shaw 2003, 2013; Sonneveld and Lindbekk 2017; Thames and Williams 2013; Valdini and Shortell 2016). What is needed is a cross-regional and dynamic analysis.

1.3 Explaining Women's Representation on High Courts

The literature on representation in the judiciary to date has emphasized domestic institutions such as selection mechanisms and the supply of candidates to explain women's representation on high courts. Building on this scholarship, we articulate a theory that includes these important influences but also considers how international factors influence the composition of domestic judiciaries. We do not view the inclusion of women on high courts as the result of a single process, but rather as the result of multifaceted and complex domestic and international influences, which collectively explain representation. Multiple paths can lead to the appointment of women on high courts, and these formal and informal institutions incentivize both selectors and aspirants.

Thus, we combine the old and the new to articulate an original theory that we test cross-nationally and explore in depth through case studies in subsequent chapters. As illustrated in Figure 1.2, we posit that it is the confluence of judicial pipelines, domestic institutions including selection mechanisms, and international influences that explain the appointment of women.

First, the pipeline for appointments to high courts taps into supply-side factors. While the formal structures of the legal system and court shape career paths and opportunities for appointments at the apex of the judiciary, in nearly all countries, formal barriers for women to enter the judiciary have been dismantled, and this has facilitated the inclusion of women on high courts. Women have entered law school and the professions that feed into the eligible pool from which judges are selected. In some cases, women hold a significant proportion of the judgeships in lower level courts. In contexts where high court judges are drawn from these lower courts, there can be greater gender diversity.

Yet, the inclusion of women on the highest courts does not always correspond with the number or proportion of women in the pipeline. Some high courts are not as gender diverse as one would expect based on the composition of law school graduates. In some countries, such as Canada and South Africa, the highest courts have been *more* gender diverse than one would expect based on the proportion of women in pipeline. Thus, we consider the importance of pipelines, but also their limitations in explaining the inclusion of women by examining educational and occupational springboards to high courts across our five case studies in chapter 4.

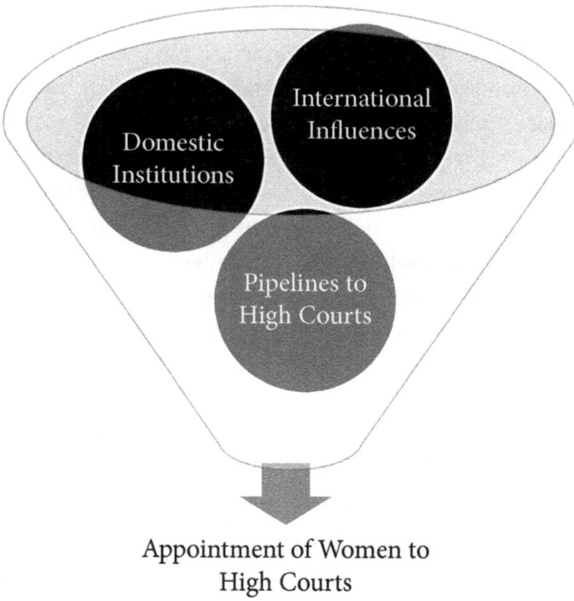

Figure 1.2 A Combination of Factors Produce the Appointment of Women on High Courts

Second, domestic institutions shape the context within which selectors make decisions about who to include (and exclude) on high courts. Past research on women's appointments to high courts has offered a number of important insights into the role of institutions, and we build on these contributions. Some explanations have emphasized the type of legal system and the role of institutional factors such as the size of the court, method of selection, and term length (Schultz and Shaw 2013; Williams and Thames 2008). Further, Valdini and Shortell's (2016) findings from industrialized democracies show that democratic institutions influence those who appoint high court justices, rendering some appointers more exposed to electoral accountability. In Latin America, changes in the political context can create multiple vacancies on high courts, at which time the ideology and motivation of selectors influences the selection of women (Arana Araya, Hughes, and Pérez-Liñán 2021).

Other institutional features might matter, and we discuss some of these further in chapter 5. For instance, in the literature on women's legislative representation, quotas have been shown to increase women's representation (Krook 2006; Franceschet, Krook, and Piscopo 2012; Tripp and Kang 2008). We are aware of relatively few instances of judicial quotas making it difficult to test their effect cross-nationally (Hoekstra 2010). We consider the influence of affirmative language in our case studies in chapter 5.

We consider both formal institutions and informal institutions such as norms, practices, and traditions. Formal institutions are more easily measured across a large number of countries, and we assess their influence in the global statistical models we estimate in chapters 2 and 3. We then more closely assess both formal institutions and informal practices and how they can contribute to women's advancement on high courts in our five case studies in chapter 5.

While pipelines and institutional structures play an important role, so too does the agency of the actors who select high court judges, and the ideas those selectors hold about who can and should serve on the high court. Selectors operate within contexts that differentially incentivize appointing women. Part of that context is shaped by their domestic support base, as well as international norms, which can exert influence as well.

The final set of factors are those that have been neglected by the literature to date: global and regional influences altering expectations of women's participation in governance. International attention to the inclusion of women in governance has flourished in recent decades. Policymakers and international organizations such as UN Women and the World Bank have raised the issue of gender inequality on governing institutions, including the judiciary, legislatures, and cabinets. International and regional treaties have spread norms of gender equality in governance and altered practices at the domestic levels.

Other work examines mechanisms of diffusion of norms of gender equality in governance, including the time since ratifying the Convention on Elimination of All Forms of Discrimination Against Women (CEDAW), regional diffusion, and memberships in international women's nongovernmental organizations (Jacob, Scherpereel, and Adams 2014; Paxton, Hughes, and Green 2006; Ramirez, Soysal, and Shanahan 1997; Berkovitch 1999). In addition to affecting the inclusion of women in cabinets and national legislatures, these norms of gender equality influence the judiciary as well.

As women's rights came to be seen as human rights, international human rights institutions have been conducive to the diffusion of norms of gender equality. CEDAW called for adding women to decision making bodies (Baldez 2014; Krook and True 2012). Over time, CEDAW has been key to improving gender equality in schools, national legislatures, and executive cabinets (Cole 2013; Jacob, Scherpereel, and Adams 2014; Simmons 2009).

Norms of women's roles in governance have not been static, but instead have shifted since the first UN World Conference on Women in 1975. As Paxton, Hughes, and Green (2006) note, the international discourse regarding "what counts as appropriate incorporation has changed over time" (902). At first, women's exclusion was highlighted, and movement organizations, treaties, and shared discourse referred to women's inclusion. After a few decades, discussion moved to gender balance and parity. In broad terms, we can think of this shift as one from equality, which emphasizes equal treatment for all, toward equity, which highlights the needs of some may be different from others. Greater emphasis on equity underpins the use of gender quotas, which are intended to help an under-represented group gain traction. We take into account this shift, examining the appointment of the first woman and moves toward gender parity on high courts in chapters 2 and 3. We trace the rise of global and regional norms of women's inclusion in the judiciary in chapter 6.

We argue that three factors—pipelines, institutions, and international norms—promote the appointment of women to high courts. Importantly, rising norms of ending women's exclusion from decision-making bodies may have a strong impact on the appointment of the first woman as these norms shine a spotlight on all-men courts. Appointing the first woman to a high court (examined in chapter 2) breaks historic patterns. Institutional and selection methods may exert greater impact on the appointment of subsequent women as they structure opportunities for appointment. After the first woman is appointed, the appointment of subsequent women represents more incremental change, and depends on open seats and sustained pressure. We consider the determinants of subsequent moves toward gender equality in chapter 3.

1.4 Research Design

To explain when, where, and why women are appointed to high courts, we employ a multi-method approach. We have built a cross-national and longitudinal dataset on the appointment of women and men to high courts. Our dataset documents the appointment of the first woman as well as the gender diversity of high courts for over half the world. Where there is a single supreme court, it is our high court of interest. In countries where there are separate constitutional and high appellate courts, we include the two in our analysis. We include both courts because we believe that determining the constitutionality of laws and serving as the highest court of appeals both constitute important functions of a country's highest court. In these split court systems, we categorize and refer to the court of last resort as the highest appellate court even if the official name of the court is supreme court.

Information collected by international entities, such as the Council of Europe's European Commission for the Efficiency of Justice (CEPEJ) Studies and the UN Gender Equality Observatory for Latin America and the Caribbean, cover only wealthy, stable democracies or one world region. Other cross-national data collection efforts, including those of the World Bank's Women, Business, and the Law Division, provide statistics on women on constitutional courts for a single point in time. Our dataset uniquely covers high, medium, and low-income countries, democracies and non-democracies, and includes a longer time series.

Our cross-national analyses first examine what influences the appointment of the first woman to the highest court, and then what explains the subsequent number of women on the bench. The appointment of the first woman to a peak court is a significant and symbolic event. The first woman high court justice receives unprecedented media coverage and scrutiny across world regions (Escobar-Lemmon, Hoekstra, Kang, and Kittilson 2016). Most courts are not large: the majority of high courts in our dataset have 15 or fewer members. Given that most high courts are relatively small, the most visible breakthrough in women's access is through the appointment of the first woman. Appointing the first woman to the apex of the judiciary system signals an end to the complete exclusion of women from the judiciary.

We then ask what determines progress toward equality by considering the composition of courts *after* the first woman has already been appointed. In particular, we are interested in determining whether the three sets of factors explain the appointment of subsequent women. By tracking the ebb and flow in the number of women on high courts, we are able to identify factors within and across countries that contribute toward progress. The countries that have come the furthest (and those which have backslid) include those with a reputation for advancing gender equality and those without it.

To compile a cross-national and longitudinal dataset, we used a variety of sources. A team of undergraduate and graduate research assistants helped us gather secondary and primary sources on the presence of women on high courts (e.g., annual reports of the judiciary, commemorative studies celebrating the anniversary of a court, newspaper articles). Depending on the country's context, we wrote to chief justices, court presidents, registrars, or ministers of justice for information on the gender composition of the highest courts to attempt to fill in gaps. For a number of high courts, we tracked the appointment and departure of individual judges. For many other courts, we were only able to collect information on the number or percentage of women on the court in a given year. Appendix 1 provides information on the data we obtained and that which, despite our best efforts, remained missing.

While the cross-national dataset allows us to identify general patterns and test several categories of explanation, five country case studies allow us to investigate the pathways and processes that facilitate women's progress through the judicial ranks. We unpack the pipeline, institutional, and international factors in Canada, Colombia, Ireland, South Africa, and the United States. We interviewed current and former high court judges, ministers of justice, high court clerks, leaders of nongovernmental organizations, members of judicial selection commissions, informed observers, and elected officials as well as collected archival data and media reports in four of the countries and rely on the extensive published literature for data on the United States. With these sources, we delineate the varied pathways leading to the appointment of men and women on high courts. The case studies help us understand the decision calculus of those charged with appointing justices.

The five countries were chosen because of important similarities, but also important differences. One difference is in level of wealth. Canada, Ireland, and the United States are high-income countries in the Global North. Colombia and South Africa are middle-income in the Global South. This mix of cases allow us to speak to women's representation on high courts outside the Global North where most of the work on this topic has been done. While there is notable variation in the level of wealth of these five countries, we acknowledge that it does not fully cover the global spectrum. A snapshot of the differences across these countries is contained in Table 1.1.

The countries selected for study also have different experiences with women's participation in the executive and legislative branches. We observe fairly low levels of women's legislative representation in all five countries except South Africa. Since 2011, Colombia has had a 30 percent quota law for legislative seats, although most political parties use open-lists that preclude a placement mandate for women. Ireland adopted a quota law in 1997, revised in 2012, mandating that women were initially 30 percent of lists rising subsequently to 40 percent of lists but did not contain a placement mandate. In contrast, neither Canada nor the United States, both of which use single-member district elections, have gender quota laws. South Africa, which uses proportional representation, does not have a gender quota law although the major party has voluntarily used one.

Of our five countries, only Ireland and Canada have had a woman head of state. Two women—Mary Robinson (1990–1997) and Mary McAleese (1997–2011)—served as president of Ireland. Kim Campbell briefly served as Canadian prime minister from June 1993 to November 1993. In three of the five countries, women

Table 1.1 The Case Studies

	Canada	Colombia	Ireland	South Africa	United States
Year first woman high court justice	1982	App: 1983 Con: 2001	1992	Con: 1994	1981
Women/Filled seats, 2020	4/9	App: 2/23 Con: 3/9	3/9	Con: 4/9	3/9
GDP per capita, PPP, 2019	$49,031	$14,722	$86,781	$12,482	$62,530
Population, 2019 (mil.)	37.6	50.3	4.9	58.6	328.2
Legal system	Common	Civil	Common	Common	Common
Women lawyers, 2010	37%	56%	40%	46%	32%
Women ministers, 2020	50%	57.9%	26.7%	48.3%	17.4%
Women legislators in lower-house, 2020	29%	18.3%	20.9%	46.3%	23.4%

Sources: Inter-Parliamentary Union (2020); Michelson (2013: Table A8); World Bank (2021).

have gained a significant share of executive branch posts as ministers, outstripping women's representation in other venues. In 2019, women held 53 percent of ministerial posts in Colombia; 50 percent of ministerial posts in Canada; 49 percent of ministerial posts in South Africa, but only 27 percent of ministerial posts in Ireland and 22 percent of ministerial posts in the United States. Women have served as Minister of Justice (or Attorney General), in almost all cases, sometimes with important consequences as we will see in chapter 5.

Strikingly, despite these differences in wealth, institutions, and women's political participation, women justices held one-third or more of the seats on high courts in all five countries by the end of 2020. Our case studies illuminate the different trajectories countries take toward reaching 33 percent women's representation on high courts.

1.5 Plan of the Book

This book contributes to our understanding of governance from a global perspective. As an institution of governance, high courts render decisions vital to their citizens and can have impact beyond their national borders. Who sits on these courts influences the perspectives and experiences brought to bear on the deliberation on cases, which can, in turn affect the outcomes of the cases themselves.[1] This book sheds light on the domestic and international factors that influence who participates in governance. Our cross-national and longitudinal lens, coupled with our case studies, yields analysis with implications for understanding how women can access the domains from which they have been excluded.

The first part of the book highlights our cross-national comparisons. The questions of when and why women first joined high courts is the topic of chapter 2. Drawing on our cross-national data set, this chapter explains why women broke through the judicial glass ceiling sooner on some courts than others. To consider the influence of multiple factors on both the timing of the first woman and the fact that some courts have never had women justices, we use event history analysis. We find that in contrast to much of the previous literature, electoral accountability does not exert a significant effect. We also find that the judicial glass ceiling is not cracked in a domestic vacuum: after countries in the region appoint a woman judge, a country appoints the first woman faster, and the first woman high court judge is appointed sooner the more civil society organizations are connected to the international women's movement. We conclude the chapter with a brief consideration of those countries that have never appointed a woman.

[1] The decisions themselves are an important topic that is worthy of study but is beyond the scope of this book.

In chapter 3 we ask and answer the question: Where have women made the most strides? Once the first woman has been appointed, what determines whether a country will move toward gender parity? This chapter draws on our dataset on the number of women on high courts. We identify which high courts have made the most progress in achieving the milestone of gender parity, and at the other end of the spectrum, where after appointing the first woman, a country has returned to having no women on the high bench. Noting differences across regions, we present over-time trends in the percentage of women on high courts across the major areas of the world. Similar to chapter 2, we explore domestic institutional explanations, comparing women's progress in the judiciaries of different legal systems and regime types. We find that global and regional influences play a significant role in explaining women's representation, more so than accountable selectors or development.

The second part of the book examines pathways and processes to investigate how and why women are appointed. Spanning four world regions (Africa, Europe, Latin America, and North America) encompassing wealthy and middle-income countries and newer and older democracies, the case studies of Canada, Colombia, Ireland, South Africa, and the United States provide nuanced information about appointment processes that can be lost in large scale analyses. In these chapters, we investigate the three main sets of explanations: the judicial pipeline (chapter 4), formal and informal institutions and mechanisms of selection (chapter 5), and international influences (chapter 6).

It is a common assertion that the more women who have the education and career backgrounds that traditionally serve as springboards to high court appointments, the more likely women are to be appointed. In chapter 4, we begin our in-depth analysis by appraising whether and how the supply of women judges and lawyers is connected to the appointment of the very first women to high courts. Understanding that the typical career path differs across our cases, we consider what the pipeline looks like in each country. We then examine the pipeline of women in the typical career path for each country (Canada, Colombia, Ireland, South Africa, and the United States). In all five cases, despite a full pipeline, women are still often blocked from gaining access.

In chapter 5, we compare formal and informal institutions that, collectively, comprise the selection process for the highest courts across five countries. Limiting the focus to formal rules of selection, as we are forced to do in the cross-national analyses, overlooks many informal institutions (norms and practices) that can affect men and women's chances differently. We examine the role formal institutions including judicial nominating commissions and affirmative language play, showing how institutions and context together shape women's representation. But, selection often rests on identifying a list of potential nominees based on informal networks, which have historically favored men. In addition, even though the formal rules do not specify the career path for promotion to the highest court, tradition and norms might favor some kinds of prior experience over others. Our case studies also reveal that gendered networks and gendered biases in selection as well as ideology work against women. Electoral accountability explains women's appointment only in cases where selectors are pressured to appoint women.

Chapter 6 examines the influence of international factors on the appointment of women to high courts in our case studies. We focus on the impact of regional trends, the ratification of CEDAW, and domestic advocacy organizations. We sketch the emergence of regional norms of gender equity in governance, including in the judiciary, in Africa, Europe, and Latin America. Drawing on UN and country-specific primary sources, we document the rise of reporting on gender diversity in the judiciary and on high courts. Our five case studies highlight the role of civil society organizations, namely, women's associations, in exerting pressure on appointers to consider women judges.

The final chapter weaves together the findings from our cross-national statistical analyses and the in-depth case studies to offer overarching arguments for when, where, and why women are appointed to high courts around the world. Our global lens allows for comparison of countries with high courts ranging in size, legal tradition, regime type, selection method, and socioeconomic context. Despite these differences, we find one common denominator: high courts are gendered. Taken together, our cross-national and cross-temporal evidence shows that women's appointment to the peak bench is not automatic, and that both domestic and international factors are influential. In general, despite relatively full pipelines, gendered selection mechanisms have limited women's advancement. In different ways, changing global norms have raised the profile of women's appointments, placing pressure on those with the power to transform the bench, although with varying degrees of success. For women to make significant and sustainable strides, it is necessary to go beyond equal treatment and access to the same opportunities. Instead, what is needed is an equity minded approach: a fundamental transformation of the processes that were built around the traditional all-men norm.

PART I

A GLOBAL AND LONGITUDINAL PERSPECTIVE

2

Breaking New Ground

The First Women on High Courts

When did women first become justices on their country's high court—supreme, highest appellate, or constitutional courts? This chapter examines when and why high courts initially break away from being all-men.[1] The appointment of the first woman disrupts conventional ideas about who can serve on the highest court. National media coverage makes the selection of the first woman justice a highly salient public event. Additionally, after the selection of the first woman, high courts rarely go back to having an all-men bench. In approximately three-fourths of our cases, once the glass ceiling was broken, at least one woman held a seat on the court thereafter. In this way, the selection of the first woman justice has long-lasting effects on the gender composition of the high court. This finding supports the "concrete floor" found in executive cabinets by Annesley, Beckwith, and Franceschet (2019).

Providing a global and longitudinal view, this chapter builds on a rich qualitative literature on the first woman trailblazers in the judiciary (e.g., Dawuni 2011; Kenney 2008; Szto 2008). This work shows that some countries had a woman on the highest court relatively early, such as China, Ghana, and Mexico. Notably, there are also cases, such as the United Kingdom, where the selection of the first woman to the peak bench took decades, if not centuries. A cross-national and over-time perspective is needed to understand why women were appointed justices sooner on some high courts than others.

As indicated in chapter 1, our book proposes that pipeline, institutional, and international factors help explain why women's representation on high courts increased in recent decades. This chapter theorizes how these three sets of explanations affect when women initially crack the judicial glass ceiling and the first woman justice is appointed to the high court. Using our dataset, we find support for supply-side explanations: the more women completing higher education relative to men, the sooner the first woman is appointed. We further find that international influences are at work. The first woman is more likely to be selected

[1] Parts of this chapter were previously published in Escobar-Lemmon, Maria C., Valerie J. Hoekstra, Alice J. Kang, and Miki Caul Kittilson. 2021. Breaking the Judicial Glass Ceiling: The Appointment of Women to High Court Worldwide. *Journal of Politics.* FirstView https://www.journals.uchicago.edu/doi/abs/10.1086/710017. The data we refer to in this chapter are available on ICPSR and our website.

Reimagining the Judiciary: Women's Representation on High Courts Worldwide. Maria C. Escobar-Lemmon, Valerie J. Hoekstra, Alice J. Kang, and Miki Caul Kittilson, Oxford University Press. © Maria C. Escobar-Lemmon, Valerie J. Hoekstra, Alice J. Kang, and Miki Caul Kittilson 2021. DOI: 10.1093/oso/9780198861577.003.0002

the more women's international non-governmental organizations are in the country, and after other countries in the region elevate a woman to their high courts, a country becomes more likely to follow suit.

This chapter begins by presenting a historical view of the appointment of the first women to high courts. Second, we outline how three sets of factors—the judicial pipeline, domestic institutions, and international influences—explain when women are first appointed. Third, we empirically examine the relationship between the three types of factors and first woman appointments using our cross-national dataset. We then note that some high courts, as of 2020, have never had a woman justice and consider what might be driving that pattern.

2.1 The First Women on High Courts

There are vast differences in when countries elevated women to high courts for the first time. Figure 2.1 uses our dataset on first women high court justices in independent countries that had a population greater than 200,000 in 2010. The figure shows the decade in which women made the initial breakthrough. In countries with a single peak bench as of 2013, we report the decade in which the first woman was selected. We refer to these single peak courts as supreme courts. For countries with two high courts—which we label as constitutional courts and highest appellate courts—we go with the earliest appointment of a woman to either entity. Among the countries with multiple high courts, if we are missing data on the first woman for one of the bodies, we code the country as having missing data (e.g., we were not able to discern when the first woman was appointed to the highest appellate court in Algeria). This gives us a map with information on 112 countries.

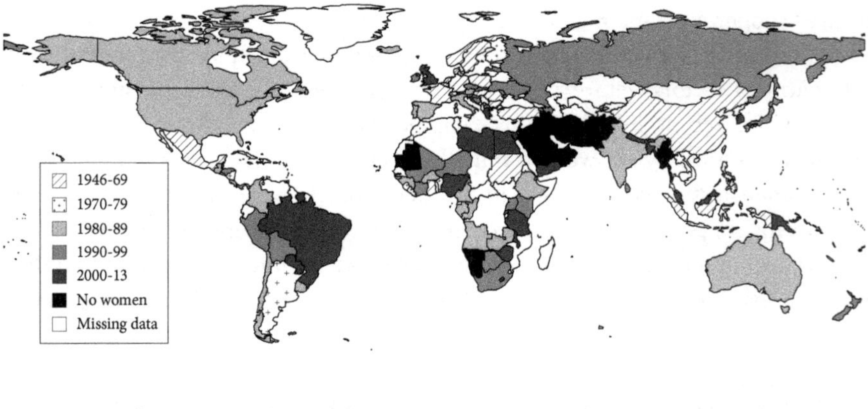

Figure 2.1 The Appointment of the First Woman to High Courts, 1946–2013
Sources: Escobar-Lemmon, Hoekstra, Kang, and Kittilson (2021); The Women on High Courts Database.

Change in terms of appointing the first woman to the high court did not happen everywhere overnight. In particular, the map shows differences within world regions. From 1946 to 1969, a smattering of countries in each region reached the milestone. In the 1970s, women were selected to high courts in countries such as Argentina, Benin, Israel, Morocco, and Switzerland. Over the 1980s, more countries joined the trend, including India, Panama, Spain, the United States, and Zambia. In the 1990s through the 2000s, the judicial glass ceiling broke in Bolivia, Ireland, Japan, and Nigeria. We next consider some of the earliest women trailblazers who were appointed before the rise of the global norm of gender equity (1945–1969) and then summarize the majority of cases that came after (1970–2013).

2.1.1 The Trailblazers, 1945–1969

Table 2.1 lists the earliest appointments of women to high courts for which we were able to obtain information. Some of these innovator countries are those in the West recognized in the women, gender, and politics literature for promoting gender inclusivity in positions of power (e.g., Denmark, Norway, and Sweden). Countries in the Global South, which are not always considered at the forefront of women's inclusion, were also part of the vanguard. For instance, Indonesia, the

Table 2.1 The First Women on High Courts, 1946–1969

Country	Name	High court	Year
France	Charlotte Lagarde Béquignon	High appellate	1946
Poland	Zofia Gawrońska-Wasilkowska	High appellate	1948
Germany	Erna Scheffler	Constitutional	1951
Germany	Gerda Kruger-Nieland and Erika Scheffen	High appellate	1951
Denmark	Bodil Dydbal	Supreme	1953
Turkey	Melahat Ruacan	High appellate	1954
Hungary	Ferencne Molnar	High appellate	1956
Taiwan	Chang Jin-Lan (張金蘭)	High appellate	1956
Bulgaria	Ekaterina Ivanova Biolcheva	High appellate	1957
Ghana	Annie Ruth Baeta Jiagge	Supreme	1961
Mexico	María Cristina Salmorán de Tamayo	Supreme	1961
China	Ma Yuan	Supreme	1963
Romania	Florica Andrei and Elisabeta Ionescu	High appellate	1965
Netherlands	Anna Augusta Leonie Minkenhof	Supreme	1967
Sudan	Ihasan Mohammad Fakhri	High appellate	1967
Taiwan	Chang Jin-Lan (張金蘭)	Constitutional	1967
Indonesia	Sri Widoyati Wiratmo Soekito	High appellate	1968
Norway	Lilly Helene Boelviken	Supreme	1968
Sweden	Ingrid Gärde Widemar	Supreme	1968

Source: The Women on High Courts Database.

world's largest Muslim country, had a woman justice, Sri Widoyati Wiratmo Soekito, on the Supreme Court in 1968.

Who were the first women in the world to crack the highest ceiling in the judiciary? Based on anecdotal evidence, these women excelled academically and met, if not exceeded, the minimum requirements for serving on the highest bench. To our knowledge, the first woman justice on a peak bench was Charlotte Lagarde Béquignon. She was appointed to France's Court of Cassation in 1946 (Arabeyre, Halpérin, and Krynen 2007: 67–8; Boigeol 2003; Rousselet 1957: 231).[2] Béquignon earned a doctorate in law in 1925, writing her dissertation on the legal ramifications of major economic crises. After her studies, she became a professor at the University of Rennes where she ascended the ranks from *chargé de cours*, to *professeur*, to obtaining an *agrégation de droit privé*, the first woman in France to do so. An expert in civil procedure, Béquignon taught civil and international private law. Women in France, however, were not allowed to be judges until 1946. This national policy of prohibiting women from judgeship was not unique to France and could be found in other European countries (Kimble and Röwekamp 2018; Schandevyl 2014; Schultz and Shaw 2003). When France changed the law so that women could join the magistrature, Béquignon was appointed to the Court of Cassation.

The first woman high court judge outside Western Europe that we know of is Melahat Ruacan, in Turkey. After serving as a judge in different parts of the country, Ruacan was appointed to the highest appellate court, the Supreme Court of Appeals, in 1954. To our knowledge, the first woman justice on a high court in Asia was Chang Jin-Lan (alternative romanization: Zhang Jinlan). Chang grew up in a family of lawyers in China; her father was a well-known lawyer and her brother also worked in the legal profession (Szto 2008). Chang ranked first in her class when she graduated from Xibei University in 1942. After taking the judicial officers' exam, she became a judge in a court in Shanxi, China. Upon moving to Taiwan, she became a judge in Tainan. She was elevated to the Supreme Court of Taiwan in 1956.

In the 1960s, women cracked the judicial ceiling in Africa and Latin America. In 1961, Annie Ruth Baeta Jiagge was promoted to the High Court of Ghana, the first woman on a high court in the British Commonwealth (Dawuni 2011). Born in 1918 in Togo, Jiagge's father was a reverend and teacher and her mother was a teacher as well. She moved from Togo to Ghana (then Gold Coast) to live with her grandmother and attend school, earning a teaching certificate in 1938. In the 1940s, Jiagge enrolled at the London School of Economics and Political Science and was admitted to Lincoln's Inn, receiving a Bachelor of Law in 1949. She was called to the Bar in 1950. In 1954, Jiagge became a magistrate in the Gold Coast.

[2] Alternative spellings of Béquignon include Bécquignon and Béquignon-Lagarde.

Beyond her work as a judge, she was active in civic, religious, and women's organizations and was an expert in the drafting of the third and fourth Constitutions of Ghana. She advocated for women's rights in her country and internationally. Jiagge co-authored the United Nations (UN) Declaration on the Elimination of Discrimination against Women, the draft of the 1979 UN Convention on the Elimination of All Forms of Discrimination against Women (CEDAW).

In 1961, María Cristina Salmorán de Tamayo became the first woman appointed to the Supreme Court of Justice in Mexico. She began her career in law through the National School of Jurisprudence and in 1953 earned her doctorate in law from the National Autonomous University of Mexico (Universidad Nacional Autónoma de México). The topic of her thesis reflected her ongoing preoccupation with the condition of vulnerable workers as it centered on the situation of women laborers. Both her grandmother and mother were profound influences on her life serving as examples of breaking barriers and supporting her career. But through their experiences she also saw and became concerned with the condition of workers, especially those who were vulnerable. In 1944 she began working as a lawyer for the Junta Federal de Conciliación y Arbitraje (Federal Board of Conciliation and Arbitration), which was responsible for the settlement of labor disputes and protection of workers. She worked her way up through the ranks being named president of the Board in 1951. In 1961, she was appointed by the President, with the concurrence of Congress, to the Labor Chamber of the Supreme Court. She served until 1986 when she retired (Bolívar Galindo 2019; Apreza Salgado 2014). Her service led to the creation of a medal awarded by the Supreme Court to an outstanding woman justice working to bring equal access to justice for all in 2016 (Corte Suprema de Justicia de la Nacion, N.d.).

2.1.2 First Women, 1970–2013

In the late 20th century and through the 2000s, the number of all-men high courts fell one by one. Figure 2.2 presents the percentage of high courts that had appointed the first woman for each year between 1970 to 2013. In 1970, women had been selected to 17.6 percent of the 108 high courts for which we have data.[3] Ten years later, in 1980, nearly a quarter of the 125 high courts in our dataset had broken the glass ceiling. By 1990, slightly more than 40 percent of 139 high courts reached this milestone, and in 2000, more than two-thirds of 195 high courts had appointed a woman justice. As of 2013, women had broken the judicial glass

[3] The figure includes courts some of which are dropped from the event history analysis due to missing data on independent or control variables.

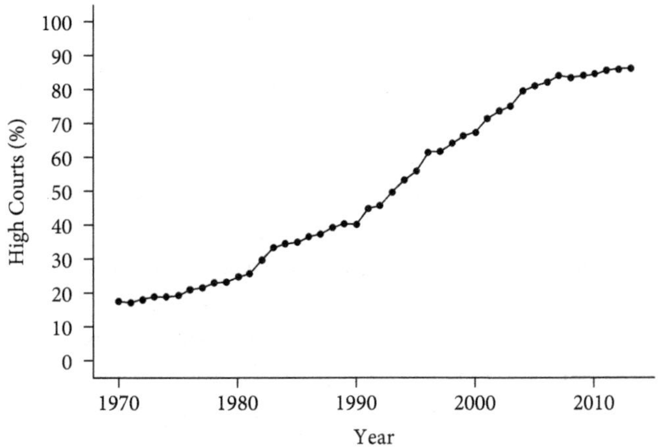

Figure 2.2 The Percentage of High Courts that Had Appointed the First Woman, 1970–2013
Source: The Women on High Courts Database.

Table 2.2 The Percentage of High Courts that Had Appointed a Woman Judge, 1970–2010

Region	1970	1980	1990	2000	2010
Africa	7.1	19.4	41.2	70.2	86.5
East Asia and the Pacific	36.4	35.7	31.3	47.1	80.0
Eastern Europe and former Soviet Asia	50.0	50.0	50.0	79.3	96.6
Latin America and the Caribbean	8.7	16.7	40.7	73.3	96.7
Middle East and North Africa	0.0	13.3	11.1	22.7	41.7
Scandinavia	80.0	80.0	100.0	100.0	100.0
South Asia	0.0	0.0	12.5	37.5	44.4
West (excluding Scandinavia)	17.4	30.4	58.3	86.1	100.0
Overall	16.8	24.2	39.9	67.0	84.5

Sources: Escobar-Lemmon, Hoekstra, Kang, and Kittilson (2021); The Women on High Courts Database.

ceiling in 86.2 percent of 208 peak courts. The selection of at least one woman justice in a high court's history has become commonplace around the world.

Table 2.2 presents the percentage of high courts by region that had appointed the first woman justice, for every 10 years and subject to available data. The initial inclusion of women on peak benches varies across region and time. In 1970, 80 percent of the high courts in Scandinavia, for which we have information, had already appointed a woman, in contrast to 0 percent in South Asia. The period of takeoff depends on the region. In East Asia, the number of high courts including the first woman more than doubled between 1990 and 2010. The number of courts having women in Africa and Latin America and the Caribbean steadily grew over the 1970s through the 2000s. By 2010, all high courts for which we have data had at least one women justice in the West, compared to 41.7 percent of high courts in the Middle East and North Africa.

In the second part of our book, we focus on five countries that varied in when the first woman high court justice was appointed. Of them, the United States was the first to appoint a woman, Justice Sandra Day O'Connor, to the Supreme Court in 1981. On the heels of the United States, Justice Bertha Wilson was the first woman named to the Supreme Court of Canada in 1982 by Prime Minister Pierre Trudeau. In Ireland, Justice Susan Denham was the first woman appointed to the Supreme Court. She was appointed in 1992. Upon the creation of South Africa's Constitutional Court in 1994, two women were appointed: Justices Yvonne Mokgoro and Catherine (Kate) O'Regan. A woman was appointed to the Supreme Court of Appeals for the first time in 1991 (Leonora Van den Heever). While the Supreme Court of Appeals was the highest court at the time, in studying South Africa in Part II, we will focus on the Constitutional Court. In Colombia in 2001, almost 10 years after the creation of a separate Constitutional Court, Clara Inés Vargas Hernández became its first woman magistrate. The first woman appointed to the Colombian Supreme Court had been Fanny Gonzalez Franco in 1984.

As shown in Figures 2.1 and 2.2, women have broken the judicial glass ceiling around the world. Most countries have had a least one woman appointed to a high court. Curiously, there are striking differences in how fast (or slow) peak courts initially included a woman on the bench. In the next section, we present theories for why the first women advanced to high courts when they did.

2.2 Theoretical Explanations for When the First Woman Is Appointed

We propose three broad categories of explanation for when women crack the glass ceiling and are first appointed to high courts and consider each in turn.

2.2.1 Pipelines to High Courts

Supply-side factors may influence women's initial inclusion on high courts. Although there really only needs to be one woman in the pool to break the judicial glass ceiling, a growing share of women with the traditional educational backgrounds may make it difficult for selectors to completely exclude them from the highest bench. The more women earning law degrees and entering the professional fields that supply the eligible pool, the more likely they will crack the glass ceiling and be selected to high courts. We anticipate that supply-side factors help explain when the first woman is appointed. The more gender-equal the composition of the pipeline, the faster a high court will have a woman justice.

The empirical findings on whether the supply of women candidates influences their appointments to high courts, however, are mixed. (Chapter 4 reviews this scholarship in more depth.) Examining the first woman on United States state supreme courts, Goelzhauser (2011) finds that the proportion of women attorneys in a state does not predict when the first woman justice is selected. Comparing 50 democracies, Valdini and Shortell (2016) find no systematic relationship between women lawyers and the percentage of women on high courts in 2012. Williams and Thames (2008) use women in the formal labor force as a proxy and find no correlation with the number of women on high courts in wealthy democracies. Focusing on high courts in Latin America Arana Araya, Hughes, and Pérez-Liñán (2021) uncover a correlation between the average number of years of women's schooling and representation, but not for the percentage of women lawyers.

2.2.2 Domestic Institutions

A rich set of research focuses on the influence of domestic institutions, including methods of selection, on the appointment of judges. Institutions are not gender neutral and can favor or disfavor the inclusion of women on high courts. Institutions encompass both formal rules and informal practices. In this chapter and the next, we focus on formal institutions. (See chapter 5 for a review of this literature.)

We build on past research on how institutions and selection methods can incentivize the appointment of women judges by considering the distinction between contexts where the appointers are elected by the public and where the appointers are unelected officials (Slotnick 1984; Valdini and Shortell 2016; Williams and Thames 2008). Electorally accountable selection methods come with public accountability, and selectors may strategize to broaden their support among groups of voters through their choices for the high court. Selectors can claim credit when they appoint justices from underrepresented groups. For example, Ronald Reagan promised during his presidential campaign that he would appoint a woman to the United States Supreme Court. Consequently, the appointment of O'Connor can be seen as part of an electoral strategy to cultivate the women's vote (Abraham 2008: chapter 11). This is not to say that countries with non-electorally accountable officials will never appoint a woman, but rather that we would expect them to be slower to do so. For instance, the first woman appointed to the high court in the United Kingdom (the first woman law lord) only took her seat in 2004.

Another key aspect of the institutional context is the use of religious law. As Htun and Weldon (2015) argue, many world religions have historically been used in ways that reproduce patriarchal structures, and a country's institutionalization of patriarchal interpretations of religion creates incentives to maintain those beliefs. In such contexts, calls for women's participation in the judiciary may be stifled or complicated. Importantly, religious law can be interpreted in different ways cross-nationally and over time. This means that countries with the same dominant religion, such as Islam, may have very different understandings about who can serve as a judge (Abdelkader 2013). For instance, women have served as judges on Islamic courts in Indonesia since the mid-1960s, whereas in Malaysia, women were not seated on Islamic courts until 2010 (Cammack 1989; Mohd Zin 2018). We expect debates over women serving as judges arising from the use of religious law will slow the appointment of the first women to high courts.

In the 1990s and 2000s, a number of countries restructured the judicial branch through constitutional revision. These changes often included the creation of a separate constitutional court. This simultaneously enhanced the visibility of the judiciary, raised the prestige of constitutional courts, and strengthened attention to the rule of law. At the same time, the international women's movement and UN Conferences on Women were raising awareness surrounding the exclusion of women from decision making structures, especially at the apex of politics. This confluence of factors—the creation of new courts and the increased necessity of including women—meant that when most or all the seats on these news courts had to be filled simultaneously, women could not be excluded. Moreover, with several seats to fill, the costs of including at least one woman were low (Arana Araya, Hughes, and Pérez-Liñán 2021). Thus, we expect that women will have a higher chance of being included on the initial court, but not necessarily on subsequent ones.

We explore these causes in our cross-national analysis because these institutional factors are discussed extensively in the judicial politics or the gender and politics literature as having an impact on women's representation. Consequently, we expect them to play a role in determining when the first woman is appointed. At the same time, we recognize that the institutional environment in any given country is nuanced and complex. There may very well be other institutional factors that influence when the glass ceiling is broken in a particular country or set of countries. In chapter 5, we examine selection mechanisms and women's appointments in Canada, Colombia, Ireland, South Africa, and the United States using more fine-grained data. This allows us to explore the conditions under which selectors can be encouraged to select women and the ways in which informal institutions act together with formal-legal ones.

2.2.3 International Influences

The transborder circulation of ideas helps explain why seemingly different countries make strikingly similar decisions around the same time (Finnemore 1993; True and Mintrom 2001; Wotipka and Ramirez 2008). We theorize that the spread of norms of gender equity in governance has influenced a broad set of countries in the appointment of the first woman to high courts.

International norms of gender equality can spread in three ways: commitment to international law; connections to the international women's movement; and the inclusion of women on the high courts of countries in the same world region. The longer a country has been committed to CEDAW, the greater their exposure to norms of gender equality. We expect this exposure to norms of gender equality renders the exclusion of women from high courts more glaring, and we expect it heightens the likelihood that the first woman will be appointed to the country's high court. By ratifying CEDAW, countries are subject to the CEDAW reporting process, submitting compliance details to an international committee of experts. This process pressures state actors to show progress on gender equality in visible ways.

Increasing communication among advocates for change may encourage the flow of new ideas about gender equality in governance. Women's organizations are often agents of political change. Through international conferences, the international women's movement promoted the discourse of gender equality (Berkovitch 1999; Paxton, Hughes, and Green 2006; Ramirez, Soysal, and Shanahan 1997). Inspired by the first UN World Conference on Women in 1975, women's groups, "vociferously demanded the admission of female judges, thereby building up political pressure" (Schultz and Shaw 2013: 8–9). Women's organizations are not limited to wealthy or Western countries, as the number and influence of women's organizations in the Global South has grown since the 1970s (Tripp, Casimiro, Kwesiga, and Mungwa 2009). Women's groups, when calling for gender equality, often do so as part of a commitment to democracy and modernization (Towns 2012).

When there is a disconnect between international norms and local norms, non-governmental organizations (NGOs) often act as intermediaries (Keck and Sikkink 1998; Merry 2006). National-level NGOs are sometimes inspired by international developments and what is happening in other countries to demand change. NGOs can themselves produce new ideas that then circulate to other countries. Women judges associations, many of whom are connected to the International Association of Women Judges (IAWJ), call for the greater inclusion of women in the judiciary among other things. For example, in 1993 the Kenya Women Judges Association called for the appointment of women judges (Kamau 2013: 185). In 1998, the first woman was appointed to the highest court of Kenya. In other instances, broader women's organizations and associations promoting the rule of law voice demands for women's representation in the judiciary. In Egypt in the 1990s, organizations such as the Alliance of Arab Women, Egyptian Center for Women's Rights, and the Arab Center for the Independence of the Judiciary pressed for selecting women to the judiciary. In the 2000s, some of them lobbied first lady Suzanne Mubarak and the chief justice to add women to the judiciary (Lindbekk 2017: 289–291). In 2003, the first woman was appointed to the constitutional court, Tehani al-Gebali. We expect the more women's international non-governmental organizations (WINGOs) in a country, the faster a woman will be appointed to a high court.

Emulation is another means by which norms of including women on high courts is spread. Goodman and Jinks (2004) define emulation as, "adopting the beliefs and behavioral patterns of the surrounding culture" (638). By extension, regional patterns may matter. Through trade, travel and media, countries situated within the same geographic area are likely to gain greater exposure to one another. Women's rights policies, including the right to vote, have spread regionally (Hughes, Krook, and Paxton 2015; Htun and Weldon 2018; Ramirez, Soysal, and Shanahan 1997). Countries are more likely, all else being equal, to share important similarities with countries in their regions and thus, comparisons are most likely to be made with regional peers. For example, Canada nominated its first woman to the Supreme Court just two years after the United States nominated O'Connor. Thus, we expect that the more courts in the region where the first woman has been appointed, the faster the first woman will be appointed.

Throughout this book we look at the confluence of pipelines, domestic institutions, and international influences affecting women in the judiciary. In this chapter, we expect that the more women relative to men in the eligible judges' pool, the faster the glass ceiling is broken. Institutional factors, such as the method of selection, the use of religious law, and the newness of the court may also influence when women are first included. Finally, we test a novel set of explanations rooted in the scholarship on international norm diffusion.

2.3 Testing Our Expectations

We now turn to testing which factors influence when the first woman is selected to a high court using our cross-national and over-time dataset on the first women justices on peak courts. We begin by discussing how we measured and operationalized each of the variables included in the model. We then discuss our modeling strategy, and finally present the results of our statistical test.

2.3.1 The Dependent Variable

In this chapter we are interested in explaining when the first woman is appointed to a high court to determine what factors are associated with it happening more quickly. Thus, the main outcome variable in this chapter can be thought of as the number of years it takes for the first woman to be appointed to a high court. We are interested only in full appointments and do not consider instances in which a woman fills a temporary vacancy or serves as an acting judge to be the first woman. In some situations, judges from other countries can serve on high courts. We are interested in when the first woman citizen of the country is appointed.

For many countries, we draw on secondary sources to identify when the first woman was appointed. For courts where we could not find adequate information in the scholarly literature, we searched court websites and state-produced primary sources such as annual reports of the judiciary and special anniversary documents. Where feasible, we also verified dates using reports from major national or international news sources. In some cases, we wrote to court presidents, court registrars, and individual judges to determine when the first woman rose to the high court. For information on where we have missing data and the range of our coverage see Appendix 1.

2.3.2 Independent Variables and Controls

Our model includes three sets of explanatory variables, corresponding with our theoretical framework.[4] The first variable is a proxy for the supply of women in the judicial pipeline. *Log women to men tertiary completion* is the natural log of the ratio of women to men completing tertiary education (Barro and Lee 2013). Data are available every five years through 2010 so we linearly impute the variable for missing years. Because judges rarely join a high court upon graduation from law school or judges' school, we lag the variable 20 years. For the time being, this variable provides the best proxy for the gender composition of the judicial pipeline for the largest number of countries and longitudinally. Other existing datasets on women lawyers or women completing judges' school, while helpful for gaining a snapshot or drawing comparisons between countries, have limited coverage over time and space (e.g., Michelson 2013).

The second set of explanatory variables focuses on the institutional context. We posit that courts with electorally accountable selectors are faster to appoint the first women. Earlier datasets code for selection methods for one point in time and mainly for democracies (Valdini and Shortell 2016; Williams and Thames 2008). Therefore, we created a new longitudinal variable based on previous and recent constitutions and secondary sources. *Electorally accountable* equals one if any of the appointers for the high court are elected (e.g., president chosen by popular vote), and zero if all the selectors are themselves appointed or hold inherited positions (e.g., minister of justice, prince). For cases where a combination of unelected and elected officials appoints high court justices, these are counted as

[4] For descriptive statistics, consult Appendix 2.

accountable (e.g., if a judicial commission compiles a shortlist from which an elected official must choose). This is a temporally dynamic variable.

Two additional aspects of the institutional context are *Religious law* and *Newer court*. The former codes whether countries recognize religious law as a valid source of law (JuriGlobe 2015). We include countries that use religion as a sole source of law and those combining it with other types (common law, civil law, or customary law).[5] *Newer court* equals one if two conditions are met: the high court was created in or after 1990 and the court was in its first year of existence. When the newer court enters its second year—that is, when the window of opportunity to appoint many justices at the same time close—the variable turns to zero. Older courts are coded as zero.

We propose that greater exposure to international norms of women's participation in governing bodies leads countries to appoint the first woman to the peak bench sooner. A longer commitment to international law should heighten the likelihood of appointing the first woman. *Log years since CEDAW* is the natural log of the years since the country ratified the convention (United Nations 2020). For countries that had not ratified CEDAW, the unlogged version equals zero.[6] To capture connections to the international women's movement, we use *Log WINGOs*, the natural log of the number of women's international NGOs to which citizens in a country belong (Hughes, Paxton, Quinsaat, and Reith 2017). WINGOs is coded for 1965 and every five years between 1973 and 2013; we linearly impute missing years.[7] Finally, countries may follow the lead of their regional peers. Using the demarcation of regions listed in Table 2.2, *Regional peer effects* is the percentage of high courts in the region that ever appointed a woman. The denominator is the number of high courts in the region for which we had data on the first woman regardless of whether they drop out of the model because of missing data on key independent variables, which increases over time if countries gain independence or create new courts.

Finally, we include a set of control variables. *Appellate court* equals one if the court is the highest appellate court and zero if the court is a standalone constitutional court or a supreme court in countries with a single peak bench. *Civil law* is coded as one if the country in which the high court is located uses exclusively civil law (JuriGlobe 2015). If the country has a common law or a mixed law system (e.g., common law and civil law, religious and civil law), the variable equals zero. Even though the scholarship on women and politics has mixed findings on the relationship between democracy and women's inclusion (e.g., Fallon, Swiss, and

[5] *Religious law* is not a proxy for the Middle East and North Africa region. Countries outside of the Middle East and North Africa that were coded as having religious law include Bangladesh, India, Indonesia, Kenya, and Nigeria.

[6] We replace zero values with 0.001 and take the natural log of years since CEDAW given significant skew. The same was done for the WINGOs variable.

[7] We use the ipolate command in Stata for this and our education variable.

Viterna 2012; Jacob, Sherpereel, and Adams 2014; Paxton, Hughes, and Painter 2010), we control for political openness in the model. *Level of democracy* for a country's given year ranges from -10 (full dictatorship) to 10 (full democracy) and is based on Polity IV (Marshall, Gurr, and Jaggers 2015). Given the traditional importance attributed to wealth, we include *Log GDP per capita* measured as the natural log of gross domestic product per capita in that year. We use Graham and Tucker's (2017) combination of World Bank and Penn World Tables values, averaging 1998 and 2000 figures for 1999, which was missing.[8] We note that we could also control for women in the legislature. In Escobar-Lemmon, Hoekstra, Kang, and Kittilson (2021), however, when we include the percentage of women in the national legislature and other measures of women's political status, we arrive at null findings.

2.3.3 How We Estimate the Model

Our dependent variable is the length of time that elapses until the first woman is appointed to a court. To appropriately model this, we employ event history analysis, also known as survival analysis. Event history models are helpful for understanding the factors associated with the timing of appointments and promotions (e.g., Barnes and O'Brien 2018; Goelzhauser 2011; O'Brien 2015). Specifically, we use the Cox proportional hazards model, which has the benefit of not requiring us to make assumptions about the shape of the baseline hazard (Box-Steffensmeier and Jones 2004: Chapter 5).[9] Because Cox models assume that the effect of covariates are constant over time, we check whether our model violates the proportionality assumption using Schoenfeld residuals (none appears to).

The unit of analysis in our model is the high court-year. Some countries have two high courts, and we analyze each separately. However, given that events in a country may affect both courts, we calculate standard errors clustered on country. We begin the observation period in 1970, five years before the 1975 UN World Conference on Women, to include years before the global emergence of a gender equity norm. From 1975 through the 2000s, attention to the inclusion of women in positions of decision-making spread through subsequent World Conferences on Women and the international women's movement. If a high court was created after 1970, the court enters at the time of its formation. For instance, Colombia's Supreme Court of Justice joins the dataset in 1970, while Colombia's

[8] In a prior version of this work (Escobar-Lemmon, Hoekstra, Kang, and Kittilson 2021), we tested the robustness of our findings to the inclusion of a host of control variables also posited as significant in the literature. These models are available in the supplemental information file associated with the article.

[9] Our findings are robust to using a cloglog specification as we do in Escobar-Lemmon, Hoekstra, Kang, and Kittilson (2021), and the findings are substantively similar.

Constitutional Court enters the dataset upon its creation in 1992. Our observation window ends in 2013. Therefore, if a high court has not had its first woman by the end of 2013, the court remains in the dataset. When we refer to a court surviving until the end of the period, we mean that the court remained all-men through 2013.

2.3.4 Empirical Results

Table 2.3 presents hazard ratios from our model estimating the relationship between pipeline, institutional, and international variables, and the appointment of the first woman. Hazard ratios are one way of interpreting coefficients from survival models. The hazard ratio provides information on the probability an observation does not survive, which in this case means fails to remain all men and sees the appointment of the first woman. A hazard ratio greater than one means that the covariate is associated with a higher probability of the first woman being appointed at a given point of time. If the hazard ratio is less than one, an increase in the variable correlates with a lower probability of appointing the first woman at a given time.

In line with our expectations about the judicial pipeline, as women complete tertiary education at higher rates compared to men, a country becomes more likely, or faster, to appoint the first woman. To visualize the impact of women to men's tertiary completion rates, Figure 2.3 plots the predicted proportion of high courts that survive (i.e., stay all-men) until a given moment in time using estimates and values from the model. In generating these predictions, we held other variables constant in the following ways: the court has accountable selectors, is older (or is a newer court past its first year), is not a high appellate court, the country does not institutionalize religious law, the country has a civil law system, is neither an autocracy nor a democracy (a polity score of zero), and has an average level of wealth. The remaining variables are held at mean values.

Figure 2.3 shows the difference between contexts where women's tertiary education completion rates are markedly lower than men's and contexts where the imbalance between women and men is less severe. In the first scenario (indicated by the solid line in the figure), the ratio of women completing tertiary education relative to men 20 years prior is at the 25th percentile, which gives us a ratio of 0.16. This is similar to the education gender gap found in Iraq in 1980. At the 10-year mark, roughly 70 percent of courts remain all-men for courts in this context of highly gender unequal educational attainment. By contrast, if the tertiary education ratio is at the 75th percentile (a ratio of 0.47, which is less gender unequal and similar to Panama's in 1980), about 60 percent of courts have not yet had a woman justice. At the 30-year mark, more than 30 percent of courts in countries with very low proportions of women completing higher education have

Table 2.3 Appointment of the First Woman on High Courts, 1970–2013

	Hazard Ratio	Standard Error
Pipeline		
Log women to men tertiary completion	1.45*	0.22
Domestic Institutions		
Electorally accountable	1.39	0.38
Religious law	0.59	0.23
Newer court	2.44	1.44
International Influences		
Log years since CEDAW	1.01	0.04
Log WINGOs	1.64**	0.29
Regional peer effects	1.02***	0.01
Control Variables		
Appellate court	0.65	0.15
Civil law	1.19	0.25
Level of democracy	0.98	0.02
Log GDP per capita	0.96	0.08
Number of appointments	114	
Number of high courts	133	
Number of countries	104	
Number of observations	2,299	
Log Likelihood	−408.3	

Note: Hazard ratios reported from a Cox proportional hazard model using the Breslow method for handling ties. Standard errors clustered on country in parentheses.

*** $p<0.001$, ** $p<0.01$, * $p<0.05$.

stayed all-men compared with 20 percent of courts in countries with a better record of gender equity in higher education.

Above, we outlined a set of institutional explanations for when the first woman is appointed. In examining a global sample of countries, we do not find that selectors who can be held electorally accountable are more likely to appoint the first woman, although the hazard ratio is greater than one. This finding contrasts with prior cross-national research that only includes democratic countries (e.g., Valdini and Shortell 2016). In a related study that we conducted, we found that among wealthy long-standing democracies, there is a positive relationship between having selectors that are subject to electoral pressure and the first woman's appointment, although caution is warranted because the sample size of country-courts was small (Escobar-Lemmon, Hoekstra, Kang, and Kittilson 2021). This relationship disappeared in countries without a history of wealth and democracy. Previous studies combined with ours suggests that the importance of having elected officials select judges in terms of the initial inclusion of women justices is context dependent.

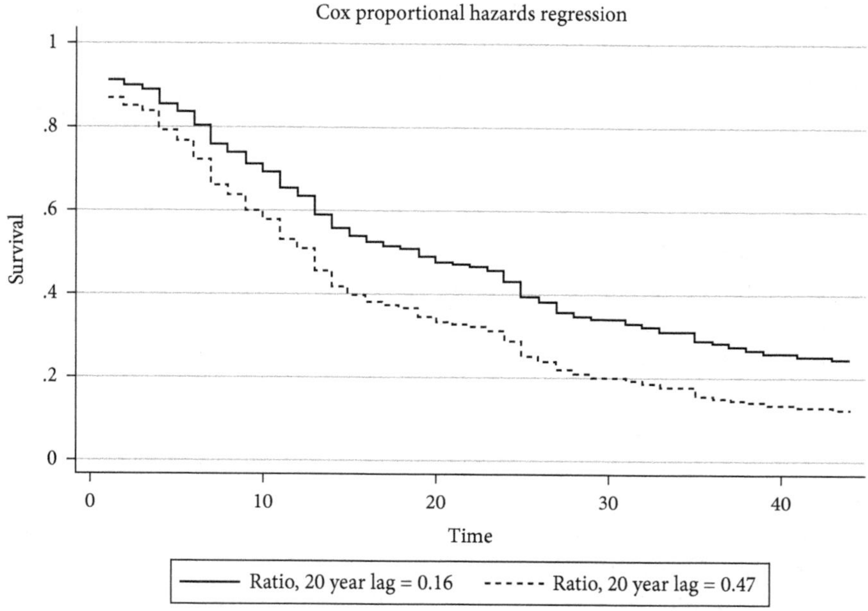

Figure 2.3 The Probability of High Courts Staying All-Men as a Function of Women to Men Tertiary Education Completion Rates

We included two additional institutional variables. The significance of both indicators varies, depending on whether we include the tertiary education measure, likely because of the cases on which we are missing education data. In the model, the hazard ratio of religious law is less than one and has no statistically significant effect. (In an alternative model that we do not report in this book, when we drop the education variable, the use of religious law has a significant and negative relationship with the appointment of the first woman.) Newer court does not attain conventional levels of statistical significance in the model, and the hazard ratio is greater than one. While our case studies in the second part of our book do not allow us to look in depth at how religious law might operate, two of our cases did create new courts in the 1990s, which we explore in chapter 5.

Our results provide support for two of our three expectations about the importance of international norms in explaining the appointment of the first women to high courts. Connectedness to the international women's movement and regional peer effects positively correlate with the appointment of the first woman on a high court. The length of commitment to international law, measured as log years since the ratification of CEDAW, does not have an effect distinguishable from zero.

The more women's international NGOs in a country, the faster it seems to appoint the first woman to a high court. Having more linkages with international women's groups corresponds with a court being more likely to have the first woman. (In models we do not report in this book, omitting the pipeline variable, however, leads the WINGO variable to lose statistical significance at the conventional level.) We explore the ways in which women's organizations do and do not play a role in chapter 6.

Figure 2.4 depicts the survival curve for two scenarios: countries with many WINGOs and countries with fewer WINGOS. Similar to that of Figure 2.3, we hold all other variables constant. The difference between the two curves is the number of WINGOs in the country, with one curve representing cases at the 25th percentile (13 organizations) and one curve representing cases as the 75th percentile (37 organizations). As shown in the figure, courts in countries with more WINGOs are more likely to "die" at a given point in time (that is, to appoint the first woman). At the tenth year of analysis time, roughly 70 percent of courts in countries with 13 WINGOs are all-men and have not broken the glass ceiling, compared with about 55 percent of courts in countries with 37 WINGOs. At the 30-year mark, the difference remains: somewhere around 35 percent of courts in the low WINGO country have survived (remained all-men) while less than 20 percent of courts in the higher WINGO country have survived.

The results support our contention that countries are influenced by the behavior of their regional peers. In Figure 2.5, we plot survivor functions to visualize the impact of regional trends on the timing of the first woman. We control for other variables as we do in Figures 2.3 and 2.4. The main difference here is in the

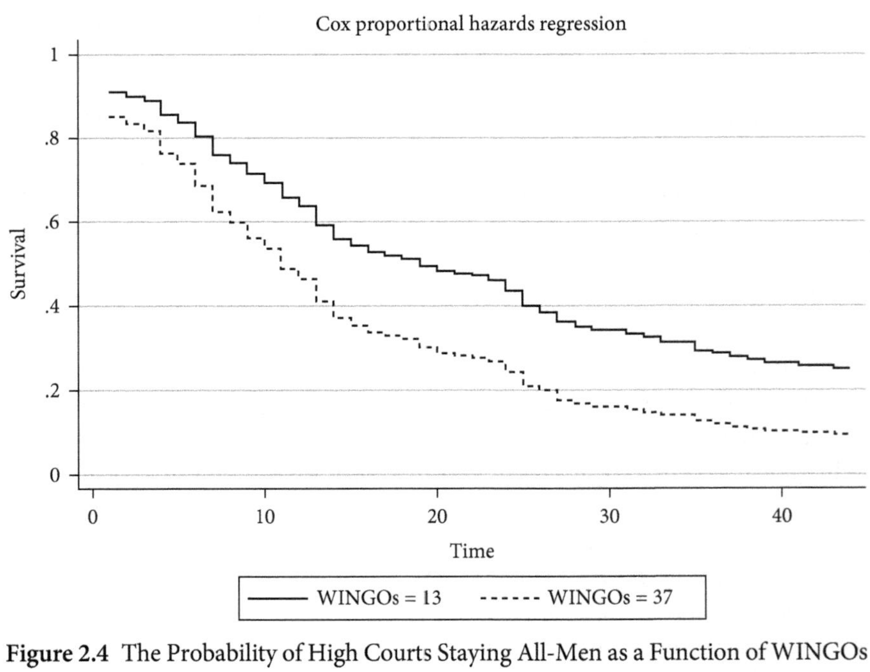

Figure 2.4 The Probability of High Courts Staying All-Men as a Function of WINGOs

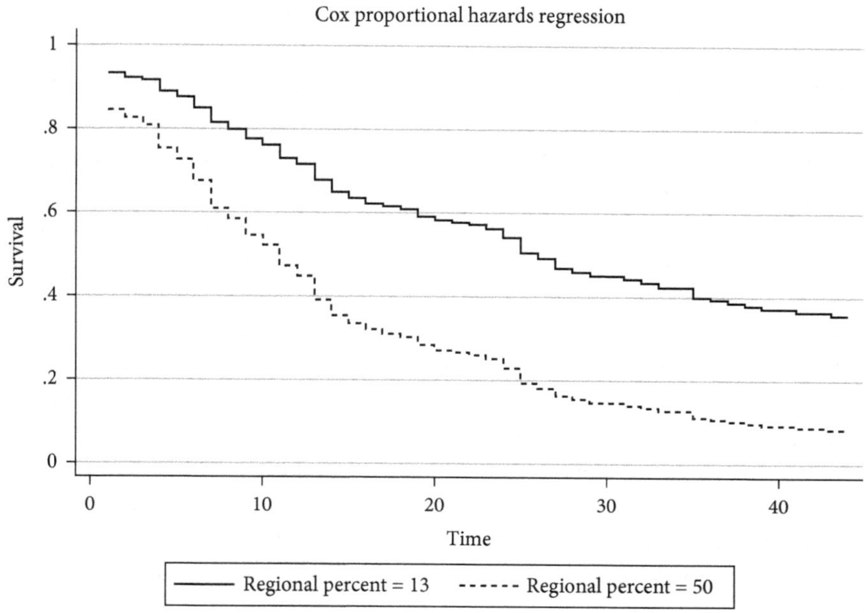

Figure 2.5 The Probability of High Courts Staying All-Men as a Function of Regional Peers Appointing the First Woman

proportion of high courts in a region that have initially appointed a woman justice. In the 25th percentile, about 13 percent of courts in a region have reached the milestone, and in the 75th percentile, 50 percent of courts have done so. At the 10-year mark, close to 80 percent of courts in the low-first women's appointments region have survived, compared with about 50 percent of courts in the region where more courts have seen the first woman. And 20 years later, at the 30-year mark, more than 40 percent of courts in regions with fewer first-women remain all-men in contrast with less than 20 percent of courts those with more first women.

Clearly, as the percentage of high courts in the region that have appointed the first woman increases, the chances a court has the first woman rise. A useful illustration of this finding is a comparison between Liberia and Sri Lanka. Liberia's first woman on the supreme court was appointed in 1977 and Sri Lanka in 1996. Neither country uses religious law nor is purely based on civil law. Seats on the countries' high courts were chosen by electorally accountable selectors, and the courts were created before the 1990s. A key difference, we propose, is that Liberia's neighbor, Sierra Leone, appointed its first woman to the high court in 1976, whereas no country in South Asia had a woman on a peak bench at that time.

The level of democracy and economic development are insignificant in our model. These null findings underscore something that we found in the first part of this chapter: women have been appointed in a variety of countries around the world and not just in wealthy democracies in the Global North.

2.4 Late and Never Appointers, 2013–2020

Using more recent information, we updated our list of women justices on high courts used in this chapter to scan for changes that occurred between 2013 and 2020. In 2013, there were 29 high courts that we knew of that had never appointed a woman. That number has since declined modestly.[10]

Between 2013 and 2020, women broke the judicial glass ceiling in Afghanistan and in countries in the Middle East and North Africa. Sally al-Saidi was appointed in 2013 to the Technical Bureau of Egypt's Court of Cassation, bringing her very close to serving on the peak bench. She earned a Master's degree in criminal law, writing her thesis on capital punishment in Egypt and the United States, and she worked for seven years in the Administrative Prosecution service before joining the Juvenile Criminal Court in 2009 (Lindbekk 2017). She was then promoted to serve on the Criminal Appeal Court in Cairo. In Jordan, Ihsan Barakat was selected to serve on the Court of Cassation in 2017, and Taghreed Hikmat joined the Constitutional Court in 2020. The first woman in Jordan to become a judge (in 1998), Hikmat previously had served on the Court of Appeal and on the International Criminal Tribunal for Rwanda.

We continue to observe the importance of international influences. International attention to women's participation in decision-making helped to keep calls for women's inclusion in the judiciary on the national agenda in Afghanistan. After Afghanistan ratified CEDAW in 2003, it eventually submitted a report admitting that there were no women on the High Council of the Supreme Court (CEDAW Committee 2011a: paragraph 134). In their evaluation of Afghanistan's report, the CEDAW Committee (2013) expressed "its concern at the . . . total absence of women judges in the Supreme Court" (7, paragraph 28). Following this evaluation, in 2015 Afghan President Ashraf Ghani nominated Anisa Rasooli to serve on the court. This nomination fell less than ten votes short in the national legislature. The president again nominated Rasooli to serve on the Supreme Court, although it remains unclear whether she sits on the High Council of the court (De Lauri 2020).[11] This is not to say that CEDAW was the cause of Rasooli's initial or subsequent nomination. Several factors were likely at play, including possibly a pre-election promise that a woman would be appointed and the organization of women lawyers and judges into the Afghan Women Judges Association, which has called for the greater participation of women in the judiciary.

[10] Countries also continued to revise their constitutions, reform their judiciaries, and create new constitutional courts. For instance, a new constitutional court was created after 2013 in the Democratic Republic of Congo. Because these courts were created after 2013, we do not include them in our dataset, and thus we may have missed newer courts with or without women during the 2013 to 2020 window.

[11] There is disagreement across sources regarding the date of her appointment. According to one government decree, Rasooli was appointed judicial councilor in September 2020.

Table 2.4 lists high courts that have never appointed women between 1945 (or the year the court was created, if made after 1945) and 2020. Readers may first observe that despite the gains mentioned above, many of the courts listed in Table 2.4 are in the Middle East and North Africa. This region has 13 never-women courts that we are aware of, accounting for about half of our list. Yet, we are cautious not to make sweeping generalizations as there is marked variation in the region. While women have not been seated on the peak court in Oman or Saudi Arabia, women justices have served on high courts in North Africa (e.g., Algeria, Morocco, Tunisia) as well as in Syria on the highest appellate court (Cardinal 2008; Saad-Zoy 2010). A productive question for the future is why women's inclusion in governance and in the judiciary varies within the Middle East and North Africa (Tripp 2019).

As shown in Table 2.4, a number of the no-women cases are relatively low population countries that have connections with the Commonwealth, an international organization of countries, many of which are former British colonies. Members include Canada, India, Nigeria, Uganda, and the United Kingdom and also 32 small states. A woman justice—more precisely, a woman judge who is a citizen of the country—has not been appointed to high courts in Botswana, Eswatini, Fiji, the Gambia, Maldives, Namibia, Pakistan, Solomon Islands, and Vanuatu. That amounts to nine out of 54 members in the Commonwealth (16.7 percent). This proportion of never-appointers is markedly higher than in Latin America and the Caribbean and of Scandinavia (see Table 2.2 above).

Why have these Commonwealth countries lagged behind in breaking the judicial glass ceiling? One answer could be demographic—the low population

Table 2.4 High Courts that Did Not Have Women Judges, 1945–2020

Bahrain—High appellate	Mauritania—High appellate
Botswana—High appellate (Court of Appeal)	Mauritania—Constitutional
Comoros—Constitutional	Myanmar
Eswatini—High appellate (Supreme Court)	Namibia
Egypt—High appellate (Court of Cassation)	Oman
Fiji	Pakistan
Gambia	Qatar—High appellate
Iran	Qatar—Constitutional
Iraq	Saudi Arabia
Kuwait—High appellate	Solomon Islands—High appellate
Kuwait—Constitutional	Syria—Constitutional
Lebanon—Constitutional	United Arab Emirates
Maldives	Vanuatu
Total: 26	

Note: This table includes only courts we could definitively confirm that no woman citizen had been appointed; if it was unclear or missing the court is excluded.
Source: The Women on High Courts Database.

size of small countries—but we do not think this tells the whole story. While fewer people means fewer women lawyers and judges, this also means there are fewer men to appoint. Another answer could be institutional, namely, the norm of bringing in judges from other countries to serve on high courts. This norm encompasses a range of practices and justifications. In general, it involves the appointment of foreign or expatriate judges, the vast majority of whom have been men. Selectors can ask the Commonwealth to advertise a vacancy on a court, and judges in Commonwealth countries can apply. Sometimes these appointments are short-term, but in the case of Botswana's Court of Appeal, foreign judges can renegotiate their contracts and continue their service for an extended period.

Some scholars contend that the practice of appointing expatriate judges discriminates against would-be citizen judges (e.g., Bauer and Ellett 2016 39; Ellett and Mafukidze 2013). If judges in the Commonwealth who are willing and able to serve in another country tend to be men, then relying on such a pool of expatriate judges could slow the appointment of the first woman citizen to a high court. In recent decades, there have been more women expatriate judges than before, such as Kate O'Regan (of South Africa) and Mabel Agyemang (of Ghana), but bringing in a woman judge from another country is not the same thing as selecting a woman to serve on her country's peak bench.

By and large, high courts around the world have had at least one woman justice. Although there are countries that have never had a woman citizen fully appointed to one or both high courts, the number of exceptions to the general trend has been on the decline.

2.5 Conclusion

The appointment of the first woman to a high court ends the historical exclusion of women from the highest ranks of the judiciary, eroding conventional expectations of who can and should sit on the peak bench. This chapter showed that countries in the West were not necessarily the fastest to appoint the first high court woman justice. In the vanguard were France and Germany, but also Turkey and Taiwan. We then outlined and empirically examined three sets of influence on the appointment of the first woman.

A combination of factors explains why women justices joined the high courts sooner in some places than in others. Women's ability to complete their tertiary education relative to men appears to be important. When more women relative to men graduate from university, 20 years down the road, it is more likely that the country's high courts have a woman justice. Domestic institutions exert less influence over the appointment of the first women, all else equal. Two of the international factors set out in this chapter emerge as significant correlates. Women's international NGOs are linked to earlier appointments of women to the highest courts. And the behavior of a country's regional peers correlates with the timing of the appointment of the first woman. This suggests that one country's appointment of a woman to its high court has implications for the diversification of the judiciary beyond its borders.

The selection of the first woman justice on a high court is a historic event, but it is not the end of the story. Once a woman is seated on the peak bench, selectors may consider the job of promoting gender equity done and revert to the older practice of picking men thereafter. In rare cases this leads to a return to an all-men court. Indeed, a number of high courts peak in our period of observation (through 2013) in having one sole woman justice. Other courts, after the first woman is appointed, have more women justices as vacancies open up and achieve gender parity.

In the next chapter, we look at what happens to high courts once the first woman has been appointed. Getting the first women on the high court involves a confluence of factors. To reach gender parity on high courts, a different set of factors may be influential. We explore in more depth the factors which determine the number of women (or gender composition) of the highest court. This allows us to test the effect that pipeline, institutional, and international factors have in determining the composition of courts as well as when the glass ceiling is cracked. It also allows us to explore in more depth the countries that backslid into all-men courts as well as those which progressed toward gender equality.

3

Where Have Women Made the Most Strides?

The first woman was appointed to the highest courts in Ghana and Mexico relatively early, in 1961. Yet, despite breaking the glass ceiling in the same year, in 2013 women held 38.5 percent of the seats on Ghana's Supreme Court but only 18.2 percent of the seats on Mexico's Supreme Court. Clearly, being an early country to appoint the first woman did not propel Mexico toward gender parity. In 2013, women were close to achieving parity on the Australian Supreme Court (holding 42.9 percent of the seats), but in that same year women were a mere 6.7 percent of the Italian Constitutional Court. In fact, like nineteen other country courts that have broken the glass ceiling (and for which we have data), the Italian Constitutional Court has never had more than a single woman justice at a time. This variation is not explained by stereotypical accounts that paint women as progressing more rapidly and to greater levels in the Global North than the Global South.

Where have women made the largest strides on high courts? Why has women's representation increased beyond having a single woman justice on some high courts and not others? We know that globally the percentage of women on high courts has steadily increased, although women are still numerically underrepresented on these bodies. In chapter 1, we proposed three sets of influence on the appointment of women to high courts: pipelines to high courts, domestic institutional context, and global influences. In chapter 2, we tested specific hypotheses within each category to explain the timing of the appointment of the first woman to a high court. In this chapter, we revisit these three categories to examine the gendered composition of and number of women on high courts.

We are interested in the overall composition of the court and the appointment of subsequent women as a court moves (or does not move) toward gender parity. Therefore, timing is less of an emphasis for this chapter. Instead, our lens is primarily cross-national with a focus on the overall presence of women shaped by cumulative appointments. For each of the three sets of explanations, we detail our expectations for further growth in women's appointment to the highest bench. We find that women hold the most seats on some of the largest courts, suggesting that it is easier to balance representation in those cases. Importantly, our statistical analysis also shows the influence of international factors. Countries surrounded by neighbors with many women on their courts, as well as those that

Reimagining the Judiciary: Women's Representation on High Courts Worldwide. Maria C. Escobar-Lemmon, Valerie J. Hoekstra, Alice J. Kang, and Miki Caul Kittilson, Oxford University Press. © Maria C. Escobar-Lemmon, Valerie J. Hoekstra, Alice J. Kang, and Miki Caul Kittilson 2021. DOI: 10.1093/oso/9780198861577.003.0003

have been long-time signatories of the Convention on Elimination of All Forms of Discrimination Against Women (CEDAW) are those with higher levels of women's representation.

The organization of the chapter proceeds as follows. First, we open with a discussion of the general trends that have characterized women's inclusion on high courts, emphasizing where advances have been made. These patterns reveal both striking success in diversifying courts, with some bodies attaining gender parity or near parity, and others making limited gains. What might explain these differences? Building on the literature on diversity in courts and other national-level decision-making bodies, we next theorize how pipelines, institutional structures as well as shared international norms explain increases in women's representation. In the third section, we test these expectations using our original dataset that contains cross-national variation on high courts that had previously appointed a woman.[1] Finally, we consider the relatively rare cases of courts backsliding to having no women justices.

3.1 Women Making Strides on High Courts

This chapter draws on an original dataset containing information on the number and percentage of women on high courts between 1970 and 2013. As in the first woman dataset used in chapter 2, we set out to collect data for all high courts in independent countries with a population greater than 200,000 in 2010. We were successful in collecting between 58–71 percent of all country courts that we believe existed for a given year (see Appendix 1 for more details).

From 1970 to 2013, women's representation on high courts markedly rose. Women's representation accelerated from 1970 through 2000. While growth has continued since 2000, the rate has slowed. Figure 3.1 shows the percentage of women on high courts over time. We include both courts that had not yet appointed the first woman and those that did. On the secondary axis, we display the number of high courts for which we were able to collect information.

In the 1970 to 1972 period, women comprised only 0.6 percent of justices on 99 high courts. About a decade later, in the years 1982 to 1984, women held an average 1.9 percent of seats on 111 peak courts. This figure more than doubled to 6.2 percent women's representation on 151 high courts in the 1994 to 1996 time period. This doubled again in the 2006 to 2008 block of time, when the average representation of women on 148 high courts was 17.1 percent. In our last block of time, which displays the average for the years 2012 and 2013, women's representation on 154 high courts was 21.4 percent.

[1] The data we refer to in this chapter are available through ICPSR and our website.

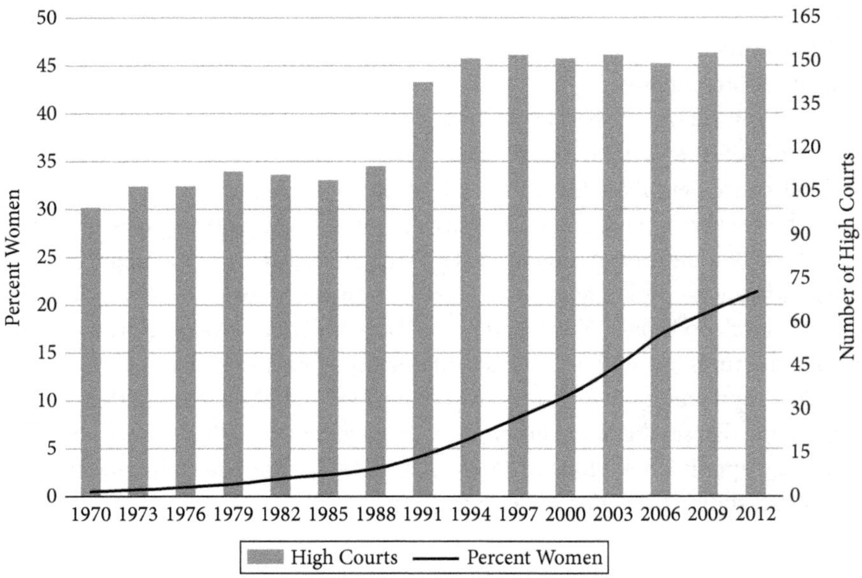

Figure 3.1 The Percentage of Women on High Courts, 1970–2013

Note: We collapsed the data into 3-year time periods and then took the global average for each period. Averages are based on all courts for which we have data at that time regardless of whether the first woman had been appointed. For more details on country courts included in the database and missing data please see Appendix 1.

Source: The Women on High Courts Database.

While Figure 3.1 displays the overall growth in women's representation on high courts over time, there is significant variation across country courts. In some countries, women's representation reached or surpassed the 50 percent benchmark. We know that women have attained gender parity with men on at least 16 courts. Table 3.1 lists the 58 country-court years of which we are aware where gender parity on high courts was achieved. This represents a small fraction of the country-court years for which we have data on the composition of a country's high court(s) after the first woman was appointed suggesting that despite having made inroads around the world, considerable progress is needed before we can speak about gender equity on high courts.

In reviewing the list of countries included in Table 3.1, it is noteworthy that they are in Africa, Central Europe, Latin America, and the Caribbean. In Africa, these include Burundi, Rwanda, Sierra Leone, and Zambia. Burundi's Constitutional Court had four women justices on a seven-person bench in much of 2001 and 2003. From October 2001 to April 2003, the court had just four justices, and all were women. Domitille Barancira was the president of the court, and the other members were Crescence Ndayishimiye, Clotilde Nizigama,

Table 3.1 Courts that Have Achieved Gender Parity, 1970–2013

Country	Court Type	Gender Parity Years
Burundi	Constitutional	2001–2003
Dominican Republic	High appellate	2011
Guatemala	Constitutional	2011–2013
Honduras	Supreme	1996–2009
Jamaica	High appellate	2010–2013
Latvia	High appellate	2006–2009; 2011–2013
Latvia	Constitutional	2011–2013
Macedonia	High appellate	2012–2013
Moldova	Constitutional	2007–2010
Rwanda	Supreme	2003; 2012
Serbia	Constitutional	2005–2009
Sierra Leone	Supreme	2009
Slovenia	Constitutional	2011–2013
Venezuela	High appellate	2012–2013
Zambia	High appellate	2011
Zimbabwe	High appellate	2012-2013

Note: A court is considered to have achieved parity if 50 percent or more of the justices are women. The listing reflects only courts for which we were able to obtain data and thus might omit other parity cases for which we are missing information.

Source: The Women on High Courts Database.

and Alice Ntwarante (Constitutional Court of Burundi N.d.).[2] This makes the Burundian peak bench the only case we know of where a high court was 100 percent women, albeit at a time when the court did not meet the required five-person minimum because the other three seats were vacant for the period. For Rwanda's Supreme Court, there are gaps in our dataset for certain years, but sources indicate that there were seven women out of 14 justices in 2003 and 2012 (Judiciary of Rwanda 2012). For Sierra Leone, we were only able to obtain information for 2009, and in that year, three of the six justices on the Supreme Court were women (CEDAW Committee 2009: 24).

The cases of Burundi and Rwanda raise the question of whether countries facing or emerging out of major armed conflict in the 1990s and beyond are more likely to have gender parity high courts. Studies by Hughes and Tripp (2015) and Tripp (2015) argue that the end of civil wars in Africa combined with rising international norms of gender equity and strong women's movements have resulted in markedly higher levels of women's legislative representation in certain countries (e.g., Rwanda). Dawuni and Kang (2015) find that a number of post-conflict African countries have since had women chief justices or women high court presidents, including Burundi, Rwanda, and Sierra Leone. Yet, one

[2] That all four judges were women was confirmed in an email between one of this book's authors and the President of the Constitutional Court of Burundi.

can also find examples of countries coming out of civil war that have been slow to appoint any or many women high court justices, such as the Democratic Republic of Congo for its recently created Constitutional Court and Colombia's Constitutional Court. The relationship between postconflict societies and women's inclusion in all branches of government is something about which considerably more theorizing and study is warranted, but which is beyond the scope of the present study.

At the same time, Table 3.1 is also a cautionary tale about the extent to which parity, once achieved, means continued gender equity. There are cases for which we have complete information through 2013 where parity is followed by backsliding and a return to fewer women on the court (e.g., the Dominican Republic's highest appellate court goes from having five to eight and then back to four women on its 16-person bench). Interestingly, Scherpereel, Adams, and Jacob (2018) find that in national legislatures, once women achieve a higher level of numerical representation, they rarely dip below that level; they refer to this continued upward climb as the ratchet effect. In executive cabinets, however, women's representation often see-saws between higher and lower levels. Some of the courts that reach gender parity see-saw between 50 percent women's representation and lower, but others appear to have ratcheted up, at least through 2013 (e.g., Guatemala's and Slovenia's Constitutional Courts).

Notably lacking from the list of parity courts are countries that were once assumed to lead the way in women's representation in other decision-making spheres. For some of these cases, women's representation exceeds 40 percent, but does not get to 50 percent. Finland and Norway both have a maximum 42.1 percent women on their highest courts in our period of coverage, and Sweden 46.7 percent. A number of high appellate courts fall in this range as well, including those in Costa Rica and Croatia. Supreme courts (in single apex court systems) where women's representation has surpassed 40 percent, but not exceeded 49 percent, include those of Canada, Israel, Mexico, Philippines, and Uruguay.

To provide a more detailed view of the differences across country courts, Table 3.2 presents the gender composition for all high courts for which we have data in 2013. Women's representation on high courts varied considerably across countries and regions. Even within regions with higher-than-average percentages of women on high courts, women's representation still lagged behind men's. For instance, women only held 8.3 percent of the seats on Belgium's Constitutional Court. In addition to the dramatic variation across countries, one observes considerable variation within countries. For instance, while the Guatemalan Constitutional Court was 60 percent women in 2013, the peak court of appeals only had one woman justice, making it 7.7 percent women.

In Table 3.2, we report not only the gender composition, but also our best estimate of the number of seats on the bench. Of the courts for which we had data, the vast majority had 15 or fewer seats. This relatively low number of seats as compared to the size of national legislatures may reflect the fact that we were

Table 3.2 The Composition of High Courts by Region, 2013

Region	Country	Court Type	Court Size	Number of Women	Percent Women
Africa					
	Angola	Constitutional	11	4	36.4
	Benin	Constitutional	7	2	28.6
	Botswana	Appellate	n/a	0	0.0
	Burkina Faso	Constitutional	10	3	30.0
	Burundi	Constitutional	7	3	42.9
	Cape Verde	Appellate	7	3	42.9
	Central African Republic	Constitutional	9	4	44.4
	Comoros	Constitutional	n/a	0	0.0
	Congo, Rep.	Constitutional	9	2	22.2
	Cote d'Ivoire	Constitutional	7	2	28.6
	Eswatini	Appellate	n/a	0	0.0
	Gabon	Constitutional	9	4	44.4
	Gambia, The	Supreme	n/a	0	0.0
	Ghana	Supreme	13	5	38.5
	Guinea-Bissau	Supreme	9	0	0.0
	Kenya	Supreme	7	2	28.6
	Liberia	Supreme	5	2	40.0
	Madagascar	Constitutional	9	3	33.3
	Malawi	Supreme	11	3	27.3
	Mali	Constitutional	9	3	33.3
	Mauritania	Appellate	n/a	0	0.0
	Mauritania	Constitutional	n/a	0	0.0
	Mauritius	Supreme	19	6	31.6
	Mozambique	Constitutional	7	1	14.3
	Namibia	Supreme	n/a	0	0.0
	Niger	Constitutional	7	1	14.3
	Nigeria	Supreme	17	4	23.5
	South Africa	Appellate	24	8	33.3
	South Africa	Constitutional	11	2	18.2
	South Sudan	Supreme	n/a	0	0.0
	Tanzania	Supreme	n/a	4	n/a
	Togo	Constitutional	9	1	11.1
	Uganda	Supreme	9	3	33.3
	Zimbabwe	Appellate	10	5	50.0
	Regional Average		*10*	*2*	*22.8*
East Asia & Pacific					
	Cambodia	Constitutional	9	1	11.1
	Fiji	Supreme	n/a	0	0.0
	Indonesia	Constitutional	9	1	11.1
	Japan	Supreme	15	3	20.0
	Korea, Rep. (South)	Appellate	14	2	14.3
	Korea, Rep. (South)	Constitutional	9	1	11.1
	Myanmar	Supreme	n/a	0	0.0
	Philippines	Supreme	14	3	21.4

Continued

Table 3.2 *Continued*

Region	Country	Court Type	Court Size	Number of Women	Percent Women
	Singapore	Supreme	16	3	18.8
	Solomon Islands	Appellate	n/a	0	0.0
	Taiwan	Constitutional	15	3	20.0
	Vanuatu	Supreme	n/a	0	0.0
	Regional Average		*13*	*1*	*10.6*
Eastern Europe & former Soviet Asia					
	Armenia	Appellate	17	3	17.6
	Armenia	Constitutional	9	1	11.1
	Azerbaijan	Appellate	32	5	15.6
	Azerbaijan	Constitutional	9	2	22.2
	Belarus	Constitutional	12	5	41.7
	Bulgaria	Constitutional	12	3	25.0
	Czech Republic	Appellate	66	12	18.2
	Czech Republic	Constitutional	15	6	40.0
	Georgia	Appellate	15	3	20.0
	Hungary	Constitutional	15	1	6.7
	Kazakhstan	Constitutional	7	1	14.3
	Kyrgyz Republic	Appellate	n/a	0	0.0
	Moldova	Constitutional	6	2	33.3
	Poland	Constitutional	15	4	26.7
	Romania	Constitutional	9	2	22.2
	Russia	Constitutional	19	3	15.8
	Slovakia	Constitutional	13	3	23.1
	Tajikistan	Constitutional	6	1	16.7
	Turkey	Constitutional	17	2	11.8
	Uzbekistan	Constitutional	4	1	25.0
	Regional Average		*16*	*3*	*20.3*
Latin America & the Caribbean					
	Argentina	Supreme	5	2	40.0
	Bahamas	Supreme	5	1	20.0
	Bolivia	Appellate	9	3	33.3
	Brazil	Supreme	11	2	18.2
	Chile	Appellate	21	4	19.0
	Chile	Constitutional	10	2	20.0
	Colombia	Appellate	23	5	21.7
	Colombia	Constitutional	9	1	11.1
	Costa Rica	Appellate	15	6	40.0
	Costa Rica	Constitutional	7	0	0.0
	Dominican Republic	Appellate	16	4	25.0
	Ecuador	Constitutional	9	4	44.4
	El Salvador	Supreme	15	5	33.3

	Guatemala	Appellate	13	1	7.7
	Guatemala	Constitutional	5	3	60.0
	Honduras	Supreme	15	3	20.0
	Jamaica	Appellate	7	4	57.1
	Mexico	Supreme	11	2	18.2
	Nicaragua	Supreme	16	4	25.0
	Panama	Supreme	9	1	11.1
	Paraguay	Supreme	9	2	22.2
	Peru	Appellate	35	6	17.1
	Peru	Constitutional	7	0	0.0
	Uruguay	Supreme	5	0	0.0
	Venezuela	Appellate	25	16	64.0
	Venezuela	Constitutional	7	3	42.9
	Regional Average		*12.3*	*3*	*25.8*
Middle East & North Africa					
	Algeria	Constitutional	9	2	22.2
	Bahrain	Appellate	n/a	0	0.0
	Bahrain	Constitutional	7	1	14.3
	Djibouti	Constitutional	6	1	16.7
	Egypt	Appellate	n/a	0	0.0
	Egypt	Constitutional	11	0	0.0
	Iran, Islamic Rep.	Supreme	n/a	0	0.0
	Iraq	Supreme	n/a	0	0.0
	Israel	Supreme	15	4	26.7
	Jordan	Appellate	n/a	0	0.0
	Jordan	Constitutional	n/a	0	0.0
	Kuwait	Appellate	n/a	0	0.0
	Kuwait	Constitutional	n/a	0	0.0
	Lebanon	Constitutional	n/a	0	0.0
	Morocco	Constitutional	12	1	8.3
	Oman	Supreme	n/a	0	0.0
	Qatar	Appellate	n/a	0	0.0
	Qatar	Constitutional	n/a	0	0.0
	Saudi Arabia	Supreme	n/a	0	0.0
	Syrian Arab Republic	Constitutional	n/a	0	0.0
	United Arab Emirates	Supreme	n/a	0	0.0
	Regional Average		*10*	*0*	*4.2*
Scandinavia					
	Denmark	Supreme	19	5	26.3
	Finland	Supreme	19	7	36.8
	Norway	Supreme	19	6	31.6
	Sweden	Supreme	16	6	37.5
	Regional Average		*18*	*6*	*33.1*
South Asia					
	Afghanistan	Supreme	n/a	0	0.0
	Bangladesh	Appellate	8	1	12.5
	Bangladesh	Constitutional	93	6	6.5

Continued

Table 3.2 *Continued*

Region	Country	Court Type	Court Size	Number of Women	Percent Women
	Bhutan	Supreme	5	1	20.0
	India	Supreme	24	1	4.2
	Maldives	Supreme	n/a	0	0.0
	Pakistan	Supreme	n/a	0	0.0
	Sri Lanka	Supreme	11	4	36.4
	Regional Average		*28*	*2*	*9.9*
West (not Scandinavia)					
	Albania	Appellate	17	4	23.5
	Albania	Constitutional	9	2	22.2
	Australia	Supreme	7	3	42.9
	Austria	Constitutional	14	5	35.7
	Belgium	Appellate	27	5	18.5
	Belgium	Constitutional	12	1	8.3
	Bosnia and Herzegovina	Constitutional	9	4	44.4
	Canada	Supreme	9	3	33.3
	Croatia	Appellate	42	18	42.9
	Croatia	Constitutional	12	4	33.3
	France	Constitutional	9	3	33.3
	Germany	Appellate	127	28	22.0
	Germany	Constitutional	16	5	31.3
	Ireland	Supreme	10	3	30.0
	Italy	Constitutional	15	1	6.7
	Latvia	Appellate	51	28	54.9
	Latvia	Constitutional	7	4	57.1
	Lithuania	Appellate	34	9	26.5
	Lithuania	Constitutional	9	2	22.2
	Macedonia	Appellate	25	14	56.0
	Macedonia	Constitutional	9	4	44.4
	New Zealand	Supreme	5	2	40.0
	Portugal	Constitutional	13	5	38.5
	Serbia	Constitutional	14	6	42.9
	Slovenia	Appellate	n/a	n/a	39.4
	Slovenia	Constitutional	9	5	55.6
	Spain	Constitutional	12	2	16.7
	Switzerland	Supreme	38	13	34.2
	United Kingdom	Supreme	12	1	8.3
	United States	Supreme	9	3	33.3
	Regional Average		*20*	*6*	*33.3*

Note: Cells with n/a indicate information was not available. Depending on the country court, court size refers to the number of filled seats or the number of seats as specified by law. Courts for which we do not have data in 2013 on number and percent women are excluded from this table.

Source: The Women on High Courts Database.

unable to collect data for a number of high appellate courts, which can be larger (see Appendix 1). There are, nonetheless, rather dramatic differences in court size among the courts in our dataset. While on average constitutional and supreme courts are smaller than peak appellate ones, in part these averages are affected by a handful of very large peak appellate bodies (e.g. Germany's highest appellate court with 127 members), although there are also large benches that we code as being constitutional courts (e.g. Bangladesh with 93 members).

A global snapshot hides trends over time that might better help us understand where women have made the most gains in accessing power through the courts. In Figure 3.2, we present our data by region to capture the extent to which there is variation over time. Women's representation in the 2000s is highest in Scandinavia and other countries in the West. In these parts of the world, women hold on average a third of the seats on high courts. The regional subplots in Figure 3.2 also indicate that women hold a sizeable percentage of the seats on high courts across Africa and Latin America and the Caribbean, averaging close to a quarter of the seats on these courts. At the same time, women's numeric representation falls well short of parity even in the regions with the highest percentages of women on high courts.

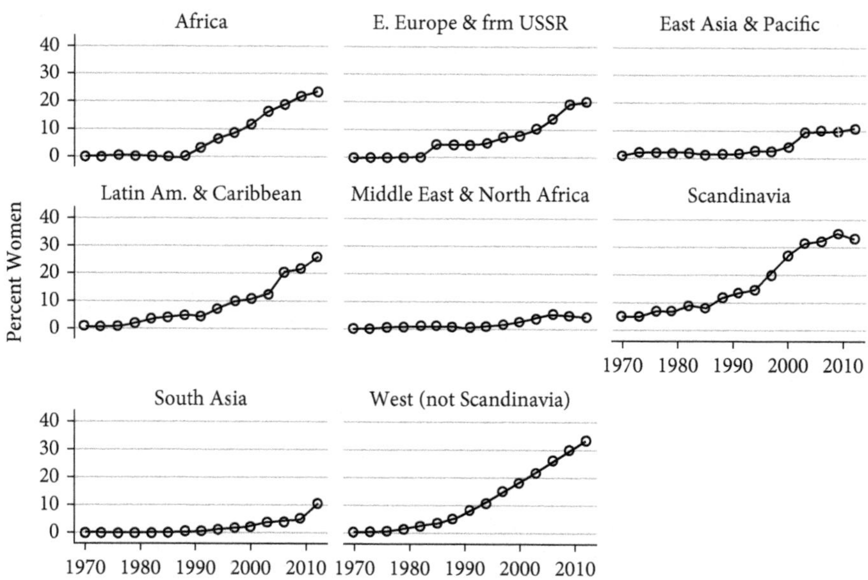

Figure 3.2 Regional Variation in the Percentage of Women on High Courts, 1970–2013

Note: We collapsed the data into 3-year time periods and then took the regional average for each period. Averages are based on all courts for which we have data at that time including those where the first woman had not been appointed. For more details on country courts included in the database and missing data please see Appendix 1.

Source: The Women on High Courts Database.

We recognize that not all high courts are the same. Different types of courts might be more (or less) favorable to the inclusion of women justices. For instance, in systems where there are multiple peak courts, women might be more likely to join the highest appellate court than the constitutional court. Peak appellate courts are often larger in size than high constitutional bodies, which can make the former a less prestigious institution (Williams and Thames 2008). At the same time, in the preceding chapter, we observed that when new courts are created during the 1990s, they were most likely to contain a woman at the time of their founding. Most of those newly created courts were constitutional courts.

In Figure 3.3, we plot the percentage of women holding seats on the high court over time by type of court. While women were slower to gain appointment to peak appellate courts in the 1970s, that pattern quickly reversed itself with women holding the highest percentage of seats (on average) on these courts by 2010. Caution should be taken here. As we discuss in Appendix 1, it was more difficult to obtain information, especially historical information, for many of the highest appellate courts in countries with multiple high courts. At the same time, it is worth pointing out that there does not appear to be marked differences among the types of courts, and the slow rise in the percentage of women holding seats on these courts holds across single peak and multiple peak courts. To the extent that smaller constitutional courts are seen as more prestigious, this alone does not appear to constitute a systematic source of disadvantage for women.

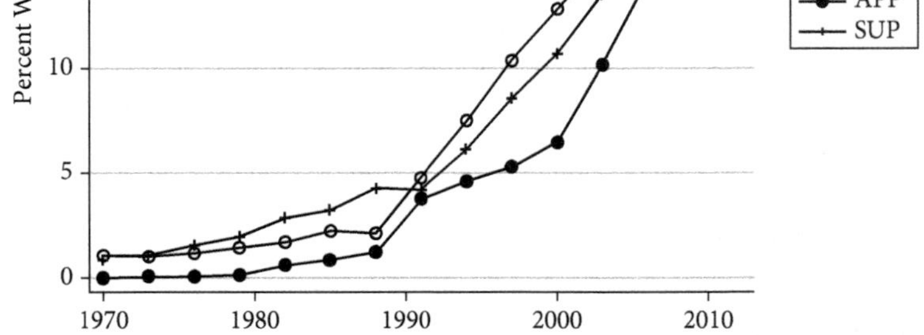

Figure 3.3 The Percentage of Women on High Courts, by Court Type, 1970–2013

Note: We collapsed the data into 3-year time periods and then took the global average for each period and court type. Averages are based on all courts for which we have data at that time including those where the first woman had not been appointed. For more details on country courts included in the database and missing data please see Appendix 1.

Source: The Women on High Courts Database.

The data presented in this section show a steady increase in the share of seats on high courts held by women in our dataset. However, we know there is variation both across time and across courts. We now turn to explaining that variation.

3.2 Theoretical Explanations for Where Women Made the Most Strides

Our argument throughout the book is that a combination of supply (pipelines), domestic institutions, and international factors explain the appointment of women to high courts. In this chapter, we examine the multifaceted processes influencing the composition of high courts by looking at the extent to which courts become more gender inclusive after the first woman is appointed. We theorize how the three sets of explanations affects the court's gender composition.

3.2.1 Pipelines to High Courts

Socioeconomic inequalities between men and women have been the most commonly cited influences on the appointment of justices. The more women with the education and career backgrounds that typically serve as springboards to high court appointments, the more likely women are to be appointed. As gender equality in higher education rises, we can expect more women to be eligible for appointment. As greater numbers of women occupy the traditional springboard positions, it becomes increasingly difficult to ignore women on shortlists and in appointments. A higher share of women with the traditional educational backgrounds may build pressure in the pipeline to the highest courts and increase the chances that when a justice is selected, she is a woman.

Some cross-national quantitative studies support the pipeline hypothesis, although the results are far from conclusive. Valdini and Shortell (2016) do not find a correlation between the percentage of women lawyers and the percentage of women on high courts in 2012. Williams and Thames (2008) use women in the formal labor force as a proxy for women in the pipeline and do not find a correlation with the number of women on high courts in wealthy democracies. In their study of women's representation on high courts in Latin America, Arana Araya, Hughes, and Pérez-Liñán (2021) find partial support for supply-side explanations. The more years women attend school in a country, the higher the percentage of women on high courts. The authors, however, do not find a correlation between a more direct measure of women in the pipeline, the percentage of women lawyers in a country, and women's high court representation.

In the United States literature, empirical studies on the relationship between women in the supply pool and women on high courts offer mixed results (Alozie

1996; Cook 1984; Solberg and Bratton 2005; Goelzhauser 2011, 2016). Arrington's (2018) analysis may help explain why the findings from the United States are inconsistent: the appointment of women judges in the 1970s and 1980s lagged behind the pool of women lawyers, but in the 1990s and 2000s, the percentage of women judges fell more in line with the proportion of women lawyers. We will consider how the eligible pool (women with educational credentials relative to men) affects the composition of the high court.

3.2.2 Domestic Institutions

Both formal and informal institutions, including the method of selecting judges, matter for women's appointments to high courts. Because domestic political and judicial institutions shape the opportunity structure, these factors may be salient for shaping gains beyond the appointment of the first woman. Where there are more opportunities and incentives for selectors to appoint women, women will make greater strides on the highest court.

Past research shows that electorally accountable selectors are more likely to appoint women to high courts (e.g., Valdini and Shortell 2016). Importantly, accountable selectors can use judicial appointments to build support among voters by selecting women and then claiming credit for the appointments. By contrast, non-electorally accountable selectors have less incentive to undercut established men powerholders. In the preceding chapter, we did not find a relationship between accountable selection and the appointment of the first women, although in a study where we differentiate between wealthy long-standing democracies and new or non-democracies, we found a correlation for the long-standing democracies (Escobar-Lemmon, Hoekstra, Kang, and Kittilson 2021). Examining the composition of the court after the first woman has been appointed, we expect institutions to play a role and courts with accountable selectors to have more women than those without.

In addition to the method of selection, another important institutional feature for creating opportunities is the size of the court. Larger courts may encourage women's appointment simply because there are more opportunities to appoint newcomers, as found by scholars of the United States' courts (both federal and state) (Bratton and Spill 2002; Hurwitz and Lanier 2003; Solberg and Bratton 2005; Williams 2007; but see Goelzhauser 2016). Similar to the effect of larger district magnitude making it easier for parties to balance gender representation on legislative lists (Norris and Lovenduski 1995; Matland and Studlar 1996; Rule 1987; Paxton 1997; Luhiste 2015; Valdini 2012), larger courts may enable selectors to obtain better representation and balance representational concerns (Arrington 2020). Consequently, we expect that larger courts will have more women justices.

The institutionalization of religious law may be another salient aspect of the domestic institutional context that shapes the inclusion of women on high courts.

Given that institutionalized religion tends to promote more hierarchical gender roles, where religion is a part of the legal process, we expect to see fewer women appointed to the high courts. In the preceding chapter, we found that religious law did not considerably increase the time to the appointment of the first woman. Nevertheless, we expect that courts in countries that recognize religious law will have a lower number of women than courts in countries that do not.

In chapter 2, we proposed that the establishment of a new high court presents several open seats to be filled. After seats on a new court are filled, however, selectors may rest on their laurels of having appointed one or two women to the bench. Courts that are born with women justices on them may see them replaced with other women, but may not necessarily see vacancies created by men justices' retirements filled by a woman. In this way, the effects of new courts may not have much impact on further increases in women's representation. Indeed, Arana Araya, Hughes, and Pérez-Liñán (2021) find that increases in the number of women on high courts are modest and limited to moments of disruption in Latin America under left-leaning governments. While the creation of a brand-new court does not guarantee that there will be a growing number of women on the bench thereafter, we consider whether newer courts have notably more women after the first woman is appointed. The literature on institutions considers a multiplicity of additional factors. We discuss this literature in greater depth in chapter 5 and examine additional factors through our case studies.

3.2.3 International Influences

The gender composition of judicial pipelines and domestic institutions may facilitate the inclusion of women on high courts, but explanations that focus only on domestic influences do not paint the full picture. As we discuss in chapter 2 and in greater detail in chapter 6, a growing ideational consensus on the legitimacy of having women in positions of decision-making power may raise expectations for appointing women to the bench. We expect these same factors that contributed to the appointment of the first woman to also matter for the appointment of subsequent women to the bench.

Countries may be influenced by their commitments to uphold international law. More specifically, we anticipate that the longer since a country ratified CEDAW, the higher the number of women justices on high courts. CEDAW is an international treaty that has heightened global awareness of gender equality on decision-making bodies. Second, the number of women on high courts may be influenced by connections to the international women's movement, as women's organizations help spread new ideas about gender equality in public life. We expect countries with more connections to the international women's movement to have higher numbers of women on high courts than countries with fewer connections. Third, the gender composition of high courts may be influenced by the behavior of other countries. For instance, if a country's peers have one or two women on the top bench, then a country may be more content with having a sole woman on the bench. Regional influences are important because countries within the same region gain greater exposure to one another through the transborder flows of goods, people, and news media. Thus, high courts in regions with higher percentages of women on high courts will have more women vis à vis high courts in regions with lower percentages of women on high courts.

3.3 Testing Our Expectations

Having identified how we anticipate pipelines, domestic institutions, and international influences to affect women's representation on high courts after the first woman is appointed, we can now test our expectations.

3.3.1 The Dependent Variable

The outcome we wish to explain is the composition of the court. While in our description of the gender composition of high courts above we focused on the percentage of the justices who are women, in this analysis we use the number of seats held by women.

We focus on a count of the number of women first because this is a more intuitive way of thinking about courts, corresponding with how courts are described in the press and likely considered by selectors. A count is a more natural unit as percentage changes are not always smooth and in no case can we discuss a court moving from 1 percent to 2 percent women—instead courts move from having one woman to two women or from having four to three women. Second, especially in small courts the appointment of a single justice can radically shift the gender composition, for instancing raising or lowering it by 20 percentage points on a five-person court. Thus, reliance on percentages can lead to incorrect inferences because a one-percentage point change does not mean the same thing in all cases, and what look like large gains might simply be the effects of court size. Using the number of women justices avoids this problem. While presenting the data in the graphs in percent form allowed us to take into account the size of the court, in a multivariate analysis we are able to do this by including a control variable for court size.

Additionally, because we are interested in explaining the composition of the court, and by extension the factors that promote moves toward gender parity, it makes sense to consider courts where the glass ceiling has already been cracked. In practical terms, this means that a peak bench does not enter the dataset that we use in this chapter's statistical analysis until after the first woman has been appointed. Thus, the courts listed in chapter 2 that had not had a woman as of 2013 are excluded. For those cases where the first woman was appointed to the high court before 1970, as listed in Table 2.1, we start observing the composition of the court in 1970 subject to data availability. For those instances where the first woman was appointed later, we start at that point in time. We end our analysis in 2013 or the last year before 2013 for which we obtained data.

Where there was a change in the number of women during the course of the year, we use the largest possible number of women. For instance, if a court with nine judges has no women January through June and one woman July through December, we report the court as having one woman for that year. If there is a woman for any part of the year the court gets credit for her presence. In cases where a sole woman justice is replaced by another woman justice, the court is credited with having one woman because the two do not serve concurrently.

We recognize that the composition of courts does not always change annually. While there may be rapid or large-scale renewal of the court in some instances, in many cases the court composition alters only every few years. To more accurately capture this pace of change, we collapse our data and take the three-year average. By averaging across a three-year period, we observe opportunities for change to take place through deaths, retirements, the end of terms, or court expansions or reductions. Thus, our dependent variable is the maximum number of women on a high court within a three-year period. In the dataset used to run our model, the number of women on a court varies from 0 to 28. We observe courts that have no women, despite the requirement for inclusion in the dataset that a court broke the glass ceiling, because after appointing the first women some benches backslide to all-men courts, something we examine later in this chapter.

3.3.2 Independent Variables and Controls

Most of our variables are measured in similar ways as described and sourced in greater detail in chapter 2, but there are key differences to lay out.[3] To proxy for the pipeline of women we include *Log women to men tertiary completion*, which is the natural log of the ratio of women to men completing tertiary education lagged 20 years. The lag helps address the fact that judges do not join the highest courts immediately upon graduation from university or law school. We collapsed the annual dataset to report the average ratio of women's to men's tertiary education across every three years.

To capture domestic institutions, we include several measures. One is whether selectors are subject to electoral pressure and thus are accountable. The model

[3] For descriptive statistics, consult Appendix 2.

uses the maximum value of *Electorally accountable* in a three-year period. *Religious law* and *Newer court* are dichotomous measures. In contrast to the newer court variable we used in chapter 2, *Newer court* here equals one if the court was made in or after 1990 and all years after that.

In addition to these variables, we made *Court size,* a variable that, to the best of our ability, measures the number of justices on the court. We use the largest court size within a three-year period. The data on court size come from a combination of court websites, constitutions and statutes, and secondary sources and reflects our best estimate. In the vast majority of cases *de facto* and *de jure* number of judges are the same, and that is what we use. When they diverge, and information is available, we use the *de facto* number of judges. This captures cases when vacancies are long-standing. In these cases, we opt to use the de facto measure of court size for several reasons. First, in these cases we know that the court was operating at less than full staff. This means that a public looking at the court saw women as the fraction of judges actually present, not as a fraction of possible judges. Legal decisions taken and signed during this period were made by those judges serving, which is not the *de jure* number. This also accounts for instances where we were not able to find constitutional clauses or laws specifying the exact number of judges on the high courts.

The inclusion of this variable is of both theoretical and practical importance. Its inclusion allows us to control for the fact that appointing one or two women may be easier when the total number of justices on a court is large as well as the fact that there may be greater pressure for inclusion in larger courts. To ensure that the effect of this variable is not skewed by a couple of very large courts, we run the analysis excluding the very largest courts (more than 52 seats). Only two courts are affected by this decision: the German appellate court, which ranges in size from 109 to 127 and the appellate court in the Czech Republic, which included 66 members.[4]

We capture the effect of international factors using three variables, similar to those employed in chapter 2. The model uses the natural log of years since a country ratified CEDAW to capture adherence to international norms; the natural log of the number of WINGOs in a country to measure connections to the international women's movement; and the average percentage of justices that are women in courts in the region, each averaged over a three-year period. While the first two are measured the same way as in chapter 2, we operationalize peer effects differently. In this chapter, we wanted to capture the extent to which neighboring courts have few or many women rather than whether they have

[4] Other large courts drop out of the analysis because we are missing data on the composition of the court after the appointment of the first woman. We know when the first woman was appointed to the Austrian appellate court (85 members) but not how many women served each year thereafter. The same is true for Bangladesh's constitutional court (91 members), France's appellate court (200 members), Greece's supreme court (200 members), and Slovakia's appellate court (77 members).

appointed the first woman. Finally, we include five control variables: dichotomous measures of appellate court and civil law; the three-year average of the natural log of GDP per capita and the country's level of democracy; and a linear variable of the time period (e.g., 1970, 1973, 1976).

3.3.3 How We Estimate the Model

To test hypotheses while controlling for other factors that might affect the number of women on the court, we use a multivariate model. Because our dependent variable is a count variable, we analyze the data using a negative binomial regression.[5] We estimate a negative binominal model instead of a Poisson regression model because there is significant overdispersion in the dependent variable. In this instance, if we used the Poisson regression the standard errors would be both biased and inefficient possibly leading to incorrect conclusions. We estimate the model with random effects. Because we have some variables that do not vary for a high court over time (e.g. appellate court) or that change slowly over time (e.g. GDP per capita), the random effects model produces less bias than a fixed effects one (Clark and Linzer 2015).

3.3.4 Empirical Results

In Table 3.3, we present the results of our model predicting the number of women serving on a high court after the first woman is appointed. One of the first things that becomes evident is that different factors are responsible for the appointment of subsequent women than for the first woman. While women's access to higher education relative to men correlates with the timing of the first woman's appointment, women-to-men's tertiary education does not appear to affect the subsequent composition of the court.

Three variables correlate with the composition of the court once the first woman is appointed: the size of the court, commitment to international law as measured by the number of years since the country ratified CEDAW, and peer effects (the gender composition of courts in the region). To illustrate the substantive effect of these three variables, we graph the predicted number of women across the range of values from the model. In these predictions, the selection method is accountable, religious law equals zero, the court existed before 1990, the court is not a high appellate court, the country is classified as having a pure civil

[5] The Stata command we used is xtnbreg, similar to Schumacher and Giger's (2018) study.

Table 3.3 The Number of Women on High Courts after the Appointment of the First Woman, 1970–2013

	Coefficient	Standard Error
Pipeline		
Log women to men tertiary completion	−0.05	0.07
Domestic Institutions		
Electorally accountable	−0.11	0.14
Religious law	−0.23	0.21
Newer court	−0.08	0.12
Court size	0.05***	0.01
International Influences		
Log years since CEDAW	0.04*	0.02
Log WINGOs	−0.10	0.11
Regional peer effects	0.02***	0.01
Control Variables		
Appellate court	−0.16	0.15
Civil law	−0.09	0.12
Level of democracy	0.003	0.01
Log GDP per capita	0.004	0.05
Time period	0.02	0.01
Constant	−14.08	191.16
Number of high courts	101	
Number of observations	746	
Wald chi-square	340.87	
Prob > chi-square	0.000	
Log likelihood	−1192.80	

Note: Coefficients and robust standard errors reported from a negative binomial model. Unit of observation is the average over a three-year period for the country court.

*** p<0.001, ** p<0.01, * p<0.05.

law system, and the other variables are held at the sample mean. These plots are presented in Figures 3.4, 3.5, and 3.6.

The only institutional factor in our model that significantly correlates with the number of women holding seats is the size of the court. As might be expected, the number of women justices increases with the size of the court. Figure 3.4 shows that there is a steady increase in the number of women on a court as the size of the court rises. For a large high court with 49 judges, we would expect more than 13 of the seats (or some number between 7.3 and 19.6) to be held by women.[6] On the other hand, for the smallest courts we observe with only four members, we would expect that at most one of the seats (between 1.1 and 1.6) to be held by a woman.

[6] We report an estimated number and a range. The estimated number is the closest integer to the marginal estimate. The range reflects the 95% confidence intervals allowing us to say with a five percent chance of error that the true predicted number of women on the court would fall between those values.

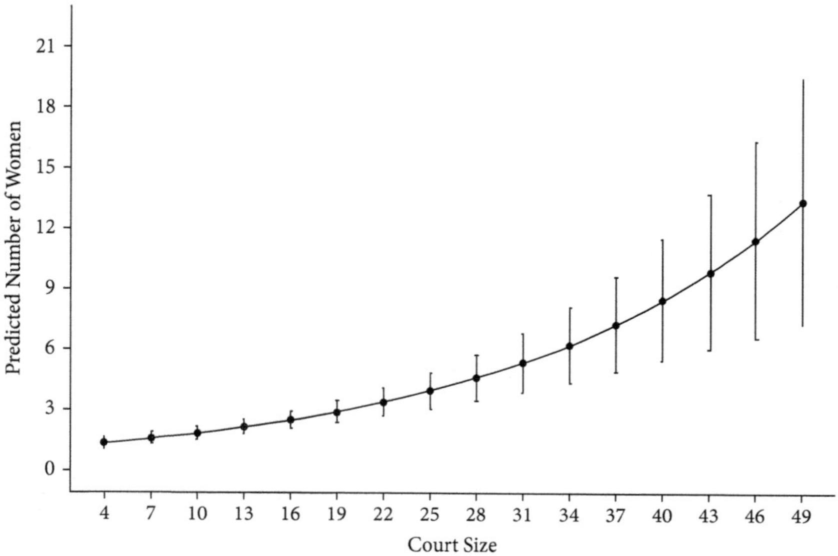

Figure 3.4 Court Size and the Predicted Number of Women on High Courts

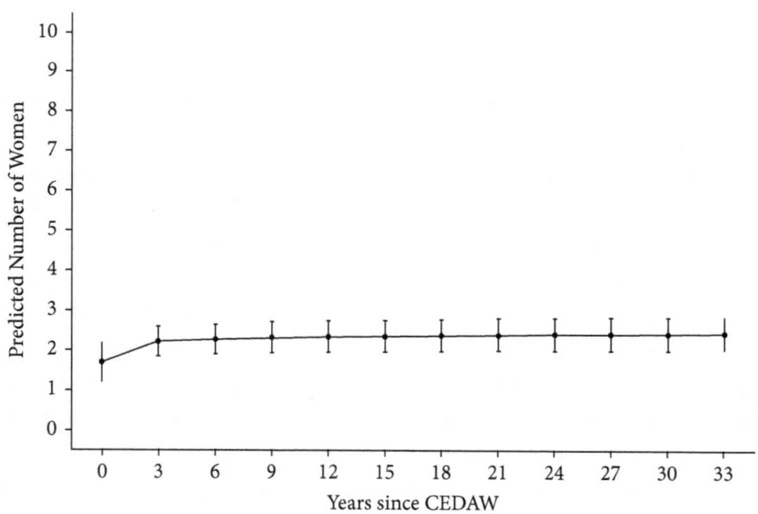

Figure 3.5 Years since Ratifying CEDAW and the Predicted Number of Women on High Courts

The average court size in our sample from the model is 13.9; for a high court composed of 13 judges, we would expect to see about two women (between 1.8 and 2.5).

That women are able to make greater inroads on courts with more seats is likely because with an increasing number of seats it becomes easier for appointers to

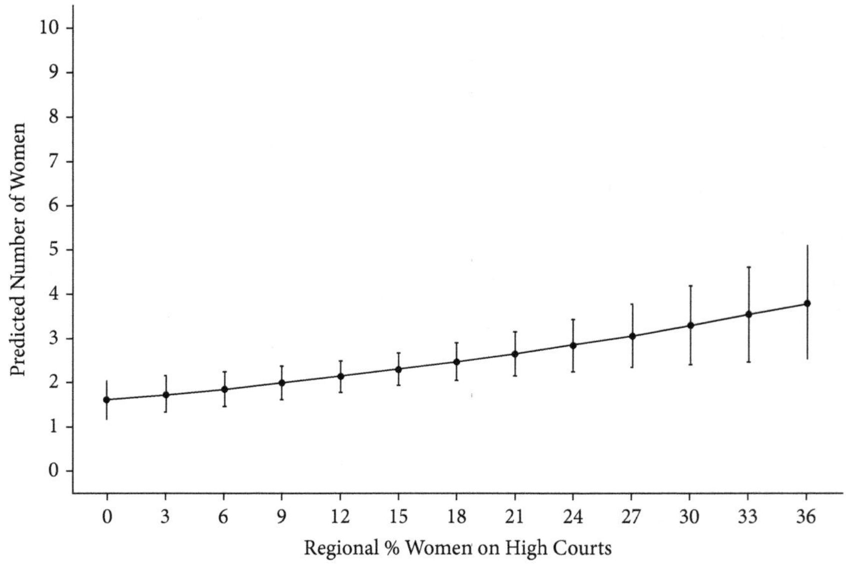

Figure 3.6 Regional Percent Women and the Predicted Number of Women on High Courts

balance a host of representational concerns. This is consistent with Arrington's (2020) finding that in larger courts balancing is easier. It is possible that large courts follow the same logic of balancing that has characterized legislative elections in which representatives are elected from closed-list multimember districts. As Valdini (2012) has shown, those with high district magnitude tend to have greater proportionality.

In our analysis, and in contrast to Valdini and Shortell (2016), we do not find any difference in the gender composition in courts where selectors are electorally accountable and in courts where selectors are not subject to electoral pressure. We are cautious in drawing the conclusion that this means how judges are picked does not matter for our dependent variable. Selection may matter in ways that are context dependent. Having been elected might not be enough, on its own, to induce selectors to promote women; the appointment of women must be made salient by events and the situation in that country. Accountable selectors may be aware that their judicial picks will be considered by voters, but if voters will not hold them to account for failing to pick a woman and instead hold them to account on other dimensions (e.g., ideology), then having electorally accountable selectors in and of themselves may not serve to diversify the courts.

While adherence to international law does not seem to affect a country's propensity to appoint the first woman, it correlates with the subsequent number of women on high courts. Figure 3.5 plots the relationship between the number of years since a country ratified CEDAW and the number of women on the court after the glass ceiling is broken. For an average sized court, we would expect only one or two women (1.2 to 2.2) to serve on the bench holding all other factors constant if the country has not yet ratified CEDAW. As Figure 3.5 shows, the expected number of women on the high court rises only modestly as time passes. Even 33 years after ratifying CEDAW, we would only expect there to be between two and three women on the same high court (2.0 to 2.8). This suggests that while adherence to international norms has an effect upon shifting domestic behavior, the impact may be subtle. The importance of ratifying CEDAW is something we consider in greater detail in the case studies in chapter 6.

In chapter 2, we found evidence for a strong demonstration effect as countries were influenced by the behavior of their neighbors and peers in the region to appoint the first woman high court justice. We also find that while leaders may not admit to putting more women on the courts because neighboring countries do so, there is nonetheless compelling evidence that the number of women on a high court is influenced by the gender diversity of high courts in the region. Figure 3.6 illustrates the strong and positive relationship between the behavior of regional peers and the number of women on a high court after the glass ceiling is broken.

On the average sized high court, if the rest of the region has few or no women—averaging say 3 percent women's representation—we would expect one or two women judges on the court (between 1.3 and 2.1 judges). If the average level of women's representation on high courts in the region rises to the middle of the observed range—say 18 percent—the number of women would be expected to increase to two or three, holding all else constant (2.0 to 2.9). In regions filled with more gender diverse courts, those where the regional average is 36 percent, courts would be expected to have about four women judges (2.5 to 5.1). Regional effects may be a result of shared flows of goods, people, and information as well as within-region linkages between civil society organizations. In our case studies in chapter 6, we explore the extent to which regional effects operate.

3.4 Backsliding: When Do Courts Return to Being All-Men?

Progress is not linear, and increases in women's numeric representation on high courts have not been constant nor automatic over time. Indeed, in some courts, initial gains were followed by setbacks. Our analysis above identified the positive role that commitment to international law, progress toward gender equality by regional peers, and domestic institutions can have in increasing the number of women on the highest bench once the first woman has been appointed. But, despite the global increase in the number of women occupying seats on the highest court there are some courts that after breaking the glass ceiling returned to being all-men entities.

Table 3.4 Courts that Return to Being All-Men after the Appointment of the First Woman, 1970–2013

Country	Court Type	First Woman	Number of Years without Women	Years
Albania	Constitutional	1992	4	1995–97; 2003
Argentina	Supreme	1970	29	1974–2003
Armenia	Appellate	1991	12	1997–2008
Armenia	Constitutional	1996	6	2004–2009
Australia	Supreme	1987	1	2004
Belgium	Constitutional	1984	5	2002–2006
Bosnia and Herzegovina	Constitutional	1998	4	1998–2001
Bulgaria	Constitutional	1991	10	1995–1996; 2001–2008
Colombia	Appellate	1983	14	1986–2000
Costa Rica	Appellate	1984	1	2000
Costa Rica	Constitutional	1993	5	2009–2013
Denmark	Supreme	1953	1	1981
Egypt	Constitutional	2003	2	2012–2013
Guatemala	Constitutional	1995	4	2002–2005
Guinea-Bissau	Supreme	1996	1	2013
Hungary	Constitutional	1999	4	2007–2010
India	Supreme	1989	4	1993–2009
Japan	Supreme	1994	3	1998–2000
Kenya	Supreme	1998	6	2003–2010
Korea, Rep. (South)	Constitutional	2003	4	2007–2010
Lithuania	Constitutional	1993	2	2003–2004
New Zealand	Supreme	1993	11	1993–2003
Peru	Constitutional	1996	11	1998–2013
South Africa	Appellate	1991	6	1997–2002
Spain	Constitutional	1980	11	1987–1997
Taiwan	Constitutional	1967	7	1987–1993
Uruguay	Supreme	1981	13	1990–2013
Zambia	Appellate	1982	8	1983–1996

Note: To be included in this table the country court must have had the first woman justice.

Source: The Women on High Courts Database.

Using our annual dataset, Table 3.4 lists 28 country courts which after the first woman was appointed, reverted to being all men. In some instances, these gaps are relatively short and reflect either a delay in filling a seat or the appointment of a woman at the first opportunity.[7] The table includes several country courts where the court only lacked a woman for one or two years. For example, in Australia,

[7] We remind the reader that our compositional data set contains appointments from 1970 to 2013. Thus, we do not know if countries that appointed the first woman very early (i.e., in the 1940s) reverted to all-men courts before 1970.

there was a gap in 2004 when Mary Gaudron retired in 2003, and Susan McClennan was appointed in 2005.

We observe some instances where the reversion to an all-men court was connected with broader political changes. In Iran, women served as judges in the 1970s until the 1979 revolution. After the revolution, the state passed a law in 1982 that prohibited women from holding judgeships (Abdelkader 2013). In Egypt, Tehani al-Gebali made history in 2003 when she was appointed to serve on the Supreme Constitutional Court. She served until 2011, when, following the 2011 revolution, political changes occurred in the country. As part of those changes the size of the court was reduced from 17 to 11 justices. The six judges with the least seniority, one of whom was al-Gebali, were removed as part of this process. Brown (2016: 108) argues that the removal of al-Gebali was not a result of her being a woman, but instead was a political move. Regardless of the motives, the result was a court composed of only men justices.

There are a few instances where after the court appointed the first woman it reverted to and remained all-men for an extended period. Two cases are worthy of some contrast and discussion: Argentina and Colombia. In 1970, Justice Margarita Argúas was appointed by President Levingston to the Supreme Court in Argentina, becoming the first woman appointed to the high court in that country. The government of Levingston was not a democratic one; he came to power following a military coup on June 28, 1966. In contrast to prior military governments, the courts continued to function and the Supreme Court supported military policy, although there were some prominent exceptions (Castagnola 2018). Justice Argúas remained on the bench until the entire Supreme Court resigned when the military government returned power to civilians following elections in 1973. The Argentine Supreme Court did not have a woman again until 2005 when Carmen Argibay and Elena Highton de Nolasco joined the court. Interestingly, much of the media coverage that surrounded their nomination and confirmation referred to them as "the first women" or the first woman to be nominated by a democratic government (Escobar-Lemmon, Hoekstra, Kang, and Kittilson 2016), as if the glass ceiling had not been broken previously.

Colombia presents another interesting case of a country where following the early appointment of the first woman the court returned to and remained all men. The first woman appointed to Colombia's Supreme Court was Fanny Gonzalez Franco who joined the Labor Chamber in March 1984. Prior to her selection, she had been a magistrate with the Superior Tribunal in Pereira. Less than two years after taking office, on November 6–7, 1985, Magistrada Gonzalez, along with 10 other justices (including the president of the court and all members of the Constitutional Chamber), was assassinated when the M-19 guerilla movement seized the Palace of Justice. In the wake of this tragedy, it fell to the vice-president of the court, Magistrate Alfonso Reyes Echandria, who was not in the court at the time of the attack, to rebuild the court. One might plausibly assume that the appointment of Fanny Gonzalez did not result in the creation of a "women's seat" in Colombia because of the violent circumstances surrounding her death, as well as the overall political situation in which the court found itself. At the time of the M-19 seizure of the Palace of Justice, which came on the heels of the assassination of Minister of Justice Rodrigo Lara Bonilla because of his hardline stance in seeking to prosecute traffickers, the court was debating requests from the United States to extradite drug-traffickers. Attempts to re-integrate the Constitutional Chamber in particular were stymied because distinguished persons would not accept the nomination. As Cajas Sarria (2015: 328) writes, "In the air was the risk signified by assuming a judgeship in the Chamber… From night to morning, to be a magistrate of the Court ceased to be an honor and had become a risky and heavy load that few wanted to bear." Cajas Sarria (2015) and Uribe Restrepo (2006: 30) argue that this situation, combined with the problems of heavy workloads, low pay, and minimal recognition for the work meant that only around 20 percent of those nominated accepted the appointment. This is the situation that characterizes the Colombian Court when it returns to being all men and remains so until 2001, when Isaura Vargas Diaz was appointed to Labor Chamber of the Supreme Court, the same year that Clara Inés Vargas joined the Constitutional Court.[8]

Most of the time, courts that backslide into being all-men quickly bounce back. For those that do not, high degrees of political uncertainty and volatility are at work. Most high courts are fairly small bodies, at least relative to parliaments. Just one or two new appointments can considerably alter the composition of the court. That the amount of backsliding to zero women is not overwhelming suggests that once a woman has broken the glass ceiling of the highest court, the presence of women becomes a more widely accepted expectation.

3.5 Conclusion

In this chapter, we examined cross-national trends in women's representation on high courts, finding that substantial strides have been made in nearly all regions of the world. Underneath the overall acceleration in women's appointments in recent decades lies substantial variation among country courts. This variation does not seem to be explained by the size of the economy nor the degree of democracy. In fact, the high courts that have achieved parity come from a variety of regions and are not necessarily in the wealthiest countries. Nor is progress linear. Backsliding occurs, although in reversions to an all-men bench, most courts bounce back.

[8] Prior to the 1991 constitution, the Constitutional Chamber was located within the Supreme Court. When the new constitution was adopted the Constitutional Court was created as a separate entity.

The factors that mattered for breaking the glass ceiling differ from the factors that matter for levels of women's representation. Pipeline explanations seem to offer little leverage for explaining women's subsequent gains on high courts. Among institutional explanations, the size of the court is key. Larger courts present more opportunities to appoint newcomers, and this often translates into more women on the court, all else equal. International factors play a vital role: regional peer effects and the length of time since ratifying CEDAW advance women's numbers on high courts.

Across the world, women's representation on the highest courts has grown, and both international factors and opportunities to appoint women matter. We have proposed a number of hypotheses within each of our three sets of explanation. However, we are not able to uncover the ways these factors operate in a detailed way in a cross-national analysis. In the next part of the book, we turn to each of the three sets of explanations and how they play out in our five case studies.

PART II

PATHWAYS AND PROCESSES TO HIGH COURTS

4
Pipelines to High Courts

In this section of the book, we conduct a more in-depth examination of each of the sets of explanations to assess how they have contributed to (or impeded) the inclusion of women on the high courts of Canada, Colombia, Ireland, South Africa, and the United States. This chapter focuses on one of the oldest explanations for the ability of women to break into the highest ranks of any group: a sufficient number of members in the eligible pool. These supply-side explanations suggest that the number of women in the pipeline is an important factor toward promotion to the apex positions of their profession. However, it is not always transparent as to what the pipeline is, especially when we consider advancement to high courts. In this chapter, we use our case studies to explore the different pathways to the high courts across our five cases, whether women were well-positioned in the pipeline, and how the pipelines vary across our case studies. We find that while the pipeline explanation appears important in some of our cases, in other cases, pipeline explanations do not fully capture the dynamics for either the first woman elevated or for the overall composition.

In Part I, we examined the factors that are associated with increased women's representation on high courts in a global sample over time. In those analyses we examined the roles that pipelines, domestic institutions, and international influences have upon the selection of the first woman to a high court and upon the composition of the court. We used women's tertiary education as a proxy for women in the judicial pipeline to study a global sample of high courts. Chapter 2 showed that as more women completed tertiary education relative to men, high courts become more likely to have the first woman justice. In chapter 3, we found that after the first woman is appointed, women's tertiary education completion rates surprisingly do not correspond with the number of women on high courts. This suggests that the supply of women relative to men in the pipeline is relevant for explaining the timing of the initial breakthrough, but not later gains for women. Our statistical analyses, however, only gauge the supply of women at a general level (all tertiary education) and do not include women's share of lawyers or judges due to lack of global and over-time data.

We look at the pipelines for five courts. In Canada, Ireland, and the United States we focus on the pipeline to the Supreme Court. For Colombia and South Africa where there are multiple high courts, we study the Constitutional Court. This decision was made to allow for a cleaner comparison across the five countries. We selected the constitutional courts rather than highest appellate courts

Reimagining the Judiciary: Women's Representation on High Courts Worldwide. Maria C. Escobar-Lemmon, Valerie J. Hoekstra, Alice J. Kang, and Miki Caul Kittilson, Oxford University Press. © Maria C. Escobar-Lemmon, Valerie J. Hoekstra, Alice J. Kang, and Miki Caul Kittilson 2021. DOI: 10.1093/oso/9780198861577.003.0004

because, as Ferejohn and Pasquino (2002) argue, there is expected to be a different composition of constitutional courts. Constitutional courts exercise the role of adjudicating constitutionality, which gives them law-making power and might make them more comparable to the supreme courts in our other three countries.

Across our five countries, the removal of barriers for women to enter the judiciary facilitated the inclusion of women, but did not have the same effect on high courts. Official laws in some of our cases that prevented women from joining the pipeline as lawyers and judges were overturned and antidiscrimination laws prohibited some of the practices that gave advantages to men over women. Interestingly, however, there are notable differences in the time it takes from women first joining the legal profession to when the first woman is appointed to the highest court. Among our case studies, there was a lag of 59 years between the first woman lawyer to the first woman Constitutional Court magistrate in Colombia to a gap of 112 years between the first woman lawyer and the first woman on the United States Supreme Court.

After the first woman is appointed, the proportion of women in the pipeline professions does not always correspond with the proportion of women on the highest courts. In two of our cases—Canada and South Africa—the percentage of women on the peak bench was markedly higher than what one would expect based on the traditional pipeline alone. In Colombia, Ireland, and the United States, the proportion of women on the highest courts has been lower than that of women pursuing degrees in the law but corresponds with the share of women on intermediate courts.

We begin with an outline of the existing literature on judicial pipelines. Then, we examine the minimum required qualifications and pipeline of women in the typical career path from 1970 to 2017 country by country. For each case, we offer an evaluation of whether the proportion of women in the pipeline professions corresponds with the gender composition of high courts. In the conclusion, we evaluate the strength of the pipeline argument in each of the five countries and draw comparisons across the cases.

4.1 What We Know about Judicial Pipelines

The pipeline theory of women's advancement in the judiciary is that as more women enter the legal profession and serve on lower courts, more women will eventually become high court judges. Cook (1984) and others refer to this as the eligibility pool theory. As Palmer (2001a: 235) writes about the United States context, "The primary idea behind both the pipeline and eligibility pool theories is the same: there will be a time lag between increases in the number of women lawyers and increases in the number of women serving in judicial institutions." Although some past research has focused on raw numbers, we look mostly at the proportion of women in the eligibility pool in subsequent sections of this chapter. According to this theory, taking into consideration the lag, women should be represented on high courts in numbers that reflect the pool (see, for instance, Kim 2009). In an article criticizing the pipeline assumption, Sommerlad (1994) calls this the trickle-up theory.

Despite gaining access to entry-level positions, women may be blocked, overlooked, or otherwise discouraged from pursuing a path to judgeship on higher courts. Putnam (1976: 33) summarizes this as the law of increasing disproportion whereby, "the higher the level of political authority, the greater the representation for high-status social groups." In studying presidential cabinets, for instance, Escobar-Lemmon and Taylor-Robinson (2016) find that women have struggled to break into what are seen as some of the most important and highest prestige parts of the cabinet (Finance or Treasury) even as they gained access to the cabinet as a whole. Watson and his colleagues (2005: 56–56) explain women's exclusion from these posts on the basis that masculinity is seen as necessary to carrying out the work. This is consistent with research by Barnes and O'Brien (2018), which identifies women's exclusion from the post of Defense Minister as being tied to perceptions of the masculine nature of the portfolio. It is possible that this occurs in the judicial branch where even as women gain access to legal education and become appointed as lower court judges, they nonetheless struggle to gain appointment to the highest courts because those who select justices still look for stereotypically men's characteristics, or retain views about the unsuitability of women for the bench.

Numerous studies of the judiciary call into question the pipeline or eligibility pool theory. Women have been graduating from law school or judges' school in equal—if not, greater—numbers compared to men, but upon graduation they encounter systemic biases that affect their promotion through the ranks (e.g., Bacik, Costello, and Drew 2003 on Ireland; Barmes and Malleson 2011 on the United Kingdom; Bonelli 2015 on Brazil; Kalem 2020 on Turkey; Klibi 2016 on Tunisia; Masengu 2016 on South Africa; Roche 2003 on Venezuela; and Schultz and Shaw 2003). A particularly striking case of delayed inclusion is the United Kingdom, which only appointed its first woman law lord in 2004 (Kenney 2008; Malleson 2003). In Botswana, the percentage of women lawyers has been on the rise for many years, yet not a single woman has sat on the court of appeal (Bauer and Ellett 2016). Writing about the United States, Brenner and Knake (2011) note that women in the legal profession should be much better represented in positions of legal authority than pipeline theory would predict. They point to factors such as bias in media coverage, stereotyping, and "visibility bias," which is the tendency to overestimate the actual numbers of women and minorities.

Even if women are entering the legal and judicial professions, vertical segregation can keep women in lower-status positions. In some common law countries, such as Ireland, South Africa, and the United Kingdom, the legal profession is split between lower-status solicitors and higher-status barristers. Women are more likely to be solicitors who can rise up to be magistrates on lower courts, while men constitute the majority of barristers from which judicial appointments for higher courts are drawn (e.g., Andrews 2006; Cowan 2006; Malleson 2003). Vertical segregation in the legal and judicial fields can take other forms. In some civil law countries, such as France, women have come to make up the majority of judges on ordinary courts, but court presidents continue to be men (Boigeol 2013; Celis and Erzeel 2017).

Scholars of gender and the judiciary have enriched the discussion arguing that judicial pipelines are themselves socially constructed and gendered (Malleson 2006a; Sommerlad 2015; Thornton 2007), and in chapter 5 we consider reliance on unwritten "qualifications" as part of a complex set of informal institutions. From this viewpoint, the important question is not whether women constitute a large proportion of the eligible pool for judgeships. Instead, the imperative is to think more broadly about the pathways that can lead to appointment to the highest courts. Rather than reproducing the same sets of backgrounds and experiences, courts can benefit from robust sets of skills derived from alternative paths. At issue is the criterion by which selectors pick judges. Selectors in a number of countries state that they choose judges based on "merit," but merit is often code for upper-class men who have followed a particular career trajectory. The notion of merit as constructed by men elites narrows the field of candidates rather than including a diverse pool of contenders. In this sense, the exclusion of women need not be conscious, rather the uncritical valuation of characteristics men are more likely to possess, combined with the unexamined devaluation of more feminine traits, can produce glass ceilings at various levels of the judicial hierarchy reducing the number of women. This reliance on men's templates especially penalizes women and other individuals who take non-traditional careers into the judiciary or come with different backgrounds. As we show below in the case of South Africa, selectors can expand conventional ideas of who is "qualified" to serve on the highest court.

Interestingly, scholarship from North and South America looking at the more recent decades of the 1990s and 2000s provides some support for the pipeline theory. Arrington (2018) finds that in the 1970s and 1980s, the proportion of women lawyers on average significantly exceeded that of women on United States state supreme courts. However, starting in the mid-1990s, the average proportion of women on state supreme courts corresponds more closely with the average percentage of lawyers who are women. Arana Araya, Hughes, and Pérez-Liñán (2021) find that the more years women attend school, the higher women's representation on national high courts in Latin America. But, they do not find a significant relationship between the percentage of women lawyers and the percentage of women on high courts. As discussed in Part I, we find that the ratio of women completing tertiary education relative to men helps explain some gains (the first woman), but not others (the number of women after the first woman is appointed). However, women's tertiary educational attainment is a blunt measure of the eligible pool. By evaluating what traditional careers look like in each of the five countries, we are better able to judge the importance of pipelines.

4.2 The Rise of Women Lawyers and the First Women on High Courts

Whether an official requirement or an unwritten assumption, individuals who are appointed to the highest court in our five countries are typically law graduates and lawyers. In some of our cases, married women were formally banned or legally restricted from entering into law school, becoming lawyers, or even working in the public sector. The loosening of formal barriers and the passage of antidiscrimination legislation permitted women to join the legal profession and judiciary.

4.2.1 The First Women Lawyers: 1900s to 1969

In the United States, women had to fight for the right to enter law schools, take the Bar exam, and join Bar associations in the 1800s (Drachman 2001). In 1869, the first woman was admitted to a Bar, and in 1870, a woman served as a judge (justice of the peace). In 1928, Genevieve Rose Cline became the first woman judge on a federal court, and in 1932, Florence Allen became the first woman judge on a federal appeals court. But, as many legal historians, including Drachman, document, men elites and men-dominant institutions continued to discriminate against women in law school admissions, the legal profession, and the judiciary in the 20th century. If we take 1869 as a starting point, there was a gap of 112 years between the first woman lawyer and the first woman on the United States Supreme Court. The removal of formal restrictions by universities and Bar associations is important in getting women into the judiciary, but unblocking the opening of the pipeline is not enough. The path to the appointment of the first woman United States Supreme Court justice was a slow and long one.

In Canada and Ireland, there is also a long period between the emergence of the first women lawyers and the elevation of a woman to the Supreme Court. The first woman graduated from law school in the late 1800s in Canada, and the first woman was admitted to the Bar in 1895 (a lag of 87 years until the first woman on the Supreme Court) (Kay and Brockman 2000). In Ireland, the 1919 Act lifted official barriers against women entering British and Irish universities although women had been attending university prior to this (Bacik, Costello, and Drew 2003). The 1919 Act, however, also specified that women could hold public positions, including being a judge, as long as they remained unmarried. Once a woman married, she had to step down from her post. In 1973, the marriage ban was finally abandoned. Ireland had its first two women barristers in 1920. If we start with the first women barristers, there is a 74-year lag to the first woman Supreme Court justice in Ireland.

In 1923, South Africa passed the Women Legal Practitioners Act 7, which allowed White women to become advocates, attorneys, and other members of the legal profession. The first White woman advocate admitted to the Bar was Gladys Steyn. In 1969, Leonora van den Heever became South Africa's first woman judge and in 1991, the first woman to serve on the Supreme Court, 68 years after White women could become advocates. While Black men were advocates and attorneys in the early 1900s, and while there were no formal bans against Black women entering the Bar, it was not until the 1960s that South Africa had Black women lawyers. The first Black woman admitted as an advocate was Zainunnisa "Cissie" Gool, in 1962. In 1967, Desiree Finca and Navi Pillay were admitted as attorneys (Ngcukaitobi 2018).

In Colombia, upon graduation with the first doctorate in law in 1942, Rosa Rojas Castro sued the state to recognize the political right of women to hold public office. Yet 40 years elapsed between her appointment as the first woman justice in 1943 and the appointment of Fanny González Franco to the Supreme Court of Justice in 1983 and 58 years until Clara Inés Vargas Hernández was appointed to the Constitutional Court in 2001.

Allowing women to become lawyers is important for unblocking the judicial pipeline, but as the five cases show, the path from first woman lawyer to first woman justice on a high court was slow.

4.2.2 The Rise of Women in the Law: 1970s to 1990s

In the one to two decades prior to the appointment of the first woman, the percentage of women pursuing degrees in law or women in the legal profession doubled or even tripled. In the United States, women's enrollment in American Bar Association (ABA) approved law schools increased dramatically over the 1970s and 1980s. By prohibiting discrimination based on gender, the passage of Title IX of the Higher Education Act in 1972 pushed law schools to rapidly improve gender equality among the students they admitted, and the proportion of women among law school graduates has increased at a rapid rate (Martin and Jurik 2006).

In 1970, about 8.5 percent of law school students in the United States were women. By 1980, the number was approximately one-third (33.6 percent). In Canada, women comprised 15.5 percent of lawyers in 1981, three times the figure of 5.2 percent in 1971 (Kay and Brockman 2000). In Ireland, 12 out of 253 barristers were women (5 percent) in 1970, and by 1980, the number of women barristers jumped to 63 out of 429 (15 percent) (Bacik et al. 2003: 72–73). South Africa also witnessed substantial growth in the proportion of women obtaining undergraduate law degrees. In 1980, women comprised 22.4 percent of LLB students at the University of Witwatersrand. By 1989, that figure had doubled to 44.5 percent (Kahn 1989). In Colombia, women constituted 7.1 percent of lawyers in 1964 (Michelson 2013), a number that grew steadily, and by 1992, 39.2 percent of all lawyers were women (CEDAW Committee 1993). By 2010, the next year for which we have data for Colombia, 56 percent of lawyers were women (Michelson 2013). A 2017 newspaper article mentioned that more women than men were graduating from all the most prestigious law schools (Universidad la Sabana, el Rosario, Externado, la Javeriana, and los Andes) (El Espectador 2017). That women were obtaining an education in the law or entering the legal profession was undeniable in the five cases. Some observers thought it signaled the end of gender inequality!

By the 1980s, selectors could no longer use the excuse that women were not obtaining law degrees. At the most fundamental level, this suggests that women have been members of the eligible pool (lawyers) much longer than they have been judges, and yet they still struggled to enter the highest ranks of the judiciary. This suggests that the problem was not getting into the initial pool (graduating with a law degree), but somewhere on the steps between entering the initial pool and being on the short-list for a high court appointment.

4.3 The Typical Pipeline to High Courts in Five Countries

The usual paths to the high court vary across our cases. In Figure 4.1, we identify the most common path to appointment to the peak court based on the training of and previous positions held by high court justices in each of our countries. The figure shows the typical starting point in a legal career and then the positions that serve as steppingstones to the next steppingstone and finally to the highest court. We acknowledge and discuss exceptions to the general rule in the case studies that follow, but for the purposes of evaluating the pipeline theory on its own terms, we focus on the proportion of women in the usual feeder professions.

In Figure 4.1 we summarize, in a highly stylized way, the typical career path of a high court justice in each of the five countries. This stylized representation of the typical career path allows us to illustrate the different rungs on the career ladder as an individual moves toward appointment to the high court. That is not to say that this is the only route as both men and women may follow non-traditional paths (although in the United States Palmer (2001a) has shown women are more likely to do so). Additionally, a justice might skip steps or add rungs in their own career ladder. However, capturing the typical progression of judges allows us to assess the supply of women available for appointment at each stage. Evaluating the validity

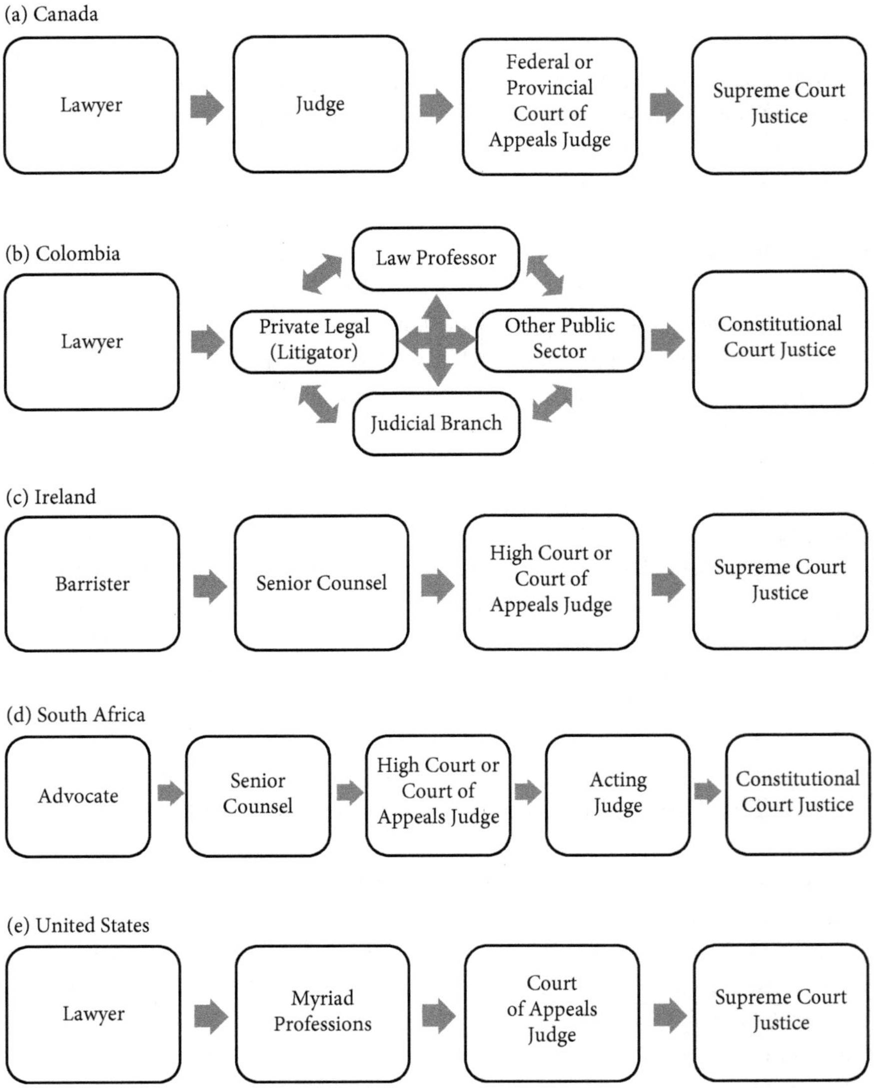

Figure 4.1 The Typical Pipeline

of pipeline explanations means assessing whether the bottleneck occurs as women try to enter the highest courts or if the supply is restricted earlier. However, we also recognize that this career progression does not happen overnight but instead takes place over the span of years.

For each case study, we examine whether the initial appointment of women to high courts quickly or slowly follows the loosening of legal restrictions on women serving as judges and present details on the eligibility pool around the selection of the first woman high court justice. This helps us look more closely at the patterns (or lack thereof) that we found in chapter 3.

Second, we consider the extent to which the proportion of women at each major rung parallels that of the high court. We compare the percentages of women at various rungs on the career ladder with the composition of women on the highest court. Where possible, we take into account lags in time. The pipeline theory suggests that women's appointments to high courts should follow some delay in gains at lower rungs on the career ladder. In the case studies, we also assess whether there is an obvious point where the pipeline leaks or women are stopped from advancing.

To assess the validity of our statistical findings from Part I, we gathered the best quality data on the gender breakdown of the pipeline professions for each country. The availability of historical information and the way each country measures gender equality in the pipeline professions, however, varies. This means that we present information on slightly different years and for slightly different educational and career categories across the case studies.

4.4 The Pipeline to the Supreme Court of the United States

The United States is a case where the gender composition of the peak bench after the appointment of the first woman has been in the range of what one would expect based on the pipeline theory.

Although there are no formal educational or professional requirements for United States Supreme Court justices, there have been typical career paths. The modal career path for justices to the Supreme Court is displayed in Figure 4.1. The pipeline to service on the United States Supreme Court, as documented by Epstein, Segal, Spaeth, and Walker (2015), has significantly changed over time. We focus on the period from the 1970s to 2017.

The first rung on the career ladder is obtaining a legal education and becoming a lawyer. Every justice appointed to the Supreme Court between 1970 and 2017 received a law degree and was admitted to the bar.

A typical step up on the ladder is service on one of the United States courts of appeals (also known as the federal courts of appeals). Prior to the 1970s, presidents appointed individuals from the legislature, executive cabinet, or private practice. In the 1980s, 1990s, and 2000s, most of the nominees were justices on one of the courts of appeals. Of the 16 justices appointed between 1970 and 2017, 12 had served on a court of appeals. The elevation of judges from the courts of appeal is one that is not always observed, and the exceptions include two women. Prior to serving on the United States Supreme Court, Justice Sandra Day O'Connor had been a legislator in the state of Arizona, and when President Reagan picked her, she was a judge on the Arizona Court of Appeals. Elena

Kagan, one of President Obama's nominees, had no prior judicial service. Before her appointment, she served as President Obama's Solicitor General. Nevertheless, in 2017, eight of the nine justices of the United States Supreme Court previously sat on one of the federal appellate courts, suggesting that serving on these courts is the most promising career path to the Supreme Court. The path from being a lawyer to judging on the federal appellate courts, however, is a black box. Between obtaining a law degree and being appointed to a federal appellate court, there are a myriad of career trajectories.

Working our way through the typical pipeline, we compare the proportion of women law students and proportion of women on the Supreme Court, taking into consideration a lag in time. Among the nominees successfully appointed to the Supreme Court between 1970 and 2017, the average number of years between the last year of law school and becoming a Supreme Court justice is 27.9 (Epstein et al. 2019). Therefore, one way to assess the pipeline theory is to compare the proportion of women in law school in 1989 with the proportion of women on the Supreme Court in 2017.

As shown in Figure 4.2, in 1989–1990, women constituted 43 percent of total enrollment in law school (American Bar Association 2015). The 42.7 percentage for 1989–1990 is not substantially higher than the 33.3 percent of judges on the Supreme Court who are women in 2017. The proportion of women associates in private practice in 2001, 41.9 percent, is also consistent with women's representation on the Supreme Court in 2017 (American Bar Association 2001).

Next, we consider whether the proportion of women on federal appellate courts, the most likely steppingstone to the highest court, parallels that of the

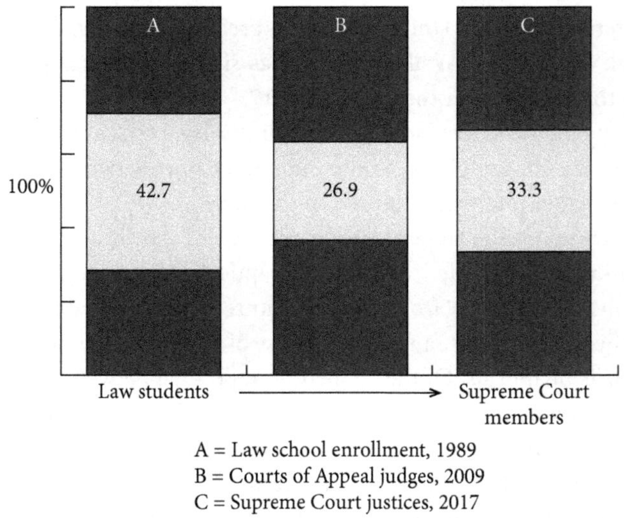

Figure 4.2 United States: Women's Representation in the Pipeline, %

Supreme Court, taking into account a time lag. Some judges sat on the appellate court for one or two years before being nominated to the highest court (David Souter, Clarence Thomas and John Roberts). Others served for 10 or more years on an appellate court (Harry Blackmun, Anthony Kennedy, Ruth Bader Ginsburg, Stephen Breyer, Samuel Alito, Sonia Sotomayor). The average years of service on appellate courts is 8.2. Working backward from 2017, we should examine the percentage of women on appellate courts in 2009. Women constituted 26.9 percent of judges on federal courts of appeal in 2009 (American Bar Association 2009). The representation of women on federal courts of appeal increased from 19.8 percent in 1999 and 9.6 percent in 1985 (Hurwitz and Lanier 2001). The 2009 figure, however, is slightly lower than the one-third proportion of women on the Supreme Court.

In sum, in the United States, women's representation on feeder courts is not markedly lower than the eligible pool of practicing attorneys. There is a noticeable gendered drop off between working in private practice and becoming a judge on an appellate court. In this way, the pipeline theory partially holds for the United States Supreme Court. Looking at the percentages of women in law school and in private practice, and taking into account a time lag, the proportion of women on the highest court does not meet expectations based on looking at this section of the pipeline. If we consider the feeder profession to be judgeship on an appellate court, then the representation of women on the Supreme Court meets the expectations of the pipeline theory.

Given the relevance of the pipeline in the United States, we can look to the future. It is important to note that the career path has become narrower in that service on a district court has become a clearer steppingstone. If this is the case, the proportion of women on the district courts may be a good indicator of the gender composition of the appellate courts and the supreme court in the next years to come. On United States District Courts in 2017, women made up about 33 percent of the sitting judges. In the same year, on the United States Courts of Appeal, 60 of the 167 sitting judges were women (35.9 percent) (Royzman and Hassett 2018). If selectors pick nominees for the Supreme Court from the appellate courts and if the pipeline theory holds, then the proportion of women on the Supreme Court will likely hold at the one-third level in the near future.

4.5 The Pipeline to the Supreme Court of Canada

Formally, the qualifications for Supreme Court judges in Canada are that they must have at least 10 years of experience since being called to the bar. The law also requires that three judges on the Supreme Court come from Quebec. Beyond the formal requirements, typical educational and professional experiences can be identified.

In Figure 4.1, we simplify and depict the modal career path to the Supreme Court of Canada. At the starting point of the pipeline is the minimum qualification: being a lawyer. In Canada, judges are drawn from the ranks of lawyers and do not receive any specialized training. The next step on the typical career ladder is judicial service in the provinces in superior courts (McCormick and Greene 1990). At this rung, lower court judges are drawn from among the ranks of law practitioners, especially those in private practice.

Moving up the ladder, the most common steppingstone before advancement to the Supreme Court of Canada is service on the highest courts at the provincial level. In most provinces, the Court of Appeals is the top court. Appointments to the provincial courts of appeal are made by the executive branch of the federal government, in a similar fashion to the Canadian Supreme Court appointment process. Based on the backgrounds of current and former justices published on the Supreme Court of Canada website, among the 37 justices appointed to the Supreme Court of Canada since 1970, 28 had previously been appointed to a provincial or territorial court of appeal. A less common route to the Supreme Court is by way of the Federal Court of Appeals, with three of the 37 appointees since 1970 taking this route. Among the few not stepping from the courts of appeal, previous professional positions include past leaders of the Canadian Bar Association, legal counsel to Prime Ministers, law professors, and lawyers in private practice.

The pipeline theory leads us to expect that as more women graduate from law school and become lawyers, more women will be drawn into the ranks of lower court justice. From there, the growing pool of women judges should provide more potential nominees to provincial supreme courts and courts of appeal, and for federal courts. Finally, as the pipeline of women on provincial and federal courts grows stronger, women will be appointed to the Supreme Court. We can expect a lag of about a decade between rungs on the ladder as women gain experience. McCormick and Greene's (1990) study of Canadian judges reveals the average age of federally appointed judges to be 60 years old. Taken together, we expect a growing proportion of women in the legal profession in the 1970s and 1980s. From there, we expect women's appointments to lower courts to grow in the early 1990s, and their appointments to the higher courts of appeal to rise by about 2000, leading up to a culmination of 44.4 percent by the end of our time frame.

The percentages defy common assumptions about the pipeline. In 1970, women made up only 5 percent of Canada's lawyers (Kay and Brockman 2000). Census surveys of Canadians show that by 1991, women made up about 14 percent of judges nationally. More specifically, in 1990 women comprised 7.5 percent of judges on Canadian Superior Courts (McCormick and Greene 1990).[1] By contrast, in 1991 women comprised 33.3 percent of the Supreme Court—more

[1] Data on women's presence on lower court benches are not widely available. However, anecdotal evidence supports these figures from the Census. Canada's Royal Commission on the Status of Women reported that in 1969 there were 14 women judges (out of 889 total) across Canada, and only one was a member of a superior court.

than double the percentage of lower courts. By the year 2000, women made up 13 percent of the Federal Court of Appeals and 19 percent of the Quebec and Ontario Courts of Appeal (the two courts for which lists of former judges are posted on court websites over time). From 2000 to 2017, the average percentage of women on the Canadian Supreme Court was 44.4.

The percentage of women lawyers starts off as the arena with the greatest share of women, growing rapidly from 5 percent in 1970 to 15 percent by 1980 and nearly 30 percent by 1990. Strikingly, in 1990, the percentage of women on the Supreme Court rises above the percentage of women lawyers. For several years, women's share of Supreme Court seats is higher than the percentage of women lawyers. The pipeline theory is not equipped to explain why the eligible pool grows at a slower pace than women's appointments at the top of the ladder.

Women's presence among the mid-level career positions grows slowly as well, trailing women's advances on the Canadian Supreme Court. The Quebec, Ontario, and Federal Courts of Appeal are common springboards to the Supreme Court bench. Women's share of the Federal Court of Appeals rose from 0 in the 1970s and 1980s to nearly 7 percent in 1990 and only 13 percent by the early 2000s. In similar fashion, the Ontario and Quebec Courts of Appeal saw a slow rise to 5–10 percent women in 1990, and 23 percent and 15 percent respectively in 2000, with faster growth toward parity in the 2000s.

Importantly, women's appointments to the Supreme Court of Canada have outpaced the theoretical pipeline of lower court appointments until 2010, when the Ontario Court of Appeals climbed to gender equality. The jump past 30 percent women for the Supreme Court occurred around 1990, with the courts of appeal not passing 30 percent until after 2005.

In Figure 4.3, we show the percentage of women on the Supreme Court in 2017 as compared to the gender composition of the pipeline professions, using lags in time. Women's share of lawyers in 1990 and federal appellate judges in 2010 matches fairly closely to that of the Supreme Court. In summary, women's participation on the highest court led the way, with women's share of the eligible pool following. Rather than a pipeline, Canada's pathway for women on the Supreme Court has been led from the apex, potentially with women at the highest levels serving as role models.

4.6 The Pipeline to the Supreme Court of Ireland

In Ireland, there is a set of qualifications for appointment to the Supreme Court, but it allows for a great deal of leeway. The following persons are qualified for appointment to the Supreme Court: 1) the President of the Court of Appeal, 2) an ordinary Judge of the Court of Appeal, 3) the President of the High Court, 4) an ordinary judge of the High Court, 5) a Judge of the Circuit Court who has served

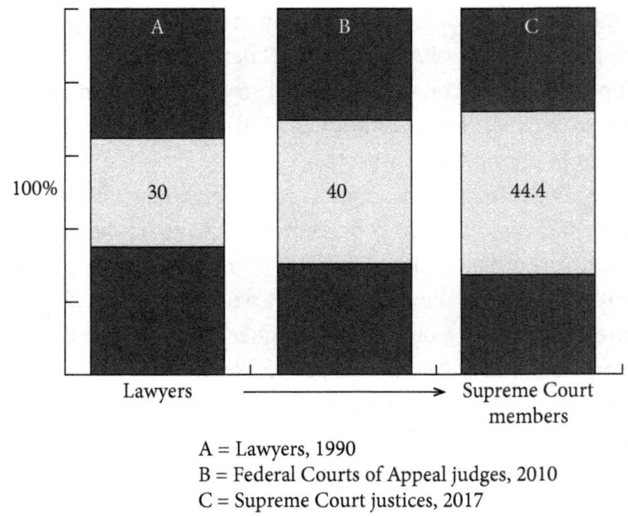

Figure 4.3 Canada: Women's Representation in the Pipeline, %

in that court for no less than two years, 6) a person who, at any time during the two-year period immediately before the appointment, has served as a Judge or Advocate General of the European Court of Justice, a Judge of the European Court of Human Rights, a Judge of the International Court of Justice, a Judge of the International Criminal Court, a Judge of an international tribunal, or a barrister or solicitor of not less than twelve years standing who has practiced for a continuous period of not less than two years before such appointment (Supreme Court of Ireland 2017). After a 2002 reform, barristers or solicitors of 12 or more years met the requirements to become a justice (Courts and Court Officers Act 2002).

Understanding the pool of eligible candidates begins with the percentage of women obtaining legal education, the percentage of women in the legal profession, and the percentage of women who have served in the feeder courts. The modal career path is presented in Figure 4.1. Becoming a barrister begins the pipeline. Ireland is one of the common law countries that divides its legal profession into solicitors and barristers. The career training for both solicitors and barristers typically starts on the same course, with an undergraduate degree in law. After undergraduate training, solicitors and barristers take separate educational and training programs. Barristers argue cases and represent clients in the courts, whereas solicitors do the bulk of work drafting documents and interacting with clients. Barristers are required by law to be independent, and thus, they cannot develop partnerships and must act as solo practitioners. This is to avoid any conflicts and to keep the profession and the individual barristers independent. However, since so much of the work of barristers is done on behalf of the state, it was common for barristers to get involved in partisan campaigns and party politics to help secure future work (McAuley 2012). Research suggests that this is less of a concern in later years (Carroll 2005). Solicitors, on the other hand, often develop partnerships or work for larger firms.

One significant implication of this split in the legal profession is that, according to numerous interviewees, having to work solo puts a burden on women barristers who may want to have children, but have fewer options for taking leave time. Solicitors can more easily take advantage of family leave policies (if they are in place), or at least will not face the same hurdles as women barristers when they reenter the workforce. Women's numbers among solicitors have long surpassed the number of women barristers, and this is an important aspect of the pipeline to consider.

Prior to reforms in 1995, all appointees to the High Court and the Supreme Court had to be practicing barristers. In 1995, important reforms included the creation of the Judicial Appointments Advisory Board (JAAB) and eliminating the requirement that all judges must be practicing barristers. Since then, appointees to the circuit courts can be solicitors, and they can be promoted from there to higher courts. In reality, however, according to interviewees, there still exists a strong bias against solicitors. Looking at the biographies of the justices of Ireland's Supreme Court in 2012, McAuley (2012) found that all were barristers. Moreover, the vast majority of judges on the Supreme Court of Ireland in 2012 were senior barristers (also known as senior counsel or silks). Membership in the exclusive club of senior barristers is another steppingstone to the Supreme Court.

From being a senior counsel, the next step to the Supreme Court is serving as a judge on an intermediate court. The vast majority of the justices on the Irish Supreme Court are elevated from the High Court or the Court of Appeal. McAuley (2012) found that Supreme Court justices in 2012 became senior barristers an average of 14 years after admission to the Bar, and from admittance to the Bar waited 27 years for their first judicial appointment. So, an optimistic time lag would be approximately 27 years from the time of entering the Bar to joining the highest court.

Figure 4.4 displays the best data we were able to obtain on women at various stages of the judicial pipeline in Ireland, with appropriate lags in time. We first compare the proportion of women in undergraduate law programs with the proportion of women on the Supreme Court, taking into account an expected interval of 27 years. There has been a dramatic increase in women students. In 1975, approximately 31 percent of undergraduate enrollees in law were women. As early as 1990–1991, women made up more than a majority (53 percent), and by 2001–2002, two-thirds of the students (66 percent) were women (Bacik, Costello, and Drew 2003). There are proportionally more women pursuing undergraduate degrees in law in 1990 than there are women on the Supreme Court in 2017.

Next on the ladder is becoming a barrister. In 1990, the percentage of women admitted to the Bar was 28 percent (Fair Trade Commission 1990). There is a drop

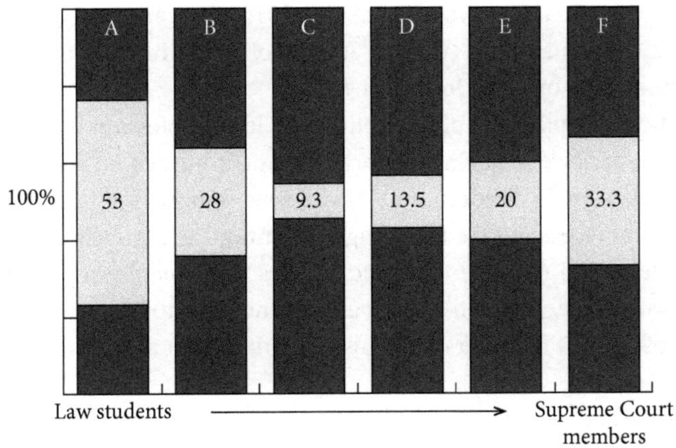

A = Undergraduate law enrollment, 1990
B = Admitted to Bar, 1990
C = Senior counsel, 2002
D = High Court judges, 2010
E = Court of Appeal judges, 2014
F = Supreme Court justices, 2017

Figure 4.4 Ireland: Women's Representation in the Pipeline, %

off in the percentage of women pursuing undergraduate degrees in law and becoming barristers. This decline from 53 percent to 28 percent will not be surprising to researchers of the legal profession of Ireland given the barriers women face in entering the Bar. If one's focus in the judicial pipeline is on women joining the Bar, the percentages of women at this rung of the career ladder and the top rung are commensurate.

Another way of exploring the judicial pipeline in Ireland is to compare the proportion of women that were senior counsel with that of the Supreme Court. In 2002, 9.3 percent of senior counsel were women (Bacik, Costello, and Drew 2003: 72). Research for the Irish parliament reports a lower figure of 5 percent women at the rank of senior counsel in 2002 (Ní Liatháin 2019). For those women who are able to become barristers, rising to the high rank of senior counsel is difficult. The rung of senior counsels has been slower to include women than have universities and the Supreme Court. The percentage of women on the Supreme Court of Ireland is higher than what one would expect based on the eligible pool of women senior counsel.

Further, we compare the proportion of women on the High Court and Court of Appeal and women's representation on the Supreme Court. In 2010, women comprised 13.5 percent of High Court judges. In its first year of operation, in 2014, two of the 10 judges on the Court of Appeal were women (20 percent). Both figures are slightly but not substantially lower than the 33.3 percent of women judges on the Supreme Court in 2017. The representation of women on the highest court is commensurate with what one would expect looking at the Court of Appeal.

It is clear that the pipeline offers opportunity for women's appointments to the Supreme Court. Women have been obtaining legal educations in large numbers for the last four decades, and the statistics show that women were a majority of the undergraduate students in law (53 percent) in the early 1990s. Yet, moving through the pipeline, the number of women barristers and senior counsel relative to men narrows. In recent years, while men still comprise a majority of the barristers, women are closely behind at about 40 percent of the profession (Liathain 2019).

4.7 The Pipeline to the Constitutional Court of South Africa

The South African case is one in which the proportion of women on the highest court has exceeded what one would expect based on pipeline theory alone. Figure 4.1 sketches the typical men-oriented career trajectory from being a law graduate to serving as a Constitutional Court justice.

While South Africa's Constitution does not specify minimum qualifications in terms of education or work experience to be a Constitutional Court justice, in practice, before getting on the first rung of the judicial ladder, individuals earn a degree related to the law.[2] All individuals appointed to the Constitutional Court between 1994 and 2017 received a Bachelor of Laws or equivalent (LLB, BJuris, or BProc). The next typical rung in the career ladder is being an advocate. Similar to Ireland, South Africa's legal profession has a vertical separation between attorneys and advocates. (In Ireland, the terms are solicitors and barristers.) Advocates are able to argue cases in front of the high courts, whereas attorneys cannot appear in high courts. There is also a hierarchy within the advocate profession, between junior counsel and senior counsel. To become a senior counsel, advocates must have 10 or more years of experience. From the 1970s to the 1980s, judges on South Africa's then highest court, the appellate division of the Supreme Court, were primarily drawn from the pool of senior counsels (Corder 2011). After the filling of the inaugural bench, 12 of the 15 justices appointed to the Constitutional Court between 1995 and 2017 were advocates, and of those, seven were senior counsel.

After becoming an advocate, the next step on the typical career path to the Constitutional Court is serving as a judge on a lower court. Of the 15 justices appointed to the Constitutional Court between 1995 and 2017, 14 had previously sat on a provincial appellate court (called High Courts), Labour Court, or Land

[2] A 2001 amendment to South Africa's Constitution specifies that four or more justices on the Constitutional Court must have been judges at the time of their appointment.

Court. The exception is Zak Yacoob, a noted architect of the South African Constitution. Nine justices had served on upper tier courts such as Supreme Court of Appeal, Labour Court of Appeal, or Land Court of Appeal.

Previous studies and interviewees state that there is an additional steppingstone to the highest court: serving as an acting judge on the Constitutional Court (e.g., Masengu 2016). The president of the country selects acting judges to the Constitutional Court upon the recommendation of the Minister of Justice and Chief Justice. Opportunities to be an acting judge arise between the time that a justice retires and he or she is replaced, or if a sitting justice takes a temporary leave. For instance, Nonkosi Zoliswa Mhlantla served four terms as an acting judge on the Constitutional Court before she was appointed as a "permanent" justice on the court. Six of the 15 justices appointed to the Constitutional Court after 1994 served on that court in an acting capacity.

We compare the proportion of women in the pipeline professions and the percentage of women on the Constitutional Court, taking into consideration a time lag. According to our calculations, the average time between graduating with a degree in law for the post-1994 judges and appointment to the Constitutional Court is 26.6 years.

Starting with the bottom rung of the ladder, we look at the proportion of women lawyers in South Africa using the available data. According to the 1980 South African census, 5.5 percent of lawyers were women (Statistics South Africa 1980).[3] The pipeline theory would predict the percentage of women on the Constitutional Court in 2006 to be about five percent. To smooth over yearly fluctuations, we examine the gender composition of the court averaged for the years 2005 to 2009. In this period, 24.5 percent of the court were women, higher than one would expect from the pipeline hypothesis.

Given the history of systematic discrimination based on the intersection of gender and race in South Africa, it is important to examine whether pipelines explain patterns for Black women. In 1980, 27 of 7,721 lawyers were Black women, or less than 0.4 percent, although these numbers should be taken with a large grain of salt (Statistics South Africa 1980).[4] In 2005–2009, 18.2 percent of the justices on the Constitutional Court were Black women. This suggests that factors other than the racial and gender composition of lawyers explain the racial and gender composition of the highest bench.

Figure 4.5 shows the proportion of women in the pipeline professions with lags in time, ending with the proportion of women on the Constitutional Court in

[3] The occupation in 1980 statistic was generated using the command, tab SEX if OCCUP80==40. According to the census, there were 7,721 lawyers. There were 1,281 judges: 4.5% women.

[4] In the 1980 census, race is broken down into several dozen categories. We divide them into White, Coloured and Asian, and Black (Black=1 if RACE>=9 & RACE<=20). The statistic for Black women lawyers was generated using the command, tab SEX Black if OCCUP80==40.

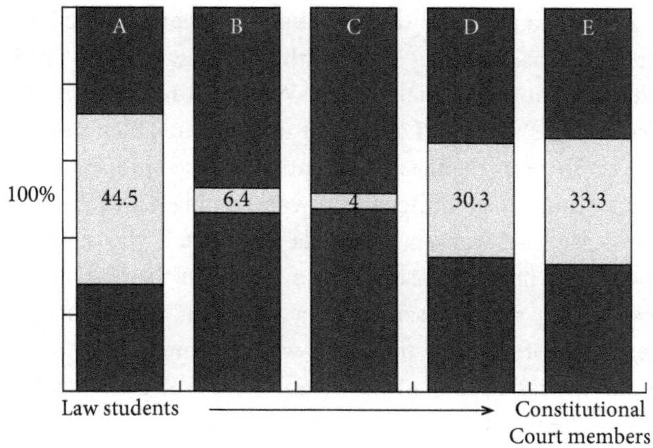

A = LLB students, Univ. of the Witwatersrand, 1989
B = Practising advocates, 1990
C = Senior counsel, 2004
D = Provincial and other High Court judges, 2013
E = Constitutional Court justices, 2017

Figure 4.5 South Africa: Women's Representation in the Pipeline, %

2017. In 1989, women constituted 44.5 percent of LLB students at the prestigious University of the Witwatersrand (Kahn 1989). There is a decrease in the representation of women law students and women becoming advocates. In 1990, women made up 6.4 percent of practicing advocates (Blum 1990). It takes 10 years or more for advocates to rise up to the level of senior counsel. Drawing on the available data, 4 percent of senior counsel in 2005 were women (Institute for Democratic Alternatives in South Africa 2005). For broadly Black women (African, Coloured, and Indian), their inclusion in pool of advocates is low. In 2004, Black women were 6.2 percent of advocates, and in 2009, they made up only 1.2 percent of senior counsel (Institute for Democratic Alternatives in South Africa 2005; Masengu 2016: 5). The pipeline from being a law student to a high-level advocate takes the shape of a funnel, narrowing at each level.

Strikingly, the share of women on provincial high courts and other intermediate courts is noticeably higher than the share of women senior counsel. In 2013, for instance, 30.3 percent of High Court judges were women (62 of 204) (Albertyn 2014: 284). (High Courts in the context of South Africa generally exclude the Supreme Court of Appeal and Constitutional Court.) This percentage parallels that of women's presence on the Constitutional Court four years later, in 2017 (33.3 percent). At the end of 2017, three of the nine fully appointed justices were women.

Behind these numbers is an important story about the social and gendered construction of pipelines. Many of South Africa's women Constitutional Court judges did not come to the court through the men-oriented pipeline, but through alternative career paths. In filling seats on the inaugural bench, President Nelson Mandela did not want to install an all-White all-men court. Composing a White men court after the fall of apartheid was unthinkable to those who fought for freedom. The previous regime almost entirely denied judgeship to Black South Africans and to women. Given the lack of women judges and the commitment to appointing at least one woman, Mandela broadened the field of candidates to include those who had never served as a judge. Of the first 11 justices on the Constitutional Court, six had served as a judge on a provincial court or on the Supreme Court of Appeal; those six were all men. The two women who were appointed, Justices Yvonne Mokgoro and Kate O'Regan, were law professors. (Since serving on the bench, Mokgoro and O'Regan have been lauded by the legal profession and peers for their contributions to constitutional jurisprudence.)

After the installation of the Constitutional Court, however, in the latter half of the 1990s and in the 2000s, appointers returned to picking judges from the typical pipeline professions, selecting from among those who had served as judges. It was during this period that the appointment of women to the Constitutional Court stagnated. Starting in 2009, with the selection of Justice Sisi Khampepe, selectors became more willing to appoint individuals who were not previously advocates. As mentioned above, the percentage of women advocates and senior counsel, while growing, has been low. Khampepe, along with women Justices Mhlantla and Leona Theron and man Justice Ray Zondo, came from the attorney's profession where there is greater gender and racial diversity.

In sum, the proportion of women, including Black women, on the Constitutional Court exceeds expectations based on the pipeline theory when considering the pool of advocates and senior counsel. In the next chapters, we trace how and why women came to join the highest court in South Africa, highlighting the role of changing gender norms in governance and pressure by women's organizations to improve gender diversity in the judiciary.

4.8 The Pipeline to the Constitutional Court of Colombia

At the minimum, one must have been a lawyer to join the Constitutional Court. Nominees also need to have at least 10 years of experience practicing law either in the judicial branch, in a ministry, as a lawyer, or as a university law professor. As Corporación Sisma Mujer (2007: 8) notes, these requirements should not block women because there are many women in law, and even if there are not as many women with experience in the judicial branch, coming from a judicial career is not required. If the formal requirements do not stop women are there other points in the pipeline that present a problem for gender inclusion?

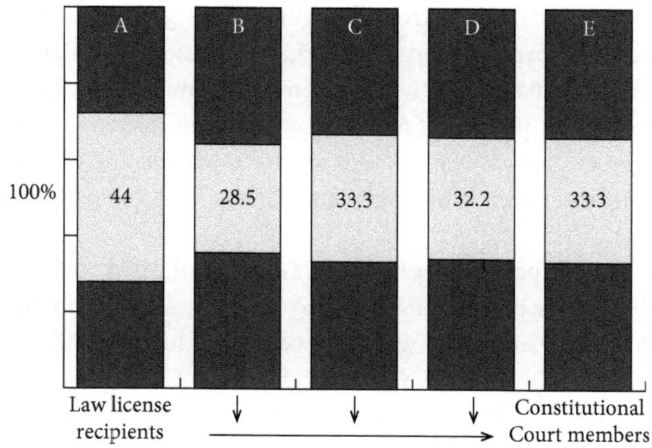

A = New law license recipients, 1987
B = Higher district court judges, 1996
C = Magistrados auxilares, 1996
D = High-level officials in the executive branch, 2003
E = Constitutional Court magistrates, 2017

Figure 4.6 Colombia: Women's Representation in the Pipeline, %

Recall that the Constitutional Court in Colombia was created with the 1991 constitution. Based on our cross-national findings (chapter 2) we would have expected women to have been included from its inception. Yet, the first woman was not appointed until 2001, and it was not until the late 2010s that the proportion of women on the Constitutional Court met expectations based on the supply of women in the pipeline professions and was in line with the 30 percent administrative quota. Figure 4.6 presents common career milestones on the route from being a lawyer to sitting on the Constitutional Court.

It is important to acknowledge that there is no single career path to the Colombian Constitutional Court. For instance, in a study of all 82 individuals (on 27 lists) nominated for the Constitutional Court from 1992 through 2009, Montoya (2013) found that almost all those nominated had careers in at least two of four following sectors: judicial branch, public sector, private sector, or academia. A list of three individuals (who we refer to as nominated) is sent to the Senate. Senators cast votes for one individual; the individual obtaining a plurality is elected to the court. Among our cases, Colombia is unique in that we actually observe a large number of high court nominees who do not become judges. More than 51 percent of those elected to the court (and 40.4 percent of those not elected) had experience in three of the four areas. For this reason, our pipeline analysis looks at some of the most common career elements but admittedly excludes others.

If the average age at the time of nomination is approximately 51 years (Montoya 2013: 71) and we are interested in the composition of the court in 2017, then it would be appropriate to look at women entering the pipeline approximately 25 years prior (around 1992) as they graduate law school.[5] We know that women's participation in the legal profession in Colombia has been increasing. In the 1970s women held 11 percent of law licenses, but by the early 1990s women held 34 percent of all law licenses in the country. Additionally, in 1987, 44 percent of new law licenses were issued to women and after 2014 women became a majority of new licenses recipients (García Villegas and Ceballos Bedoya 2019: 103–104).

Moving to the next part of the pipeline, we examine the percentage of women in the judicial branch as judges roughly 10 to 20 years after graduation (between 1997 and 2007). In 1996 women were 28.5 percent of higher district court judges and 28.9 percent of administrative court judges (CEDAW Committee 1997a: 65). Data from 2007 indicate that women constituted a majority of family court judges (56 percent), and there was near gender parity on Civil, Criminal, Courts of First Instance (Family, and Juveniles), Labor Courts (43 percent), and Courts of First Instance (42 percent). But, women constitute only 20 percent of the judges on Civil Agrarian courts and 30 percent on Specialized Criminal Tribunals (Corporación Sisma Mujer 2007: 5–6). Moreover, between 2011 and 2013 the average percentage of women judges on the country's 18 district courts (a level below high courts) ranged from a low of 33.5 percent in Villavicencio to a high of 59.5 percent in Bucaramanga y San Gil (Correa Henao 2013). This parity is important because one of our interviewees described the dominant path for judges as coming from the judicial branch. Multiple judges—men and women—also described their personal trajectory as including work as a municipal judge and advancing through to the department (state) courts.

Another common aspect of background—again for men and women justices—was that they had previous served as *magistrados auxiliares* in the high courts, a finding confirmed by Montoya (2013).[6] In 1996, women were six of the 18 *magistrados auxiliares* in the Constitutional Court (33 percent) (CEDAW Committee 1997a: 65). According to an interview with one women *magistrada auxiliar*, the relatively high numbers of women at this stage in the pipeline are

[5] In Colombia, one can practice as a lawyer providing legal services, in a university or private consultation with only an undergraduate degree. However, to represent clients before a judicial body or to hold a public post as a lawyer necessitates a professional license (*tarjeta professional, TP)* from the National Registry of Lawyers. Prior to 2018 one simply needed to fill out a form and pay a small fee to obtain a *tarjeta professional.* While not all law graduates apply for a *tarjeta,* because having one is a requirement to litigate or serve as a judge this constitutes a good measure of the eligible pool (García Villegas and Ceballos Bedoya 2019: 101–104).

[6] Cepeda Espinosa and Landau (2017: 15) translate *magistrado/a auxiliar* as law clerk and describe them as: "highly paid and generally very experienced; many of them are also professors at top universities in Bogotá. Clerks often stay at the Court for a number of years; moreover, it is fairly common for incoming justices to maintain the law clerks of their predecessors, or otherwise to draw on clerks who have had previous experience on the Court." However, one *magistrado auxiliar* interviewed resisted translating the title as law clerk explaining that they had considerable autonomy and seniority and that beside the magistrate they were the most senior staff in the office.

consistent with fewer barriers to appointment as assistant magistrates, but making the jump to the next level seems accompanied by more hurdles. Another interviewee, a man assistant magistrate, even recognized that a glass ceiling might exist remarking that he knew many good women assistant magistrates with longstanding service who had not advanced.

However, interviews with justices and *magistrados auxiliares* also suggest that while an assistant magistrate might be named an acting justice (*encargado*), it was highly unlikely they would be nominated. Indeed, men and women said it was necessary to leave and do something to distinguish one's self. This presents problems for identifying the supply of women as the other careers involve everything from university professorships, to appointed government positions, to private sector litigation, or some combination (Montoya 2013).

The necessity of possessing multiple qualifications is best illustrated by comparing the backgrounds of the three judges on the list nominated in October 2015: Alejandro Linares, Magdalena Correa Henao, and Catalina Botero. Magdalena Correa was a lawyer and doctor of law (PhD) with expertise in economic constitutional law. She had served as a *magistrada auxiliar* in the Constitutional Court and various public sector posts. At the time of her appointment she was director of the department of constitutional law at the Universidad Externado de Colombia. Catalina Botero was also a professor of constitutional law at the Universidad Externado. She had previously served as an adjunct judge on the Constitutional Court and worked as a legal advisor for UNESCO and the Electoral Tribunal for Judicial Power in Mexico. Alejandro Linares (the one ultimately elected) was a doctoral candidate in law at the Universidad Externado with a legal degree and specialization in finance from Universidad de Los Andes. He had been legal vice president for Ecopetrol (the state-owned oil company), worked in the office of the presidency of the republic, been vice-minister for agriculture in 1992 and minister plenipotentiary in the Colombian Embassy in France, and worked in the ministry of finance and public credit and the national department of planning (El Tiempo 2015).

Because of the challenge in identifying the pool in other areas, we focus on one highly visible area—public posts—as the next step in the pipeline. In 2000, Colombia adopted Act 581 of 2000 which established a 30 percent gender quota for discretionary appointments in higher-level decision-making posts (Jaramillo 2000). In 2003, women occupied 32.2 percent of high-level posts (managerial, executive, and advisory positions) and 37.8 percent of middle-level (professional and technical positions) in the executive branch (CEDAW Committee 2005a: 45).

In 2017, one-third (three out of nine justices) of the Constitutional Court were women. However, it is worth noting that this surge in including women was very recent. In 2013, there was just one woman magistrate on the court. The pipeline is full in Colombia, suggesting that there is an ample number of qualified women, and it raises questions about whether pipeline explanations are sufficient.

4.9 Conclusion

The efficacy of the pipeline argument varies substantially across these five countries. In different and complex ways, our case studies call into question the assumption that as more members of underrepresented groups join the legal profession, the bench will naturally diversify over time. There is a great deal of variation in the supply of eligible women as defined in the most traditional sense, from a low in South Africa to a high in Ireland. This variation does not provide much leverage in explaining women's presence on high courts. In some cases, we find that women are making great strides along the typical career path, but are still not being nominated to the highest bench.

In some regards, Ireland fits with the pipeline theory. The filters along the pipeline begin early though, with women being more likely to become solicitors than barristers, with the latter being the bouncier springboard to higher courts. Similarly, in Ireland the percentage of women among senior counsel has been low, relative to men's share. The United States case lends some support to the pipeline theory, displaying some of its basic contours. Even with a narrow vision of who is eligible, the number of women on lower courts in the United States provides a rich pool. At the same time, there is a drop off in women's share from working in private practice to being appointed to a federal court of appeal.

In Colombia, the pipeline is healthy in the sense that women enter the legal profession and populate the lower ranks of the judiciary in reasonable numbers. Women, however, have traditionally struggled to make significant inroads at the highest levels. In Colombia, there are many qualified women, but not many are selected. The insular and political nature of the process, especially for the Constitutional Court, may contribute to leaks (or kinks) in an otherwise full pipeline.

In a different way, the Canadian and South African cases illuminate the limitations of focusing on pipelines alone. Women's appointments to the Canadian Supreme Court outpaced the theoretical pipeline of lower court appointments for several years, until women comprised larger proportions of the eligible pool in more recent years. Similarly, in South Africa, the appointment of Black women to the Constitutional Court outpaced the pipeline of Black women advocates. The first women South African Constitutional Court judges did not come to the court through the typical pathway. Selectors in democratic South Africa shed the apartheid-era tradition of appointing lower court judges to join the highest court, expanding the idea of who can serve to include law professors.

Importantly, the highest courts in our case studies have nine to 11 seats. Not everyone can reasonably aspire to be a judge on the supreme or constitutional court, as being picked is like getting hit by lightning. Most judges do not get selected for high courts. Therefore, having a certain percentage of women in the pipeline is not necessary, as exemplified by Canada and South Africa. Nor is having a strong eligible pool sufficient for women's appointment to the high courts, as shown by the Colombian case.

If we consider the pipeline analogy in all five countries, today there is a rich eligible pool of women with the minimum qualifications. Women have been and are obtaining legal educations. Women are holding positions as judges on the lower courts. Where women made early gains, the necessary ingredient was for a selector to remove the filter and act as a promoter. Consequently, our next step is to investigate whether certain formal and informal selection rules encourage the appointment of women to the top bench.

5

How Institutions Influence the Appointment of Women to High Courts

In this chapter, we examine how domestic institutions affect women's advancement to high courts by looking into the five case studies of Canada, Colombia, Ireland, South Africa, and the United States. We build on the longitudinal cross-sectional work presented in chapters 2 and 3 on the appointment of the first woman and the move toward gender parity. In those chapters, we found that the type of selector—whether they are elected or unelected officials—does not appear to systematically influence women's representation. Although the variable for newer courts (courts created in or after the 1990s) did not attain statistical significance in chapters 2 and 3, many of them do typically have a woman justice from the start. Because accountable selectors and newer courts may matter in ways that are context dependent, we explore them in greater detail in this chapter.

In our quantitative analyses, we were limited to examining formal institutional factors. By focusing on five countries in this chapter, we are able to consider the role of not only formal institutions but also informal rules, norms, and practices in increasing women's representation on high courts. An important qualitative literature finds that both formal and informal aspects of appointing high court judges matter for diversity on courts (e.g., Bauer and Dawuni 2016; Kenney 2013; Malleson and Russell 2006; Schultz and Shaw 2013; Schultz and Masengu 2020; Sonneveld and Lindbekk 2017). Limiting the focus to the formal rules of selection overlooks informal norms and practices that can affect men and women's chances of appointment differently. Therefore, we consider the formal and informal institutions that, collectively, comprise the selection process. Within those institutions, we hone in on the practices of selectors and their inner circle.

Formal institutions are the written rules regarding selection enshrined in the constitution or in law. These include structures and the prescribed roles for governmental offices and committees in nominating and appointing judges. As part of the set of formal institutions, we examine whether selectors are electorally accountable; whether there is a nominating commission; whether the court was created whole cloth during our time frame; and whether there is affirmative legal language for the composition of the court. Informal institutions are commonly shared ideas and unwritten practices and norms that surround building the list of potential nominees or appointees. Some of these informal institutions are publicly known, such as the ideology of selectors, which encompasses shared ideas about

Reimagining the Judiciary: Women's Representation on High Courts Worldwide. Maria C. Escobar-Lemmon, Valerie J. Hoekstra, Alice J. Kang, and Miki Caul Kittilson, Oxford University Press. © Maria C. Escobar-Lemmon, Valerie J. Hoekstra, Alice J. Kang, and Miki Caul Kittilson 2021. DOI: 10.1093/oso/9780198861577.003.0005

gender equality. Many informal institutions work behind closed doors and are only visible through in-depth investigation. These gendered informal institutions include the traditionally men-biased ideas among selectors about what constitutes "qualifications," the reliance on gendered social networks from which shortlists are often drawn, and the role of men advisors in promoting potential appointees.

Using information collected through archival research and interviews that we conducted in Canada, Colombia, Ireland, and South Africa, and primary and secondary sources in the United States, we find that institutions can act as filters and promoters in women's pathways to appointment. When selectors perceive electoral benefit from selecting a woman, and can be held accountable by their electorate, they are more likely to do so. Our findings on the role of ideology are mixed and suggest that ideas about gender equality are only sometimes rooted in political party affiliation. Whether judicial nominating commissions encourage the appointment of women is less clear. Both affirmative legal language and new courts can promote the selection of women. Our case studies further suggest that the selection process often rests on identifying a list of potential nominees based on informal networks, which have historically favored men. In this way, gendered networks and gendered ideas about qualifications (also see chapter 4) act as filters to hinder the appointment of women. When selectors or their key advisors decide to do so, they can disrupt reliance on these traditional networks by looking beyond the usual suspects as they draw up their shortlists.

5.1 Formal Institutions and Women's Representation on High Courts

A wide variety of institutional factors, particularly the method of selection, have been suggested as influencing the appointment of women on high courts. Much of the quantitative research examining how the mode of selection affects the appointment of women looks at state high courts in the United States. That research tests the relationship between the selection of judges by election and the selection of judges by executive appointment on the presence of women and minorities on the bench (e.g., Bratton and Spill 2002; Goelzhauser 2011, 2016; Holmes and Emrey 2006). Cross-national quantitative studies also take into account selection methods, particularly in wealthy democracies (Thames and Williams 2013; Valdini and Shortell 2016; Williams and Thames 2008).

Scholars have theorized that selectors who can be held electorally accountable are more likely to select women to serve on high courts (Slotnick 1984; Valdini and Shortell 2016; Williams and Thames 2008). If selectors are elected officials, then they can claim credit for diversifying the bench by appointing women and potentially attract women voters to the party. If the appointers are unelected, such as ministers of justice, there could be less incentive for them to appoint women. In another study, we propose that the effect of credit-claiming on appointing the first woman to the high court is particularly germane in long-standing democracies (Escobar-Lemmon, Hoekstra, Kang, and Kittilson 2021). Valdini and Shortell 2016 refer to the credit claimers as "exposed" and the non-credit claimers as "sheltered." In this chapter, we use the term accountable for those exposed selectors.

Formally, the selection of high court justices could include both electorally accountable and non-electorally accountable actors. Accountability is more difficult to assign in these mixed-selection systems. Electorally accountable selectors can claim credit for appointing women, but they can also shift blame to the nonelected selectors for thwarting the promotion of women judicial candidates.

This "clarity of responsibility" created by political institutions was first theorized by Powell and Whitten (1993) in studying economic voting in comparative perspective. In elections, voters are expected to assign credit or blame to an incumbent government where the government has a high degree of unified control over choices. By contrast, where the institutional configuration allows for a larger set of actors able to exert control along the way, responsibility is less transparent. In short, electoral accountability is ensconced in a complex set of political institutions, and the context matters for understanding how this electoral accountability works.

Many countries have created judicial nominating commissions with the assumption that they will improve transparency and limit cronyism in processes that typically rely on a tap on the shoulder. Greater transparency and less politicization are assumed to improve the diversity of the judiciary in general and high courts in particular. Members of independent judicial bodies, however, can themselves be biased against women. Judicial nominating commissions include and are often led by senior members of the judicial or legal profession who are not looking to challenge status quo gendered hierarchies. Partiality, patronage, and power dynamics are prevalent in judicial commissions, just in a different form, and illustrate how efforts to build transparency may fail (Masengu 2020). Indeed, Goelzhauser (2018) finds that in the United States, women candidates are less likely to be chosen by merit commissions for judicial short lists than are men candidates.

Case studies offer mixed findings on whether judicial nominating commissions improve women's representation on the bench. On the one hand, Malleson (2006a: 43) finds that commissions can make a difference, but the outcome depends on whether the commission is charged with appointing more women or members of other underrepresented groups. For example, England, Wales, and Northern Ireland created appointment commissions with the explicit goal of increasing diversity by increasing the transparency of the process (Macneill 2015; Malleson 2006b). On the other hand, appointment commissions can discriminate against women candidates, as Kamau (2013) finds in the case of Kenya's Judicial Service Commission (JSC) and as García Goldar (2020) observes of Spain's men-skewed General Board of the Judiciary.

Another institutional factor is whether a high court is installed whole cloth. When selectors have the opportunity to fill many seats at the same time, this facilitates the appointment of at least one woman justice. The scholarship on legislatures shows that when presenting a slate of candidates, as parties do in proportional representation electoral systems, parties often operate on a "logic of inclusion" by adding women to the party list to broaden the party's appeal among groups of voters (Beckwith 1992; Kittilson 2006). Arrington (2020) extends this insight about group selection to the judicial context and shows that individuals notice and criticize the selection of all-men slates, more so than the selection of men judges one-by-one. The opportunities for newcomers when governments fill a large number of seats on the bench at one time is also illustrated by judicial reshuffles in Latin America (Arana Araya, Hughes, and Pérez-Liñán 2021). With multiple vacancies at one time, selectors may install women, although other factors must be at work as well.

Constitutional revisions in the third wave of democratization often called for the creation of standalone constitutional courts (Ferejohn and Pasquino 2002; Ginsburg 2003). Across Latin America, there was an expansion in the power and independence of these constitutional courts including their ability to limit the power of executives (Ríos-Figueroa 2011; Rodríguez-Raga 2011). Importantly, the creation of these new courts coincided with the rise of the international norm of gender equity in decision-making and UN conferences on women. The opportunity to fill multiple seats, combined with the mainstreaming of ideas surrounding women's inclusion, encouraged the appointment of at least one woman justice on the new high court.

One formal institutional factor that we were not able to include in chapters 2 and 3 is whether there is affirmative legal language for women's appointments to high courts. In some cases, countries have judicial gender quotas. These are less common than are quotas for the legislature, although they are growing in number (Hoekstra 2010). Quotas are argued to be more effective than relying on the goodwill of selectors and pose no problems in terms of "merit" because there are a sufficient number of women in the eligible pool of justices (Malleson 2014). In its 2009 constitutional reform, Bolivia adopted a gender quota that requires 50 percent of candidates for judicial elections be women and that each list include a person of indigenous descent. Sometimes gender quotas address all executive appointments in the government writ large, including, but not limited to, appointments in the judiciary, as can be found in Colombia, Kenya, and Niger. Positive language for the inclusion of women and gender targets are also found in treaties that govern international courts, such as the International Criminal Court (Chappell 2015; Dawuni 2020; Grossman 2016).

Some constitutions include aspirational clauses for the inclusion of women in the judiciary. These clauses may act as important symbols of national principles and values, and they may "name disadvantage, recognizing those who have been excluded or rendered legally 'invisible' in the past" (Irving 2009: 24). Such aspirational language does not specify a target number or percentage of women to be judicial candidates or appointees. As we discuss below, South Africa's constitution calls for the judiciary to reflect the racial and gender composition of the country.

5.2 Informal Institutions and the Appointment of Women to High Courts

The written rules and policies that specify selection procedures are complemented with a complex set of ideas, norms, and practices that influence who is ultimately selected for these prestigious positions. Broadly, Helmke and Levitsky's (2006) distinction between formal and informal institutions strengthens our ability to compare complex selection methods. Formal institutions are codified, and consequently more transparent and widely understood.

In contrast, informal institutions are unwritten, sometimes known only to those inside the selection process, and allow for discretion among actors. At the same time, informal institutions can constrain actors in consistent ways. Our consideration of informal institutions includes three broad sets of informal institutions: 1) ideology of selectors, 2) gender biases in "qualifications," and 3) gendered networks of advisors and eligible appointees. Not all of these informal institutions matter in every case study, and we highlight them where we have evidence to suggest that they operate.

In chapters 2 and 3, we did not account for the ideology of the selector due to the challenges of measuring the selector's ideology across countries, world regions, and time. This chapter allows us to explore the role of ideology in conjunction with theories of electorally accountable selection and the role of advisors. In contexts where the selector is electorally accountable and seeks to appeal to loyalists or attract new voters, the partisan affiliation or ideology of the selector may be influential. Leftist selectors may hold more egalitarian ethos and perceive greater pressures from women's organizations in and outside their parties to advance women to high courts (Arana Araya, Hughes, and Pérez-Liñán 2021). The role of party ideology figures prominently in the literature on courts in the United States. Starting with President Jimmy Carter there has been a greater tendency for Democratic presidents to appoint women and members of underrepresented groups (Diascro and Solberg 2009; Segal 2000; Spill and Bratton 2001; Slotnick, Goldman, and Schiavoni 2015; Solberg and Diascro 2020).

The cross-national research on women in parliament and women in cabinets, however, is less conclusive on the role of party ideology. On the one hand, leftist parties have been associated with candidate gender quotas and greater gender equality within their parliamentary delegations and cabinets (Davis 1997;

Duverger 1955; Escobar-Lemmon and Taylor-Robinson 2005; Htun 2005; Kittilson 2006; Lovenduski and Norris 1993). On the other hand, the explanatory power of ideology does not seem to hold across all world regions such as Africa (Arriola and Johnson 2014; Kang and Tripp 2018). Further, the influence of ideology on the inclusion of women may wane over time. In recent years, right-leaning parties have made strides in promoting women for office. For example, in Europe, the British Conservative and German Christian Democratic parties have advanced women within their ranks (Childs 2008; Childs and Webb 2012; Wiliarty 2010). Across Latin America, Htun (2005) suggests a similar trend, as major right-wing parties have gained ground in promoting women for office, with several women candidates coming from the right.

If formal qualifications for selection are written into constitutions or the law, they are in most cases quite minimal and render a large pool of potentially eligible appointees. Informally, selectors and their inner circle often have in mind an unwritten set of qualifications. For Malleson (2006b), merit is a broad and actively constructed set of principles, which must be translated into concrete qualifications in the selection process. This process requires interpretation on the part of the selectors and is always tied to the backgrounds and characteristics of the eligible pool. Based on this, selection most often defaults to the candidates who are most similar to past appointees and the selectors themselves.

Selectors may tell themselves that the qualities they are looking for are gender neutral, when in fact these ideas about what constitutes qualifications are built on exclusively men-dominant career paths. As Annesley, Beckwith and Franceschet (2019) note for selection processes for cabinets, the small number of formal qualifications leaves open much room for discretion in deciding which experiential qualifications are most important, and many of these conventions surrounding qualifications were built by men for men.

In countries such as Australia, the United Kingdom, and the United States, selectors use the term "merit" to describe those ineffable qualities that justices of high courts must possess. What constitutes "qualifications" or "merit," scholars argue, is gendered and privileges a much narrower subset of society (Thornton 2007). In chapter 4, we outlined how in countries with a split bar, barristers often have had an edge over solicitors in being appointed to high courts. Yet, as Malleson (2006b) points out, ideas about who is "qualified" or possesses the most "merit" can change over time. As we argue in this book, rising expectations about appointing women judges can improve gender diversity on high courts.

Networks of insiders and outsiders are crucial to understanding who is ultimately shortlisted and selected for high courts (Kenney 2012). Professional networks include the selectors and those they regularly interact with, and they operate on the basis of informal norms and practices. Not only are selectors more likely to be aware of potential nominees in their networks, but also over time these dense networks can serve to supply support, advice, and the "inside scoop" on little known selection criteria. These networks are often gendered, disadvantaging women as potential appointees. For example, in Turkey, men judges more easily arrange "Ankara visits" where they meet members of selection committees and exchange professional information through informal meetings such as dinners, or even Friday prayers (Kalem 2020).

The gender of participants in the selection process may either support or disrupt the reliance on traditionally men-dominant networks. Individuals who are close to the selectors may themselves demand the appointment of more women on high courts. Research suggests that women are more likely than their men counterparts to take up the role of promoting other women. Evidence from interviews and surveys of political elites from Europe, Latin America, and the United States shows that women tend to place greater value on women's rights and gender equality than their men counterparts do (Carroll 2001; Schwindt-Bayer 2006). Thus, when women gain top leadership positions, they can either select or pressure selectors to add women to the shortlist of candidates. More specifically, Kittilson's (2006) research on political parties in Europe finds that having women among the party selectorate is a powerful mechanism for increasing the share of women candidates on party lists. By extension, women in a position to advise selectors in appointing high court justices may select more women. Other studies, however, find that the gender of selectors is not associated with the selection of women (Krook and O'Brien 2012). O'Brien, Mendez, Peterson, and Shin (2015) find that women prime ministers are no more likely to have women in their cabinets.

5.3 Domestic Institutions in Five Countries

Our five cases studies allow us to gain insight into how formal and informal institutions affect the advancement of women to high courts. We chose cases to ensure at least some level of variation in institutions. We sought a certain degree of variation among legal systems: Canada, Ireland, and the United States all use common law, whereas South Africa employs a mixed system of common and customary law, and Colombia is a civil law country. We also chose courts of different sizes. The Colombian Constitutional Court and the Supreme Courts of the United States, Canada, and Ireland all contain nine judges. The South African Constitutional Court contains 11 justices. The Colombian Supreme Court is our largest with 23 justices. There is some variation in term length. The United States appoints high court justices for life. Canada and Ireland appoint justices for life, but have a mandatory retirement age. In contrast, justices on both the Colombian Supreme Court and Constitutional Court are limited to a non-renewable 8-year term. South Africa's Constitutional Court justices serve a 12-year non-renewable term or until they reach age 70, whichever comes first.

Above, we theorized that accountable selection, the newness of the court, the creation of judicial nominating commissions, and affirmative legal language influence women's high court representation. Table 5.1 compares the formal institutions for our case studies. While all five countries have an accountable mode of selection for at least one of their high courts, justices on Colombia's highest appellate court are chosen by non-electorally accountable selectors.

Our cases vary in the use of nominating commissions both across country and over time. Canada until 2016 did not have a commission to compile a shortlist of judicial candidates (we end our case study analysis in 2017). The United States does not have a judicial commission for Supreme Court appointments. Ireland reformed its system in 1995 to create a judicial nominating commission, as did South Africa in its transition to democracy. Colombia does not use a standalone nominating body to select judges to any of its high courts.

Major institutional changes took place in Colombia and South Africa with the creation of constitutional courts in 1992 and 1994, respectively. At its inception, the South African court contained 18.2 percent women. In contrast, it was a full decade after its founding, in 2001, that the first woman was appointed in Colombia, although the first woman joined the Supreme Court in 1983.

In each case study, we highlight factors that come up frequently in the scholarly literature on each country and that arose in our interviews. This means that the case studies will vary in the institutions that matter most or appear the most relevant.

5.4 The United States

The evidence for the United States suggests key formal and informal institutional factors played dynamic roles in advancing women's representation on the Supreme Court: electorally accountable selectors, party ideology, gender biases in evaluating qualifications, and gendered networks.

Formally, the Constitution of the United States mandates that the president nominates a person to fill a Supreme Court vacancy. The president selects by considering a list of potential jurists drafted with the assistance of legal advice within his or her administration, senators from potential nominees' home states, and other sources. Ultimately, it is up to the discretion of the president. After selecting a nominee from this initial vetting process, the name is submitted to the Senate. From there, the confirmation process begins as the Senate Judiciary Committee conducts hearings and votes on the nominee. Notable exceptions include Harriet Miers who withdrew her nomination after conservatives questioned her commitment to a conservative ideology and general questions about her qualifications and the Senate's decision to not act on President Obama's nomination of Judge Merrick Garland. If a nominee receives a majority vote from the committee, their name is forwarded to the full Senate. Because the

Table 5.1 Formal Institutions for Selection across Five Countries

	U.S. Supreme Court	Canada Supreme Court	Ireland Supreme Court	Colombia Supreme Court	Colombia Constitutional Court	South Africa Constitutional Court
Accountable selector	✓	✓	✓	No	✓	✓
Nominating commission	No	No	After 1995	No	No	✓
Newer court	No	No	No	No	✓	✓
Affirmative legal language	No	No	No	After 2000	After 2000	✓
Term length	Life	Life	Life	8 years	8 years	12 years or until age 70
Court size	9	9	9	23	9	11

main actors in the process, the president and the Senate, are elected, we regard selectors in the United States as electorally accountable.

The formal process, however, does not adequately describe how informal practices have affected the appointment process and how they have evolved over time. Much research has focused on the informal aspects of the nomination and confirmation process in the United States (Davis 2017; Epstein, Lindstadt, Segal, and Westerland 2006; Nemachek 2008; Peretti 2007; Rogowski and Stone 2019). While politics have always been a part of the process, recent decades have witnessed increasingly political confirmation hearings including threats to filibuster, failed nominations, significant delays, and significant interest group mobilization in support or opposition of judicial nominees. Critical to the increasing partisan and ideological polarization was the removal of the filibuster for Supreme Court nominees in 2013. Since then, nominees need only 51 votes for confirmation. Thus, recent confirmations have received only the barest margin of votes.

For the first stage of selection, there is a great deal of emphasis on presidential advisors' informal networks. Usually, the Attorney General and other members of the president's legal staff compile a list of names for Supreme Court nominees as part of the transition to presidency in anticipation of having the opportunity to make at least one nomination (Nemachek 2008).

Presidents vary considerably in their approaches to selection. For example, President Obama's administration is known for using a less formalized selection process in which there was constant coordination between the Justice Department and White House Counsel's Office in drafting and vetting lists of names (Slotnick, Goldman, and Schiavoni 2017; Solberg and Diascro 2020). Often, those who rise to the attention of the legal staff have been known personally to the president or were active in party politics. Recently, Republican presidents have increasingly found their nominees among the ranks of the Federalist Society, an organization of conservative lawyers, judges, and professors.

That presidents are accountable to the electorate clearly made a difference in selecting the first woman to the Supreme Court. President Ronald Reagan's campaign promise to appoint the first woman to the United States Supreme Court came to fruition with the nomination of Sandra Day O'Connor in 1981. For Reagan, and the Republican Party, this was largely a maneuver to attract women voters to the Republican Party. Yet, she lacked some of the prior judicial experience of many other Supreme Court nominees having served on the appellate court of the state of Arizona and not on the state supreme court or on a federal court.

Ideology in the form of the party of the president has had a significant impact on nominations to federal courts in the United States. Moreover, since it is the lower courts in recent decades that serve as a main supplier of men and women to the Supreme Court (for more on this, see chapter 4), party ideology may indeed be a key promoter of women's representation on the United States Supreme Court.

The removal of the filibuster for Supreme Court nominees seems to have increased the importance and salience of ideology.

While Ronald Reagan is widely acknowledged for his nomination of O'Connor, most observers credit the efforts of President Jimmy Carter to diversify the federal judiciary. Although Carter did not have the opportunity to make any appointments to the Supreme Court, his efforts to improve women's representation on lower-level federal courts not only bolstered the pipeline of eligible nominees with more women, but also began chipping away at some of the preconceptions and practices that had hampered women's progress in selection processes.

Starting with President Carter there has been a greater tendency for Democratic presidents to appoint White women, women of color, and men of color to federal courts (Segal 2000; Diascro and Solberg 2009; Segal and Spaeth 2002; Spill and Bratton 2001; Slotnick, Goldman, and Schiavoni 2015). While Republican presidents in the 1980s through 2000s have done better on this account than prior Republican administrations (Haire and Moyer 2015), overall, Democratic presidents have a much better record of appointing women to the federal courts. Looking at the proportion of women judges appointed to the federal courts, Carter appointed 16 percent, Reagan 8 percent, Bush 19 percent, Clinton 28 percent, George W. Bush 22 percent, Obama 42 percent, and Trump 28 percent (Gramlich 2018).

Despite Reagan's nomination of the first woman to the United States Supreme Court, his administration did not make a concerted effort to appoint more women, nor to continue the efforts begun by the prior Carter administration (Martin 1987). Similarly, President George H. W. Bush and President George W. Bush eschewed active efforts to advance members of underrepresented groups on federal courts and the Supreme Court. Instead, policy and ideological goals played a larger role in selecting nominees (Diascro and Solberg 2009). President George W. Bush nominated Harriet Miers to replace Justice O'Connor on the court, but this nomination did not advance to a seat on the court. Under pressure, Miers withdrew her nomination. Although Miers lacked judicial experience, she had been the first woman to be managing partner of a large Texas law firm and the first woman to serve as president of the State Bar of Texas (Penrose 2018).

By all accounts, both President Clinton and President Obama valued diversifying the Supreme Court and federal courts to better reflect the American public on ideological grounds (Spill and Bratton 2001; Kenney 2012). For the two vacancies that occurred during his administration, President Clinton selected Ruth Bader Ginsburg and Stephen Breyer. President Obama prioritized improving representation in multiple and overlapping ways, and actualized this value by nominating the first Latina justice to the United States Supreme Court, Sonia Sotomayor. In addition, President Obama nominated Elena Kagan. For the federal judiciary more comprehensively, Obama pursued a transformation to improve gender, racial, and ethnic diversity (Slotnick, Schiavoni, and Goldman 2017).

These efforts did not stop at the Supreme Court, as the Obama administration realized the largest ever number of federal appointments of White women, women of color, and men of color (Solberg and Diascro 2020).

Given that President Carter's efforts appear to have been a catalyst in improving women's representation, what then explains Carter's actions? While ideological commitment to gender equality and diversity play a role, many also attribute President Carter's inner circle as exerting an important influence. When Carter took office in 1977, women's presence on the federal courts was almost non-existent: there was one woman federal appeals court judge and five women district court judges (Clark 2002). Many of Carter's advisors advocated for women's advancement in the judiciary. For example, Assistant Attorney General Barbara Babcock was charged with generating a list of names for vacancies on the federal courts and ensured that many women were on the list. Other advisors included Sarah Weddington (one of the attorneys who argued *Roe v. Wade*, 1973), Margaret McKenna (Deputy White House Counsel), and Carter's wife, Rosalyn Carter (Clark 2002). Especially vital was McKenna, the first woman to serve as Deputy White House Counsel. Her strategic work in President Carter's inner circle was vital to getting underrepresented groups, including women, into federal judgeships (Kenney 2012). She actively lobbied senators and federal courts of appeal nominating commissions to add women's names to the shortlist. In addition, she highlighted the American Bar Association's (ABA) proclivity for rating women as "not qualified." Thus, women in the inner circle helped to reinforce Carter's goal of diversifying the judiciary. As Barbara Babcock said, "I think that all the women judges would never have been appointed again without the strong presence of women bosses in the Carter administration" (quoted in Clark, 2002: 245).

Personal connections have also mattered for selection, both for the Supreme Court and for the pipeline feeder federal courts. Kenney (2012) notes the old adage in the United States that "a judge is a lawyer who knows a senator" (1505). In line with this saying, Slotnick's (1984) comparison of those selected to federal bench found that White men were most likely to have records of partisan political activities, relative to judges who were White women, women of color, and men of color. The Carter administration began placing less emphasis on political connections and political activity and broadened conceptions of qualifications to emphasize academic credentials, which women nominees were more likely to have (Kenney 2012; Martin 1987).

The role of qualifications in the selection process is complex, as cogently captured by a justice department memo from 1980 that states, "Because the number of capable individuals is much greater inevitably than the number of places to be filled, few nominations have occurred in which a candidate's outstanding ability alone appears to have decided his nomination" (Nemacheck 2008: 10, quotes John M. Harmon). As informal institutions, qualifications are often cited as a factor influencing who gets nominated. Among the qualifications emphasized for Supreme Court nominees, neutrality to parties in litigation, fair-mindedness, legal knowledge, logical reasoning, integrity, and judicial temperament emerge as salient (Abraham 2008). Yet, how these principles and attributes are applied is less clear.

The ABA has long played a routinized role in the selection and nomination processes for supreme court justices. Thus, at some points in time the ABA has been an institutionalized part of the selection process (despite having no official capacity in government), and at other points has acted as a domestic advocacy organization. For example, President Clinton alerted the ABA as his administration identified potential nominees (Smelcer, Navarro, Steigerwalt, and Vining 2012). Under President George W. Bush's administration, the role of the ABA was moved from being a routinized part of the process, to allowing the ABA, among other groups such as the Federalist Society, to weigh in informally (Nemachek 2008). President Obama restored the traditional role of the ABA, and President Trump reversed course on this (Slotnick, Schiavoni, and Goldman 2017).

The ABA's part in the process was tightly connected to assessing qualifications. The ABA's 15-member Committee on the Federal Judiciary rated nominees as either "not qualified," "qualified," or "well qualified" (the category of "exceptionally well qualified" was dropped). The criteria valued by the committee have included judicial experience, practicing at a law firm, and trial experience. Until more recently, academic credentials were not as highly prized (Kenney 2012).

Slotnick's (1984) research revealed that, for selection to the federal bench, the ABA had rated four times as many White men as "exceptionally well qualified," as compared to women of color, men of color, and White women. Following on this, Martin (1987) demonstrated that the ABA ratings had been biased in favor of men, applying the lowest rating to women if they had not previously served as judges, but not applying the same standard to men without this experience. In addition, the ABA also often latched their low ratings of women to not having worked for large law firms: but for many decades, women were barred from working at these firms. More recent research on the courts of appeal found these biases against traditionally underrepresented groups have persisted into recent decades (Gill, Lazos, and Waters 2011; Haire 2001; Sen 2014).

More broadly, structural inequalities in American society and the paid workforce shaped different paths to the federal bench for women of color, White women, and men of color, relative to White men. Slotnick's (1984) study demonstrated that White men were more likely to rise to the federal bench from private practice than underrepresented groups, who were more likely to have been sitting judges or law school professors. As a consequence, promoting more underrepresented groups to the highest courts required broadening the traditional path to include difference experiences and expertise.

Taken together, the evidence for the United States suggests institutions have acted as both filters and promoters of women's representation on the Supreme Court. The role of an electorally accountable selector was important for the first woman. That Reagan was the first president to nominate a woman to the Supreme Court seems largely explained by an electoral strategy to gain women's votes in a context of political realignment, when the women's vote shifted from the Republican Party to the Democratic Party. Although President Reagan was a Republican, subsequent successful nominations of women have been made by Presidents Clinton and Obama (and more recently by President Trump, although the timing of this nomination falls outside of the scope of our examination). Importantly an ideological commitment to improving nominations of under-represented groups, including women of color, emerges as an important factor in explaining both the Clinton and Obama eras. Further, informal institutions such as gender-biased perceptions of qualifications and reliance on gendered networks have hampered women's advancement at many points in time, but concerted efforts to overcome these sticky institutions paid off for the Carter, Clinton, and Obama administrations. Some evidence indicates women in the inner circle of the Carter White House helped to break these entrenched patterns.

5.5 Canada

Formally, the prime minister appoints justices to the Supreme Court of Canada. With only one formal selector, the process is relatively centralized. The prime minister is accountable to the electorate for his or her decisions. Consistent with our coding we classify this process as being electorally accountable.

For this chapter, the focus is on the pre-2016 selection methods. In 2016, Prime Minister Justin Trudeau altered the appointment process for Supreme Court nominees. With the goal of creating a more transparent process, today, an independent and non-partisan advisory board identifies the best potential candidates in a process where any practitioner or judge can apply.

Formally, ideology and partisan politics do not play a role in selection to the Canadian Supreme Court. Closer inspection reveals that party ideology may be weakly associated with the selection of women justices. Among the 10 women appointed to the Canadian Supreme Court, four were made by the Conservative Party (or its former Progressive Conservative), and six were made by the Liberal Party. Because opportunities to nominate are key, it is important to look not only at the total number appointed, but also the composition of appointments. Prime Minister Pierre Trudeau (Liberal) appointed the first woman to the Canadian Supreme Court, but during his leadership, only one of his 10 appointments (10 percent) was a woman. Among Prime Minister Brian Mulroney's (Progressive Conservative) nine appointments, two were women (22.2 percent): Claire

L'Heureux-Dubé and Beverly McLachlin. Among the eight appointments of successive Liberal Prime Ministers Jean Chrétien and Paul Martin, four were women (50 percent). Among Prime Minister Stephen Harper's (Conservative) eight appointments, two were women (20 percent). Taken together, the Liberals have been slightly more likely to appoint women to the Canadian Supreme Court.

Given the strides made by prime ministers across the party spectrum, it is clear that party affiliation does not fully explain why prime ministers select women. The prime minister operates in a broader political and legal context in Canada that create incentives for selecting women, and these incentives may change over time.

A close circle of advisors to each prime minister are often called upon in the process of identifying and vetting candidates for appointment. The actor most proximate to that decision is the minister of justice, who in most governments, draws up the short list of candidates from among which the prime minister selects. This important insider role for drawing up the shortlist of candidates and advocating for particular strengths and weaknesses of candidates empowers ministers of justice to either push for a diverse set of candidates, or to stick with the status quo.

Beyond the formal rules, interviews with former ministers of justice reveal that it is common practice for the minister of justice to advise the prime minister in the appointment of judges to the highest court. Although the norms of this process vary by prime minister, most commonly the minister of justice assembled a shortlist with fewer than 10 potential appointees accompanied by prepared dossiers. If the prime minister favors having women on that list, women will be included on the shortlist. The minister of justice also has some power to shape the agenda and can make an effort to include women on the shortlist if he or she sees fit. A dossier is created for each potential appointee, complete with news stories about the candidate. The dossiers include feedback on the nominee from the law society and bar association in the nominee's province. Together, the prime minister and minister of justice usually pare down the list to about three names, and finally the prime minister selects one person for the Canadian Supreme Court.

The inner circle of advisors proved vital during the appointment of the first woman to the Supreme Court of Canada, Bertha Wilson. Wilson's appointment was made in the context of a months-long process of behind the scenes lobbying in 1981 as sitting Justice Ronald Martland approached the age of mandatory retirement. Monique Beguin, Trudeau's Minister of Health and Welfare, called on him to appoint Wilson (Backhouse 2019). The prime minister wavered on whether to seek out a woman for the post, and he sought the advice of his former colleagues to suggest names (Anderson 2001). A former special advisor on judicial appointments, Edward Ratushny, sent Trudeau a confidential letter, stating that the prime minister would be asked why he did not select Wilson, and called upon Trudeau to "make history" (Backhouse 2019: 149). In the final moments, Trudeau called a cabinet meeting where Trudeau announced to the ministers that Wilson should be appointed. In that meeting, Minister of Justice Jean Chrétien said, "Prime Minister, the girls are right. You should appoint her" (Backhouse 2019: 150). Chrétien further announced to the cabinet that he disagreed with appointing the man on the shortlist and warned against missing the opportunity to appoint a woman. Because Trudeau had previously confided in the chief justice that the candidate who was a man would be appointed, he left it to Chrétien to call the chief justice and tell him it would be Wilson. In that phone call, the chief justice was so upset that he hung up on the minister (Backhouse 2019). Within a few days of this discussion, the appointment of Bertha Wilson was announced by the Trudeau government.

Do the characteristics of the minister of justice themselves make a difference? To date, there have been three women ministers of justice and one woman prime minister in Canada. The first woman minister of justice was Kim Campbell, who served 1990 to 1993 in the Progressive Conservative government, and later as the first woman prime minister of Canada. The second was Anne McLellan (1997–2002) and the third Jody Wilson-Raybould (2015–19), both of the Liberal Party. The women who served as ministers of justice worked to advance women in the judiciary at all levels, including appointments to the Supreme Court. Although there were no opportunities to select a justice for the peak court during Campbell's tenure as minister of justice, she made efforts to promote women to the federal judiciary and provincial courts of appeal. Her efforts laid the groundwork for the appointment of women to the Supreme Court in subsequent years. Similarly, Anne McLellan worked closely with Prime Minister Chrétien, and they sought out women candidates for the short list. During this time, gender diversity was a consideration in drawing up shortlists, in addition to other forms of representation in appointments to the bench. Advising Prime Minister Chrétien, McLellan was part of the process when two more women were selected for the highest court. At the same time, a man minister of justice (Irwin Cotler) was also cited by multiple judges and former ministers of justice as a key player in advocating for women on the bench, both at the provincial and federal levels. Taken together, Ministers of Justice McLellan and Cotler oversaw the appointment of four women to the Supreme Court. More than the gender of the selectors, the desire and determination to select a woman played a key role in the Canadian case.

In conclusion, in Canada, when prime ministers have perceived benefit in selecting women, women have been placed on the shortlist. Several ministers of justice have also worked at the lower-level courts to build up the supply of women for these appointments when the vacancies occur. One filter working against women's selection to the Supreme Court been informal norms of relying on close networks of established elites to identify candidates for the court. These networks were traditionally composed of men. A few key ministers of justice, both women and men, disrupted these gendered social networks. These close advisors of the prime minister looked beyond the traditional network to identify women to add to the shortlist. By expanding the shortlist, prime ministers were presented with well-qualified women, who also offered the benefit of credit-claiming in appointing a woman to the court.

5.6 Ireland

In Ireland, appointments to the Supreme Court are formally made by the president, who is popularly elected, on the advice of the prime minister (the Taoiseach) and cabinet (collectively, the government), members of which are also popularly elected. As part of a complex set of formal institutions, the Irish presidency is a largely ceremonial post. The cabinet is nominated by the Taoiseach, approved by the national legislature (Dáil Éireann), and then formally approved by the president. This leads us to categorize the selection process in Ireland as electorally accountable.

Following a 1995 reform, the president is presented with a list of nominees prepared by the Judicial Appointments Advisory Board (JAAB). The president is not obliged to appoint someone from that list, but in practice appointees have come from the JAAB's list. Thus, the Irish system of judicial selection is still electorally accountable because following the recommendation by the JAAB is not mandatory.

The JAAB accepts applications from barristers or solicitors interested in serving as a judge. The JAAB neither solicits applications nor interviews applicants, relying on the written materials in the application. Members of the JAAB include the Chief Justice of the Supreme Court, judges on other courts, the Attorney General, members of the legal profession, and three lay members. Unlike similar reforms (creation of a judicial commission) that took place in neighboring Northern Ireland, England, and Wales, Ireland's reform began after its ruling coalition fell apart after two controversial appointments. It was a quick fix, intended to increase transparency and reduce the former "tap on the shoulder" aspect of the process. However, the JAAB plays an important role in providing a forum for those seeking a judicial appointment to put their name forward, in evaluating candidates, and providing the president with a wider pool of candidates.

Other, potentially more significant, formal reforms also came in 1995 and then in 2002. In the Court and Court Officers Act of 1995, for the first time, solicitors became eligible to be appointed to the courts of appeal so long as they had served for 10 years. The same formal experience requirement, however, did not hold for barristers. In 2002, the Courts and Court Officers Act made the same change for appointments to the High Court and the Supreme Court. Still, solicitors had to meet the formal requirement of 10 years of experience (MacNeill 2016). Why is this formal change significant? The two professions differ greatly in their gender composition. Traditionally, women have been much more likely to become solicitors than barristers (see chapter 4).

By all accounts, party ideology has not played an obvious role in the selection of women to the Supreme Court. The two historically dominant political parties, Fianna Fáil and Fine Gael, have mostly been seen as centrist, and the Irish party system differs from some other European party systems in the issues most central to party competition (McElroy 2017). This is borne out by the data on appointments of women to the Supreme Court since 1990. It was in the first year of Mary Robinson's tenure as president of Ireland that the first woman was appointed. President Mary McAleese served from 1997 to 2011 and was a member of Fianna Fáil, and was also an Independent. She appointed 11 judges, three of whom were women. President Michael Higgins began his term in 2012. While he had been a member of the Labour Party, he resigned from it once elected president and joined Fianna Fáil. He appointed five justices, three of whom were women. Higgins has the highest percentage of women appointees, but his administration is more recent.

Gendered networks influence the selection process in Ireland. Many judges on the court have past connections to the major political parties (Mac Cormaic 2013). MacNeill (2016) contends that being known personally by one of the key players in the process of advising the president is an important factor in being appointed. Further, MacNeill's interviews with Supreme Court justices revealed that many believed their political connections benefited them in the appointment process. Given that these political networks have historically been dominated by men, women are likely to be excluded from the key professional networks from which shortlists are drawn.

Gendered networks also shape traditional ideas about what constitutes "qualifications" for selection. Virtually all judges on the high courts have come from the bar (i.e., barristers), specifically members of the Inner Bar (those who have been promoted to senior counsel). This remains true despite the formal changes that have allowed solicitors to be appointed (given 10 years of experience). Barristers often perceive that solicitors do not have the "in-court" back-and-forth experience needed to do the work of a Supreme Court justice (or high court judge). Solicitors argue that they are equally experienced—they know how to write, they often attend court proceedings with their clients, and they hire barristers for their clients. This, solicitors argue, shows that they understand what makes for quality appellate arguments.

Barristers are also a tightly connected group, often through their time in Kings Inn, where barristers are trained. Moreover, despite that recent years have seen a majority of women barristers called to the bar (approximately 60 percent), there is a precipitous decline among those who are promoted to be senior counsel, the Inner Bar. Thus, women, though formally qualified, suffer from the stickiness of prior practices of considering only barristers, and senior barristers specifically.

In some cases, women's role in the selection process as advisors may disrupt the reliance on traditional gendered networks, but we do not have clear evidence this is so in Ireland. The appointment of the first woman as Chief Justice of the Supreme Court in 2011 coincided with the appointment of the first woman as Attorney General in the same year, but connections between these two events have not been established. In its early years, the JAAB was largely made up of men, but by 2013, five of its 11 members were women (National Women's Strategy 2013). Despite the presence of women as presidents of Ireland, the prime minister and government are the effective decision-makers. Even still, there is no clear pattern of women presidents selecting more women Supreme Court justices. The record is nearly equally divided: women appointed four of the women judges and men appointed three.

In sum, we find little evidence that electorally accountable selection matters in Ireland. Compared with the United States especially, appointments to the Supreme Court in Ireland are not particularly notable or newsworthy events. Thus, it is unclear that there is much for selectors to gain electorally by selecting women. Ideology appears to play little role as well. In Ireland, the exclusion of women from barrister networks and the default emphasis on a barrister's career path as qualification build a complex set of gendered informal institutions that serve to filter women out of the elite circle considered for selection.

5.7 Colombia

At the end of a magistrate's term on the Supreme Court of Colombia, the remaining justices pick a replacement through a process referred to as co-optation.[1] This insular method of selection is not subject to any form of electoral accountability. Because justices serve an 8-year term there is awareness in advance when a vacancy will occur. Thus, prior to the end of the term, the Supreme Council of Judicature publishes a call for nominations inviting qualified individuals to submit their application materials. This results in a long shortlist containing names of all those who survive a preliminary vetting of qualifications. A former high court justice commented that women do not seem to be kept off the list at this point. Once the list is presented, interviews are held, allowing applicants to present their knowledge on a legal issue, demonstrate their mastery of the law and its application, and establish credibility in the eyes of their peers. However, both men and women justices interviewed for this project reported that

[1] This same method is used for the Council of State. While widely considered to be a peak court in its own right, we focus primarily on the Supreme Court and Constitutional Court for comparability with the other case studies.

this was not the only part of the interview process and that equally important were individual meetings with the justices on the court.

In contrast, the selection process for members of Colombia's Constitutional Court is more open to electoral pressure and includes accountable selectors as it relies on participation by the elected Senate. Constitutional Court justices also serve 8-year terms and so in anticipation of vacancies, the group responsible for nominating prepares a list of three names. This list—referred to as a *terna*—is then sent to the Senate. The Senate holds hearings and one-on-one meetings with the three nominees and then conducts a vote. The person receiving a majority of the votes is elected. So how are the lists composed? Of the nine justices on the Constitutional Court one-third each come from lists proposed by the president, the Council of State, and the Supreme Court. The Council of State and the Supreme Court use a process similar to that used to select judges to those bodies, which allows some public sense of who is being considered. In contrast, the president's list is composed in a more opaque way with the president simply putting forward a list of names.

While the selection process for the Constitutional Court involves more accountable selectors, it is not fully transparent. During the 2014 process that resulted in the selection of Gloria Stella Ortiz, Coalición Elección Visible was publicly critical of the lack of transparency in general criticizing specifically a failure to: clearly state the requirements, publicize conflict of interests among those doing the selecting, share the rules of the interview process with candidates being considered, and post complete CVs for all who applied. They argued this was critical to block the use of a "clandestine lobby" (El Tiempo 2014a). It is important to note that calls regarding the need for transparency were also echoed during the 2015 election process when the Corporación Excelencia en la Justica, among others, called for more transparency in the form of having the hearings before the Senate be open and televised, which ultimately happened. Nonetheless, Montoya (2013) argues that informal lobbying by candidates determines who is selected by the Senate. She concludes, "candidates who were not elected signaled that, even though it did not result in their election, the personal interviews with senators were key in obtaining the few votes they received" (180).

It is worth noting that the relatively open selection process has led to greater publicity and public attention to nominations for the Constitutional Court. It also led to greater pressure for transparency in the selection process being applied by NGOs (something discussed in detail in chapter 6). Looking at the composition of the Constitutional Court compared with the Supreme Court, one might be tempted to conclude that the relatively larger percentage of women on the Constitutional Court than the Supreme Court is a result of the more transparent selection process. However, this greater gender equality on the Constitutional Court is a relatively recent development (it was only in 2017 that the court achieved one-third women).

Both South Africa and Colombia created separate, standalone constitutional courts during the 1990s. However, unlike South Africa where the first woman was appointed from the start, it was not until almost a decade after its founding in 2001 that the first woman, Clara Inés Vargas, was appointed to the Constitutional Court in Colombia. When the Constitutional Court was created in 1992 the initial court was provisional and contained seven judges, three named by the president and one each by the Supreme Court and Council of State. These five judges picked the sixth and then the six of them picked the seventh together. No women were among the seven selected, and while "[s]ome judges, a minority, distanced themselves from this decision and individually went on the record as protesting against the exclusion of women it did not lead to women being included on the initial court" (CEDAW Committee Report 1993: 120).

Ironically, there are indications that this new court sitting in a new building was not prepared for women. The building that houses the Constitutional Court, Supreme Court, and Council of State was completely rebuilt in 1990 because the prior edifice was destroyed during the military's reclaiming of the building after the M-19 guerilla group seized the building and took the court hostage in 1985. "When she [Justice Clara Inés Vargas] was elected as the first female magistrate on the Constitutional Court she found that the building had bathrooms for male magistrates but not for female. '*When they designed the Constitutional Court building they never thought women would come*'" (Corporación Sisma Mujer 2007: 6, author's translation).

Colombia's constitution does not contain any gender specific affirmative language. Law 581 of 2000 establishes a 30 percent quota for women's participation in the highest decision-making posts, but it exempts judicial careers in which entry to is based on merit. This has been taken to mean that the high courts are not bound by this (Jaramillo 2000). In addition, because judges for the Constitutional Court are selected from *ternas* (or lists) many have interpreted the requirement as being met by including one woman on the list, regardless of whether she is ultimately selected.[2]

Several women working in the high courts acknowledged that this often meant that women were included on lists with no real chance they would be selected. Many described such women as *rellena* or filler. For instance, in 2007 when Mauricio González was nominated to replace Alvaro Tafur on the Constitutional Court, two women—Ilva Miriam Hoyos and Cristina Pardo—were also included. Both later withdrew and publicly criticized the connections between González and the president, suggesting that agreements to fix the election for González were in place. As Hoyos said, "The Senators themselves demonstrate

[2] This is different from the way in which the gender quota was applied in Bolivia for elections to the Constitutional and Supreme Courts, mandating women and persons of indigenous descent constitute a percentage of candidates (Driscoll and Nelson 2015).

that there were agreements, without the chance to dialogue with them, we thought the democratic conditions for a healthy debate did not exist and for that reason we withdrew" (El Tiempo 2007).

It is difficult to use the case of Colombia to assess the role of ideology. The two presidents whose list produced a woman magistrate were both founding members of the Partido de la U, a centrist-liberal party that united some dissident Liberal Party members with the various individuals who were part of the coalition that supported President Alvaro Uribe's bid for the presidency. The promotion of women was not a central part of the party's ideology.

An interesting intersection of the formal and informal aspects of the selection process is connected to the constitutional requirement that vacancies be announced and that individuals who wish to be considered submit their names and credentials. While the process seems open and competitive, one aspirant for the court noted that some people are strategically encouraged to put their name forward, meaning that if the president wanted to nominate someone they would make sure that person submitted their name. Additionally, at this self-nomination step, some women hold back. Recognizing this problem, several women's groups started contacting prominent and distinguished women jurists to not only encourage them to self-nominate, but to help them apply. One aspirant reported she received a call from a women's NGO who wanted her to put her name forward. They assembled all the documents she would need and took them to be registered on her behalf. They also provided her with background information on magistrates she would meet during the interview process so she would know their political ideology and their legal areas of expertise.

Women also refrain from self-nominating because they lack access to the power networks that are important in being selected. When asked why she didn't submit her own name for consideration, a woman aspirant stated, "If all you go with is a good CV that won't be enough. Women don't self-nominate because they know the way it works and that they need help and support. If a man has no linkages and no political godfather, that won't bother him. He will still put his name forward but women don't."

Additionally, Montoya (2013) highlights the importance of having the backing of other powerful political leaders such as party or party faction leaders or others in the process that she refers to as a "political godfather" (*padrino politico*), something echoed in interviews conducted for this project. Women who have powerful political patrons can benefit from having these connections. For instance, Gloria Stella Ortiz became the third woman to serve on the Constitutional Court in May 2014 having previously served as the right hand of the Attorney General, Eduardo Montealegre. News reports at the time referred to her as the political niece of Luis Guillermo Guerrero who was serving on the Constitutional Court (El Tiempo 2014b). The challenge is that fewer women have access to these networks than do men.

Men and women aspirants, justices, and academics all commented that the university where one earned a law degree was important, and universities are an important network. One commented that universities desire their graduates serve on the courts because it brings prestige to the university and their law program. According to one justice, when he was under consideration, his law school organized a forum where he had a chance to present scholarship, and the school invited sitting justices. This is not uncommon, and now that he has a seat on the court he has been invited to participate in these seminars, presumably to meet future aspirants for the court and ensure they are selected. In some cases, these university networks can work to the advantage of women as there is an expectation that one supports the candidacy of alumni from one's law school.

5.8 South Africa

We now turn to the role of institutions in advancing women's representation on the Constitutional Court of South Africa. With regard to formal institutions, we will focus on accountable selection, affirmative legal language, the constitutional court as a post-1990s entity, and the judicial nominating commission. The latter three were borne out of wider institutional changes that took place in South Africa's transition from Apartheid to democracy. In considering informal institutions, we will consider the use of unwritten qualifications and networks in selecting justices.

Formally, the president appoints judges to the Constitutional Court of South Africa after consulting the chief justice and leaders of parties in the National Assembly. South Africa has a parliamentary system where the National Assembly elects from among its members a president of the country. We consider the president to be electorally accountable because how he or she takes the position is the culmination of an electoral process. The president must win the approval of legislators who are themselves accountable.

Ideologically, all three South Africa's presidents between 1994 and 2017 were members of the African National Congress (ANC) party, and no one leader has a markedly stronger record of appointing women to the high court. President Nelson Mandela made 13 appointments to fill the newly created Constitutional Court (12 judges and one president of the court). He appointed two women: Justices Yvonne Mokgoro and Kate O'Regan. President Thabo Mbeki had fewer opportunities to appoint Constitutional Court justices. Of the four "ordinary" (i.e., not the Chief Justice) judges he appointed, one was a woman: Justice Bess Nkabinde-Mmono. President Jacob Zuma had eight opportunities to select justices to the Constitutional Court in addition to two chances to appoint a Chief Justice. Three of the eight were women (Justices Sisi Khampepe, Nonkosi Zoliswa Mhlantla, and Leona Theron), and Zuma only appointed the latter two after consecutively selecting four men. (President Cyril Ramaphosa appointed one woman and one man, Justices Zukisa Tshiqi and Stevan Majiedt, in 2019.)

Importantly, the reforms adopted in the early 1990s include a constitutional clause calling for the consideration of race and gender in appointing judges. Section 174 (2) in the Constitution of 1996 stipulates, "The need for the judiciary to reflect broadly the racial and gender composition of South Africa must be considered when judicial officers are appointed." To our knowledge, this inclusion of positive language on gender in judicial appointments was unprecedented for any democracy in the world. The clause helped put the issue of diversity in the judiciary in the national spotlight. Recalling the appointment of justices to the Constitutional Court in 1993, JSC member George Bizos said, "[w]e were mindful of the provisions in the Constitution that we had an obligation in appointing judges to do so having regard to racial and gender issues, and [Mokgoro] fitted the description well" (Constitutional Court Trust Oral History Project 1993). Former members of the JSC emphasized to an author of this book in interviews conducted in 2015 that the commission takes this constitutional provision seriously. (In chapter 6, we outline the role of advocacy organizations and key actors in proposing this clause.)

Since the early 1990s, selectors have interpreted and used Section 174 (2) to improve the representation of Black South Africans in the judiciary. Providing historical context here is necessary. In the move to democracy, many of the White members of the executive and legislative branches were replaced with members of the ANC through elections and other processes. The legal system and judiciary, however, did not experience such a turnover, and as Bonthuys (2013: 60) states, were "the least 'transformed' organs of government." Given the constitutional and political imperative to make the judiciary a more representative and legitimate body, it is logical that successive presidents prioritized the appointment of Black judges. Feminist thinkers, however, argue that the president as well as the JSC have prioritized racial transformation without paying due diligence to the ways in which race and gender intersect (e.g., Albertyn 2014; Masengu 2015). This lack of attention to the intersection of racism and sexism has resulted in the underrepresentation of Black women judges in the judiciary. In this way, having affirmative legal language for the selection of judges in and of itself does not guarantee the representation of women in all their diversity.

In chapter 3, we found that after the creation of a new high court, the number of women matches that of older courts. The case of South Africa's Constitutional Court conforms with this finding. As envisioned in the 1993 Interim Constitution, four of the 11 judges on the new Constitutional Court were picked from the preexisting Supreme Court, which was then almost completely dominated by White men judges. The other seven judges were selected by President Mandela in consultation with other officials. As mentioned above, Mandela appointed two women justices to serve on the new court. After the Court's creation, the number of women increased from two to three in 2006 with Mbeki's appointment of Nkabinde-Mmono. When Mokgoro and O'Regan retired from the bench in 2009, however, only one was replaced by a woman. The number of women justices on the Court dropped to two, and with the appointment of men judges in the 2010s, the court remained there until the 2015 appointment of Justice Mhlantla.

In addition to creating the Constitutional Court, one of the major reforms to the judiciary in the transition to democracy was the creation of a JSC. The JSC consists of 23 elected and unelected officials. Other members include the President of the Supreme Court of Appeal, a Judge President who is designated by the Judges President, and the cabinet member who oversees the administration of justice. Additional members are designated by the president of South Africa, the National Assembly, the advocates' profession, the attorneys' profession, law professors, the National Assembly, and the National Council of Provinces. The Chief Justice of South Africa presides over the JSC.

As mandated by the Constitution, when there is a vacancy on the Constitutional Court, the JSC compiles a shortlist of nominees "with three names more than the number of appointments to be made" (Government of South Africa 1996: Section 174 (4)). From that list, the president is to make appointments. If the president decides all the shortlisted candidates are unacceptable, the president must explain why this is the case, and the commission then provides a supplemental list of nominees. From that list, the president must select a justice. This means that the JSC plays a critical role in furnishing the shortlist, although ultimately, it is the president who chooses the justice.

Has the creation of a Judicial Services Commission improved women's representation on the Constitutional Court? The answer in the scholarship on the South African judiciary is mixed. The JSC is itself a men-dominant institution that, as Masengu (2016: 488) writes, "operates in a man's world." Scholars have found the JSC insensitive to the realities of gender inequality and discrimination against women—particularly Black women—in the legal profession and in the judiciary (Albertyn 2014; Masengu 2015). This lack of sensitivity is shown through the type of questions that the commissioners have posed to women candidates in the 2000s (Andrews 2006). In 2015, the Commission did make an all-woman shortlist for a vacancy on the Constitutional Court, but this occurred only after concerted pressure by women's and civil society groups. It may be that considerable and sustained organizing from the outside and the constitutional clause on gender in judicial appointments combined can push the JSC to include women on their lists.

Directing our attention to the role of informal institutions, it is difficult to know who in the inner circle influences presidents in choosing a particular candidate from a shortlist. Other unwritten ideas and practices, however, do emerge in the scholarship and in interviews as important in how justices are selected. These informal institutions affect women's and men's chances differently.

For one, while there is no formal requirement that justices have previously served on a court in an "acting" capacity (to fill a temporary vacancy), the JSC has informally favored candidates with such experience. This unofficial practice affects men differently than it does women. Acting positions are more likely to be given to men in part because court presidents choose who fills temporary gaps, and men court presidents tend to have familiarity with other men in the legal profession. In 2010 to 2016, women were only given 20 percent of the more than 6,000 acting positions (Masengu 2020). Further, the JSC tends to apply the informal requirement of having done an acting stint when the candidate is a woman and less so when the candidate is a man (Masengu 2015). Taking the 15 justices who were appointed to the Constitutional Court after the first bench was installed, from 1998 through the end of 2017, six had previously served in an acting capacity on that court. Two of the four women (50 percent) appointed in this period had previously served as an acting judge on the Constitutional Court compared with four of the 11 men (36 percent).

A second informal practice is the reliance on informal networks to recruit and select justices. Multiple sources indicate that judges often wait to be encouraged by a senior member of the judiciary or the president of the country before applying for a high court position. This appears to apply to both men and women. For instance, retired Constitutional Court Justice Dikgang Moseneke (2016) recounts in his autobiography that President Mbeki, former President Mandela, and former Chief Justice Arthur Chaskalson all encouraged him to leave the private sector and join the judiciary. If personal and professional networks are gendered, this practice can disadvantage women, and it makes it all the more important that the president, Chief Justice, and other senior officials ask women, including Black women, to apply for vacancies on high courts. Presidents and Chief Justices, however, have all been men. South Africa has had a woman Minister of Justice and Constitutional Development, Brigitte Mabandla, a vocal advocate for women's rights. From April 2004 to September 2008, Mabandla held this post, and she took steps such as hosting a conference on women's judicial appointments and reporting gender-disaggregated data on the composition of the judiciary to women's groups and the National Assembly (Andrews 2006; Albertyn 2014).

5.9 Conclusion

Our case studies suggest that knowing the formal mechanisms may not reveal the full story about selection processes. The formal rules are important for improving gender diversification so far as they create incentives for selectors. When selectors are motivated to choose women, either based on electoral incentives or personal conviction, they can act to place women on the shortlist and to appoint women. Importantly, informal norms and procedures also shape who is ultimately selected as a high court justice. Reliance on established networks and traditional conceptions of "qualifications" built on all-men courts have worked together to marginalize women. Shared ideas such as party ideology work in complex ways as part of a broader set of interrelated institutions to shape selection choices.

Our case studies show that the effectiveness of judicial nomination committees in advancing women's representation is context dependent and may depend on the existence of affirmative language in the constitution, for instance. Two of our five countries established judicial nominating committees: Ireland and South Africa. In South Africa, the constitutional requirement for considering gender and racial diversity seems to have contributed to the nominating committee being more responsive to putting women on their shortlists. In Ireland, where there is no formal rule guiding diverse selections, the opposite has occurred as the insulated selection process has not often led to diversity in selection, especially as it is not mandatory to pick from the committee's list. Interestingly, by 2017, the high courts in both countries reached the benchmark of having one-third women justices reinforcing our argument that there is no single pathway to women's representation on peak courts.

It is also not clear that selectors who are electorally accountable are more likely to appoint women. The Canadian and United States cases point toward the importance of electoral accountability. Yet the first woman joined Colombia's Supreme Court (our only instance of a non-electorally accountable process) in 1983, just three years after women joined the United States Supreme Court (an electorally accountable selection process). And while the mixed-selection process in South Africa led to a Constitutional Court that included women from its founding, it took a decade after Colombia's was created for a woman to be selected. In short, our findings reinforce that formal institutions are only part of the story. Electoral accountability may only be important in cases where selectors are actually pressured to appoint women, something that we explore in detail in the next chapter.

Supporting the findings of Annesely, Beckwith, and Franceschet (2019) on cabinet appointments, we find that the formal rules intersect with informal institutions in complex ways that make it harder for women to gain appointment. One common theme from the case studies is women not being among the "usual suspects" because of the concentration of women in professional networks that are less typical of the previous high court justices. For example, in South Africa and Ireland the members of both sides of the split bar are formally eligible to be nominated. However, in practice, barristers (in Ireland) and advocates (in South Africa) have had an advantage. They are more likely to appear before the high courts and are therefore part of the network most visible to the selectors. This is problematic in Ireland as the differences in professions has made a career as a solicitor more attractive to women than a career as a barrister.

Only in particular contexts are selectors from liberal or left-leaning parties more consistent in appointing women, namely the United States. Selectors from conservative or right-leaning parties display less consistent patterns, with some regularly appointing women, as in the case of Canada. The influence of party ideology is difficult to examine given that in our three remaining cases (Colombia, Ireland, and South Africa), the ideology of the selector's political parties does not markedly vary after the first woman is appointed to a high court. In South Africa, ideology plays a role in the long sweep of history, but since the 1990s, the same party has held power.

Although party ideology does not yield a strong and consistent effect, individual selectors who prioritized having women on the court were able to appoint women. In the United States, President Reagan chose to fulfill his campaign promise and appoint a woman to the Supreme Court. And in Canada, significant strides toward gender parity occurred under Prime Ministers Chrétien and Martin when their ministers of justice pushed for selecting women. Further, it is not just selectors who are elected who play an important role. For better or for worse, the candidacies of women justices in Colombia have been much aided by "political godfathers" who have helped their appointment. Both in the United States and Canada, the role of close advisors is key in reminding selectors of the efficacy of appointing a woman to the court. Yet, across Colombia, Ireland, and South Africa, the role of inner circle advisors in demanding the appointment of women is less clear.

Throughout this chapter we have highlighted the way formal rules regarding the selection of high court justices intersect with informal norms and practices. It is the intersection of those two that produces some of the greatest opportunities for the advancement of women and that simultaneously pose as some of the most persistent barriers. When motivated, selectors who have sought to include women on high courts have been successful. Where they have not felt compelled to act, they have not done so. In the following chapter, we take up the question of what might encourage selectors to be motivated to act and to appoint women by exploring the role of civil society and international norms.

6

International Influences on Women's Representation on High Courts

Those with the power to appoint judges to high courts operate in a broader context of shifting norms of gender equality in governance. Gender equality on decision-making bodies has emerged as an international norm, most often discussed in reference to national legislatures (e.g., Bush 2011; Krook 2006; Hughes, Krook, and Paxton 2015; Towns 2012). International organizations such as the United Nations (UN), international meetings such as the UN world conferences on women, and women's movements forged a global consensus about the importance of women's equal presence when and where decisions are being made.

This chapter takes a closer look at international influences and domestic advocacy organizations on the appointment of women to high courts in our five case study countries. We argue that women are more likely to be selected when traditional images of high courts fade as a consequence of rising new ideas about gender equality. Importantly, we also find that the spread of internationally circulating ideas on the appointment of women plays out differently within country contexts.

In chapters 2 and 3, we found, all else being equal, that women's organizations, time since ratifying the Convention on the Elimination of All Forms of Discrimination Against Women (CEDAW), and regional peer trends help predict women's appointments to high courts. Behind these statistical relationships lie nuanced and context-specific processes in which norms are co-created and transmitted between the local, regional, and international levels over time. These processes are not easily quantified and measured across a large number of cases. Further, our cross-national measures of international influences forgo richness for more easily quantifiable dimensions of multi-faceted concepts. This chapter's in-depth investigation allows us to consider the broader national context and the salience of domestic advocacy organizations, commitments to CEDAW, and regional norms.

In this chapter, we first trace some broad contours of the rise of the global norm of gender equality in the judiciary. Second, we present three linkage mechanisms through which the international norm of gender equality in the judiciary is transmitted between the international and domestic levels: domestic advocacy organizations, CEDAW commitments, and regional norms. Then, for each of our cases, we consider the relationship between women's appointments and the three

Reimagining the Judiciary: Women's Representation on High Courts Worldwide. Maria C. Escobar-Lemmon, Valerie J. Hoekstra, Alice J. Kang, and Miki Caul Kittilson, Oxford University Press. © Maria C. Escobar-Lemmon, Valerie J. Hoekstra, Alice J. Kang, and Miki Caul Kittilson 2021. DOI: 10.1093/oso/9780198861577.003.0006

linkage mechanisms. We find these mechanisms vary in their salience across our cases, resulting in different processes at play.

Heightened international expectations for gender equality draw attention to the inclusion of women in the judiciary as a problem that needs addressing and give individuals and groups something to leverage. To clarify, our argument is not that international factors cause women to be appointed to high courts or are the origin of women's appointments. Rather, international factors can catalyze change by altering ideas and expectations about who can and should be a judge.

6.1 The Rise of the Global Norm of Gender Equality in the Judiciary

Before examining mechanisms through which norms of gender equality spread, we first sketch the rise of the global norm of women's equal participation on decision-making bodies, focusing on the judiciary. The ideal of gender equality in the judicial branch emerged in the UN World Conferences on Women in Mexico City, Nairobi, and Beijing and have spread to international courts and regional organizations.

In the 1950s to the 1970s, international women's activists and international organizations articulated and spread the idea that women's rights are human rights and that women ought to be included in political and public life. In multiple declarations and treaties, which were widely signed and ratified, the issue of women in the judiciary was for the most part implied and not addressed in-depth (or at all). One of the earliest explicit mentions of the importance of including women in the judiciary, that we know of, arose in 1975. In that year, the World Conference of the International Women's Year in Mexico City adopted a World Plan of Action for the Implementation of the Objectives of the International Women's Year. The Mexico City Plan of Action states that participation in political life "implies participation as voters, lobbyists, elected representatives, trade-unionists, and public officials in the various branches of government, including the judiciary" (United Nations 1975: paragraph 59). In 1979, the UN adopted CEDAW, which demands that party states "take all appropriate measures to eliminate discrimination against women in the political and public life of the country," but no direct reference to the judiciary is made (United Nations 1979: Article 7).

Over the course of the 1980s, international women's activists and organizations shifted the framing of women's participation on decision-making bodies from inclusion to gender equity. In general, discussions on the global stage about women in the judiciary or high courts remained less visible than those based on the legislative branch. Even so, some global calls explicitly mention the judiciary. The Nairobi Forward-looking Strategies for the Advancement of Women, which was adopted at the UN's Third World Conference on Women in Nairobi in 1985, declares that, "Governments and political parties should intensify efforts...to achieve equity in the appointment, election and promotion of women to high posts in executive, legislative and *judiciary* branches in these bodies" (United Nations 1985: paragraph 86, emphasis by the authors).

The global norm of gender equity in the judiciary advanced in 1995 at the UN's Fourth World Conference on Women in Beijing. Governments attending the conference adopted the Beijing Declaration and Platform for Action, which asks governments to "[c]ommit themselves to establishing the goal of gender balance in governmental bodies and committees, as well as in public administrative entities, and in the *judiciary*" (United Nations 1995: paragraph 190, emphasis by the authors). Reinforcing this point, the Platform for Action calls upon governments to "[e]nsure that women have the same right as men to be judges..." (paragraph 232, Section m). Further, it calls for the use of affirmative measures to address men's dominance in the judiciary, which includes "setting specific targets and implementing measures to substantially increase the number of women with a view to achieving equal representation of women and men, if necessary through positive action" (paragraph 190).

From the 1990s through the 2010s, commitment to the global norm of gender equity in the judiciary deepened. In 1997, the UN body charged with monitoring the implementation of CEDAW issued General Recommendation No. 23 on Political and Public Life. The recommendation states that the elimination of discrimination against women includes removing barriers to "in particular the exercise of legislative, *judicial*, executive and administrative powers" (CEDAW Committee 1997c, emphasis authors' own). Like the Beijing Declaration, the General Recommendation states that countries ought to adopt temporary measures such as "targeting women for appointment to public positions such as the judiciary" to attain gender equity.

The international norm of gender equity in the judiciary reached supranational courts in the late 1990s with the creation of the International Criminal Court (ICC). Formed in 1997, the Women's Caucus for Gender Justice, a network of women's activists from the Global North and the Global South, advocated for gender inclusivity on the ICC (Chappell 2015; Copelon 2000; Spees 2003). A report by members of the Women's Caucus said that the women's activists "saw the creation of the world's first permanent criminal court as an opportunity to [...] implement many of the strategic objectives outlined and committed to by Governments in the [Beijing] Platform for Action" (Spees 1999). Mobilization by the Women's Caucus helped influence the treaty provision that in the selection of judges, state parties shall "take into account the need" for "a fair representation of female and male judges" (United Nations 1998, Rome Statute, Article 36(8)). The inaugural court had seven women out of 18 judges, far exceeding women's representation on previous supranational courts.

In 2015, member states of the UN adopted the Sustainable Development Goals (SDGs) as part of the 2030 Agenda for Sustainable Development. The goals are an integral part of a global action plan to end poverty and achieve enduring prosperity, and establishes targets against which countries are compared. SDG 16 sets a goal for effective, accountable, and inclusive institutions for sustainable development, and one of the target indicators is equal proportions between men and women in national and local institutions, including the judiciary.

In sum, decades of international women's activism and UN conferences forged a global expectation that judiciaries must not just include women but also achieve gender balance. But how are these global norms linked to the domestic level? Three linkage mechanisms—domestic advocacy organizations, CEDAW commitments, and regional norms—help to explain how international norms of gender equality are transmitted between the international and domestic levels as a long-term process.

6.2 Domestic Advocacy Organizations

In calling for the appointment of women to high courts, advocacy groups help create and transmit global norms of gender equality. In chapter 2 we found a positive relationship between the number of women's international nongovernmental organizations (WINGOs) in a country and the appointment of women. The cross-national measure we utilized operationalizes advocacy organizations in a very specific way, only counting the number of women's international NGOs to which citizens in a country belong. This measure provides functional equivalence across a large number of countries, but overlooks the mobilization and strategy of these groups in pressing for more women on the highest courts. Further, both domestic and international advocacy organizations may play an important role in communicating norms and lobbying for women's appointments. Our case studies allow us to consider the influence of international and domestic women's activism in a broader and more nuanced way.

Domestic advocacy organizations include women's nongovernmental organizations, legal advocacy groups, and academic research centers.[1] Previous research establishes that global advocacy movements play an important role in disseminating ideas about, mobilizing for, and placing issues of gender equality and women's rights on the political agenda (Paxton, Hughes, and Green 2006). In their cross-national study of policies combatting violence against women, Htun and Weldon (2012) find that the impact of global norms for national-level outcomes is mediated by domestic feminist organizations.

[1] We set aside independent state institutions or ad-hoc commissions charged with promoting the status of women, which may be a fourth linkage mechanism.

Advocacy organizations—specifically, women's organizations—address a wide array of issues, from representation on decision-making bodies, to labor rights, to access to reproductive health (Htun and Weldon 2018). Thus, at any point in time, the mere presence of advocacy organizations makes no assurance that women on the high court will be the most salient issue for which they mobilize. Further, Hughes, Krook, and Paxton (2015) uncover a puzzling relationship: a negative interaction between the global normative environment and the number of feminist or WINGOs on the adoption of gender quotas. That the two do not always go hand in hand leads us to inspect the role of domestic advocacy organizations in each country and then examine the broader context of international norms of gender equality in governance.

In some countries, advocacy organizations are the first to publicly highlight the dearth of women on high courts. As such, women's and other advocacy groups help put the issue of women on the bench on the national agenda, as was the case in the United States (Clark 2002). They can bring attention to the lack of women on high courts by issuing press releases, publishing studies on women in the judiciary, and organizing conferences on gender inequality in the legal profession and on courts. For instance, in the United Kingdom, the Association of Women Barristers and the Association of Women Solicitors, along with other groups, organized conferences on women and the law starting in 1995. As Kenney (2008: 729) writes, at these events, "Lord Chancellor Irvine was called to account for the low numbers of women judges and QCs, something he was rarely, if ever, called to account for in Parliament or even the press. The media covered these events, and they thus provided an opportunity to keep the lack of progress in the public eye." Advocacy groups can articulate multiple arguments for why women ought to be included on the bench: gender diversity is necessary for the legitimacy of the courts and yields better decisions. Advocacy groups, therefore, often constitute the primary source of public demand for more women judges.

At times, advocacy groups use international venues to articulate their demands. Advocacy groups can also draw on international agreements such as CEDAW, which we discuss at greater length in the next section, to call for the inclusion of more women on high courts. Women in the UK drew on regional comparisons through its membership in the Council of Europe and European Union, to show the UK as an outlier by comparison (Kenney 2008).

Advocates for gender equality also form international networks of organizations and individuals who share a goal of promoting gender equality in the law and in the judiciary. Specifically, the International Association of Women Judges (IAWJ) is an international nongovernmental organization with national chapters around the world. Members include women judges. The IAWJ and their affiliates organize national, regional, and global conferences. These conferences help inspire women to accept or apply for higher-level positions in the judiciary and help spread a norm of gender equality in judiciaries and high courts.

In certain cases, but not always, advocacy organizations may support individual women candidates for judgeship as part of a larger strategy to help diversify high courts. Advocacy groups may elect to informally or formally feed names of potential candidates to selectors and members of their inner circle of advisors. Where applicable, organizations may write nomination letters to selection committees (for instance in South Africa) or testify in confirmation hearings (as in the United States) in support of highly qualified women to encourage the diversification of high courts. In some instances, women's and other organizations may also encourage women to submit dossiers and help them assemble their applications.

6.3 CEDAW Commitment

International human rights treaties codify norms, and CEDAW is one of several treaties that has heightened global awareness of gender equality. The treaty is integral to the broader phenomenon of rising expectations of gender diversity in governance and in the judiciary. While the convention cannot compel countries to comply through sanctions, countries improve the protection of women's rights after ratifying CEDAW (Hill 2010; Lupu 2013; Gray, Kittilson, and Sandholtz 2006; Simmons 2009). Notably, it can take years, if not decades, before CEDAW can have a domestic impact, depending on the country.

CEDAW influences domestic discourse on gender equity on high courts in several ways. Merry (2006: 72) argues that engaging with the convention "does important cultural work." After a country ratifies the treaty, it is obliged to submit periodic reports to a treaty body, the Committee on the Elimination of Discrimination Against Women (confusingly, also referred to as CEDAW). These reports ought to be submitted to the committee every four years and note significant developments and obstacles in realizing treaty goals. As it considers the report, the committee poses questions to be answered by the country's representative. Merry (72–73) writes, "[t]he process of ratification, preparing reports, and presenting and discussing reports fosters new cultural understandings." We suggest that in debating, researching, presenting, and hearing feedback on reports to the CEDAW treaty body, country representatives and international experts co-create the norm of gender equity in the judiciary. The back-and-forth interaction that occurs between member states and the CEDAW Committee does not always operate smoothly. A country's leaders can ignore or react negatively to international criticism of discrimination against women. Nevertheless, the CEDAW reporting process provides one way in which both countries and international entities promote the development of the global norm of gender equity in the judiciary.

Second, after a country ratifies CEDAW, the convention can provide domestic advocacy groups an opportunity to ground, and perhaps legitimate, their claims in a broader framework (Simmons 2009). Domestic advocates may use CEDAW and other international declarations to buttress demands for more women on high courts and in the judiciary. If domestic advocacy groups mobilize and state oversight bodies take international law seriously, advocacy groups can use CEDAW in making claims upon the state. To be clear, we do not argue that advocacy groups take up this process in all countries or at all times.

Among our five countries, four have ratified CEDAW. The earliest party among our case studies is Canada, which ratified CEDAW in 1981. Colombia ratified the convention in 1982, followed by Ireland in 1985 and South Africa in 1995. Although the United States signed CEDAW in 1980, it has not ratified the convention. Canada began submitting CEDAW reports in the 1980s, and all four countries submitted reports into the 2010s. This span, covering more than 30 years, allows us to examine when countries and the committee began to bring up the issue of women on the judiciary and whether women's inclusion as judges stays on the agenda. We gathered country reports over this period of time to seek out specific mentions of women, gender, courts, and the judiciary (United Nations Office of the High Commissioner 2020).

6.4 Regional Norms

Norms of gender equity on courts may also grow within world regions. Countries in the same geographic area are exposed to each other through trade, travel, language, and media, and thus, comparisons are most likely to be made with regional peers. As such, as norms of gender balance in the judiciary rise within a region, countries may be encouraged to include more women in the judiciary to keep up with their regional peers. If countries are ahead of the curve, they may feel less pressure to appoint more women to high courts.

Norms of gender equity can flow through regional organizations. Previous studies of women's rights have found that norms addressing gender discrimination in employment, sexual harassment, and violence against women are often established and strengthened at the regional level (e.g., Alvarez 2000; Zippel 2006; Adams and Kang 2007; Friedman 2009; Montoya 2013). Regional organizations promulgate treaties on women's rights, set benchmarks on gender equality for member countries to meet, and help monitor progress toward gender equity.

The presence of women on supranational courts, many of which are regional, may heighten expectations for women to serve on domestic high courts. As former ICC judge Akua Kuenyehia notes, "Regarding women judges, one can say that we can be role models—if you can have someone on an international court, why not on the Supreme Court at the domestic level?" (Dawuni 2017: 70, quoted in Moyer 2019: 192). To varying degrees, regional bodies have taken steps to end the practice of having all-men regional courts and include women.

Regional expectations about gender equality have been codified in European Union (EU) law since its founding. EU laws, more broadly, have called for equal rights between men and women. In 1995, the EU, referring to the Beijing Declaration and Platform for Action alongside previous EU policy, called for the balanced participation of men and women in decision-making (Council of the European Union 1996). By 1999, the EU Commission had released its first report that specifically called for more women in high courts (Anasagasti and Wuiame 1999). The report urged member states to reassess the criteria used for the selection of justices to their high courts, and to limit reliance on closed networks and professional circles.

Some of the first concerns about women's exclusion from the European Court of Human Rights were raised in the early 1990s (Vauchez 2015), and the European Court of Justice seated its first woman in 1981, but it was not until 1999 that the next two women joined the bench. Since 2004, member state nomination lists for the European Court of Human Rights must include at least one candidate of each gender.

In Africa, gender equity norms flow through both subregional and continent-wide organizations. In 1997, the Southern African Development Community (SADC) adopted the Declaration on Gender and Development. Referencing the Nairobi Forward Looking Strategies and the Beijing Declaration and Platform for Action, the SADC Declaration calls for a 30 percent target of women in decision-making structures by 2005 (Southern African Development Community 1997: Section H(ii)). A decade later, in 2008, SADC adopted the Gender Protocol on Gender and Development, which challenges states to adopt legislative and other measures to ensure "that women have equitable representation on, and participation in, all courts . . . " (Southern African Development Community 2008: Article 7(f)).

At the continental level, the African Union (AU) adopted a host of laws and policies to promote gender equity. In 2002, the continental body integrated the promotion of gender equality as one of its principles in its Constitutive Act. The next year, the AU promulgated the Maputo Protocol on the Rights of Women, a treaty that encourages the use of temporary positive measures to improve women's participation in governance. In 2004, the AU finalized the Solemn Declaration on Gender Equality in Africa, with goals of spreading the principle of gender parity and tracking annual progress at the national and regional levels. And in 2009, the AU adopted a Gender Policy, which explicitly states that "[w]eak representation of women in diverse ministerial positions in many States, and even in Parliament as well as in the judicial system, is a major concern and challenge that demands prompt attention" (African Union 2009: 13).

The African regional norm of gender equity in governance extended to regional courts in the 2000s. Drawing on the Maputo Protocol, women's activists pushed the AU to ensure that the African Court on Human and Peoples' Rights, which was installed in 2006, includes gender-sensitive language for the appointment of judges (Dawuni 2020). Between 2006 and 2017, women held two of the 11 seats on the court, and in 2017, the number increased to four. Overall, 10 women out of 29 judges have been women (35 percent). Subregional courts, such as the Economic Community of Western African States (ECOWAS) Court of Justice, do not have a gender-sensitive clause, but as Dawuni (2020) reports, 30 percent of the ECOWAS Court of Justice members have been women. The East African Court of Justice (EACJ) has had five women out of 28 judges (18 percent) since its creation in 1999.

Across Latin America, regional organizations have similarly established norms of women's rights, gender equity, and non-discrimination. Friedman's (2009) research establishes the "centrality of regional institutions in setting norms" and notes the back-and-forth between regional organizations and "networks of allies in national and/or regional civil society, particularly in putting pressure on national decision makers" (371–372). Leading the way, the Inter-American Commission of Women was established in 1928: the first intergovernmental agency created to address women's rights as part of a broader human rights framework. The Inter-American Commission of Women is an autonomous body within the Organization of American States (OAS), and in 1986 called for full and equal participation by the year 2000 (Friedman 2009).

A major force in creating regional norms and putting pressure on decision makers across Latin America has been the Encuentros, begun in 1982 by CLADEM, a network of women's organizations in Latin American and the Caribbean (Alvarez 2000). In addition to regional meetings of domestic advocacy organization such as those fostered by CLADEM, there have been cross-border meetings of women high court judges. In 1999, the director of the Women, Justice, and Gender Program of the Latin American Institute of the United Nations organized a series of region-wide meetings of women high court justices to discuss the inclusion of a gender perspective in the administration of justice. The first of these was held in 2000 in San José, Costa Rica; the seventeenth in 2018 in Guatemala. Additionally, there have been three separate meetings of only women constitutional court justices. The summits are described as leading to improvement in the judicial system through the implementation of policies to ensure equal access to justice and the creation of gender equality units (Fundación Justicia y Género 2021). Each summit includes a declaration drawing attention to issues and clearly provides an extended opportunity for women serving on these courts to network and exchange ideas.

Regional organizations in Latin America long heralded anti-discrimination principles and more recently have specifically addressed women's equity and full participation in decision making. The Charter of the OAS in 1948 states that "All human beings, regardless of race, sex, nationality, creed or social status" have rights. In 1969, this was followed by recognition that "All persons are equal before the law." The Additional Protocol to the American Convention on Economic, Social, and Cultural Rights in 1988 further established the guarantee to exercise those rights "without discrimination on the grounds of race, color, sex, language" or other grounds. Established by the OAS in 1994, the Office of the Rapporteur on the Rights of Women focuses on women's rights and gender equality. Yet it was not until 2017 that a specific Declaration on Gender Equality and Women's Empowerment for the Good of Humanity was issued by the OAS (OEA/Ser.L/II.7.10). Specifically, the Office calls for women's "full and equal access, participation, representation, leadership and the influence of women in the civil, political, economic, social and cultural spheres" (Organization of American States 2021).

Similar to the European Court of Human Rights and the African Court of Human and People's Rights, the Inter-American Court of Human Rights is an autonomous court that interprets and applies the American Convention. The court itself had very few women on its bench, with one woman appointed in the late 1980s, reverting back to an all-men panel, and finally increasing to three women of the seven justices by 2007 (Corte Interamericana de Derechos Humanos 2019).

6.5 International Influences in Five Case Studies

How do the three linkage mechanisms work in our five case studies? We examine the role of domestic advocacy organizations, CEDAW commitments, and regional norms in each country over time.

6.5.1 The United States

An important influence on women's appointments to the United States Supreme Court has been domestic advocacy organizations. Advocacy organizations in the United States helped create demand for the appointment of women to the Supreme Court. Lobbying by women's organizations dates back to Truman's presidency, by the National Association of Women Lawyers (Clark 2002; Goldman 1999), and some advocated for nominating a particular woman to the Supreme Court (Cook 1982). Stepped up pressure for women's inclusion on the United States Supreme Court began in 1965 with suggestions of three women's names for the Arthur Goldberg vacancy (Cook 1982: 326). Although a woman was not selected at that time, demands for including women on the shortlist grew. In 1971, the National Women's Political Caucus (NWPC) prepared a list of qualified women judges for President Richard Nixon, and a representative of that organization also appeared in Senate Judiciary Committee hearings to call out the dearth of women in the federal judiciary, squarely linking this to growing dissatisfaction among women voters (Cook 1982). Joining in this pressure to appoint a woman to the Supreme Court were groups such as the League of Women Voters, National Federation of Republican Women, American Bar Association Committee on the Rights of Women, and the National Council of Negro Women (Cook 1982).

About the same time that President Jimmy Carter's circle of advisors was helping to push forward his agenda of appointing women, a number of advocacy groups mobilized, including NWPC's Legal Support Caucus, which aimed to "identify and assist well-qualified feminist lawyers in appointment to the federal bench" (as cited in Clark 2002: 246). The Legal Support Caucus presented the Carter administration with lists of names of women after embarking on campaigns to encourage women to consider a federal judgeship. The Caucus presented these names in the form of a letter, which was signed onto by a number of advocacy organizations, including the American Association of University Women, the NAACP Legal Defense Fund, the Women's League Defense Fund, and the Women's Division of the National Bar Association. Further, the Caucus was behind efforts to get Ruth Bader Ginsburg appointed to the DC Federal Court of Appeal (Clark 2002).

Both the NWPC and the other powerhouse women's advocacy organization, the National Organization of Women (NOW), intensified pressure for the appointment of women to the Supreme Court in the 1970s (Cook 2018). NOW's Legal Defense and Education Fund prepared data and messaging on the dearth of women in the United States judiciary for the news media to disseminate (Cook 2018). And at the local level, chapters of NOW encouraged individual women to apply for federal judge positions.

These groups did not end their efforts at the stage of selecting a nominee. Senate confirmation is also critical to the appointment of judges to the Supreme Court in the United States. Advocacy groups began to lobby members of the judiciary committee as well as members of the Senate at large, testifying at committee hearings and making rounds to the Senators' offices. This practice is well-entrenched for every nominee now, and not just for women.

Although the Carter administration partnered with advocacy organizations to boost women's nominations, the Reagan and Bush administrations pursued a less cooperative path with these groups (Clark 2002). The Clinton era ushered in a new wave of pressure from advocacy organizations for the selection of a second woman to the Supreme Court. Many of the organizations that had played a role in pressuring Carter began lobbying again, buoyed by President Bill Clinton's support for gender equality and by the fact that he had selected the first woman ever to head the Department of Justice (Davis 2005).

Other prominent domestic advocacy organizations have been equivocal about the appointment of women to federal courts, especially the Supreme Court. Most notable among them is the American Bar Association (ABA). The ABA has at times played a more institutionalized role in the selection process, as mentioned in the previous chapter. During some administrations, the role of the ABA has been largely as one advocacy organization among others, and so we discuss that aspect of its role here. Dating back to the Eisenhower Administration, presidents have relied on the ABA's Standing Committee on the Federal Judiciary's ratings for all nominees for a federal judgeship.

In addition, domestic advocacy organizations aside from women's groups testify at confirmation hearings of Supreme Court nominees and also provide names to presidents of who they view to be suitable candidates. Conservative interest groups, such as the Federalist Society, have exerted pressure in the nomination process (Nemacheck 2001). In fact, the Federalist Society provided names to then-candidate Donald Trump. On that list were Neil Gorsuch and Brett Kavanaugh.

The United States affiliate of the IAWJ is the National Association of Women Judges (NAWJ), formed in 1979 to advocate for women on the United States Supreme Court and in the judiciary more broadly, and for an end to discriminatory practices (Morrison 2002). At its founding, the NAWJ also advocated for ratification of the Equal Rights Amendment. By including women in key positions as conference speakers and attendees, the organization hoped the visibility of women judges in these events would stand as a "first hand lesson that women can be judges" (Rossman 1980: 1237).

The first resolution, passed unanimously at the first NAWJ conference, affirmed that the central challenge was ending the exclusion of women from the United States Supreme Court, and called on the next president with a vacancy to appoint a woman (Rossman 1980: 1252). Taking up an insider strategy, the group pressed for the appointment of the first woman to the ABA's Board of Governors. They also set up task forces to investigate gender biases, and established gender bias trainings (Martin 1993).

Continuing to press for the first woman to be appointed, the NAWJ teamed up with the NWPC and the NOW Legal Defense and Education Fund (Morrison 2002). The second annual NAWJ conference in 1980 in Washington, DC, included one event at the United States Supreme Court, with a welcome from Chief Justice Warren Burger, a reception hosted by Justice Lewis Powell, Jr., and a luncheon hosted by President and Mrs. Carter (Davis 1982). President Carter spoke to the members of the NAWJ and "promised that he would give full consideration to women for a Supreme Court seat" (Cook 1982: 325).

Yet President Carter did not have the opportunity to fill a vacancy, and it was not until the Reagan administration that the first woman on the Supreme Court was successfully nominated and confirmed. President of the NAWJ, Joan Dempsey Klein, appeared at Justice Sandra Day O'Connor's Senate confirmation hearing, testifying to her exceptional qualifications to serve on the Supreme Court (Davis 1982). In the following year, the annual conference honored Justice O'Connor, and she spoke to the group, thanking them for their support in her

Senate hearings (Davis 1982). More recently, the focus on women on the Supreme Court has continued. Justice Ruth Bader Ginsburg addressed or appeared at the annual conferences in 2003, 2007, and 2011. Justice Sonia Sotomayor was given an award in 2009 by the NAWJ when former Justice O'Connor spoke, and Justice Sotomayor gave the keynote speech in 2014.

In addition to the Supreme Court focus, the NAWJ has advocated for more women on all levels of courts across the country. The NAWJ first compiled a directory of women judges in the United States in 1981, at which time there were 727 women listed across 49 states (Davis 1982). The directory was provided to senators as a resource for highly qualified women to serve on federal courts.

Beyond advocating for and providing regular statistics on women on courts across the United States, the NAWJ and its annual conferences provide a forum for women judges to network with one another. Some of the original organizers dubbed this an "old girls network" to bring change (Rossman 1980). These connections encourage sharing ideas, experiences, and strategies and provide a collective voice. The 1982 conference included a men's fashion show themed "Thou Shalt Not Take Thyself Too Seriously," and the event was praised as a "delightful departure from the usual fashion show by women for judges' wives" (Davis 1982: 20).

International influences appear to play little direct role in women's appointments to the Supreme Court in the United States. Because the United States has yet to ratify CEDAW, there is no reporting process to act as a linkage mechanism. Although 187 countries around the world have ratified the treaty, the United States stands alone among industrialized democracies in not having ratified. Several context-specific explanations have been offered for this, including domestic United States politics, disagreements among women's organizations, and the geopolitical hegemonic power of the United States (Baldez 2014).

Regional influences do not appear to exert notable influences. Advocacy organizations in the United States have not buttressed their claims for more women on the United States Supreme Court with mentions of CEDAW or other international treaties. Therefore, the linkage mechanism that played the strongest role in the United States was domestic advocacy organizations, overshadowing any regional or CEDAW effects. Domestic advocacy groups in the United States have lobbied for the advancement of women in the judiciary and Supreme Court and will likely continue to do so.

6.5.2 Canada

Taken together, domestic advocacy organizations, CEDAW commitments, and regional effects have all played an important role in translating and transmitting norms of gender equality in governance within Canada. Importantly, domestic organizations rarely advocate for particular women judges in public ways. Among the judges and former ministers of justice interviewed by one of the authors of this book, several stated that it is frowned upon to lobby for the selection of any particular justice. Behind the scenes, there may be efforts, but these are difficult to document.

Overall, the role of advocacy organizations in Canada has been more instrumental in publicly raising the issue of women's underrepresentation on the Supreme Court of Canada (SCC) and in the judiciary more broadly. To understand the broader context for the saliency of women on the high court, it is necessary to take a step back to examine fundamental constitutional changes in Canada that coincided, partly, with the rise of the international women's movement.

Domestic advocacy organizations in Canada were pivotal to getting the issue of women's equality into the Canadian Charter of Rights and Freedoms. Commissioned in November 1980, the Canadian Advisory Council on the Status of Women advocated for women's rights in the Canadian Charter of Rights and Freedoms (Ruth 2012). Based on their discussions with women's organizations across Canada, the Council proposed "new wording for Section 15 and other provisions of the Charter" (Ruth 2012). The Charter was enacted in 1982, and it was not until 1985 that the equality provisions came into effect, further intensifying scrutiny of what was, at the time, a SCC with only one woman.

The enactment of the Charter of Rights and Freedoms in 1982 turned a spotlight onto the SCC as the court geared up to adjudicate on a new set of rights and freedoms that had not previously been enshrined in the Canadian Constitution. The Canadian public was aware that the SCC would now adjudicate on a host of new issues, and among the set of increasingly salient issues was women's rights. The near absence of women's faces among the justices on the bench stood in stark contrast to the Charter with its calls for equality and non-discrimination.

Concomitant with this new constitutional shift, the Canadian feminist movement extended its demands to call for more women on the SCC (Backhouse 2019). The National Action Committee on the Status of Women, a coalition of domestic women's organizations, "struck a 'Women are Persons' medallion and vowed to store it for safekeeping until it could be presented to the first female appointed to the Supreme Court" (Backhouse 2019: 147). Behind the scenes, women's advocacy organizations pressured for the appointment of the second woman to the SCC (Backhouse 2019). Their efforts centered on Prime Minister Mulroney, a Conservative. The Prime Minister wanted to announce Claire L'Heureux-Dube's appointment on the fifth anniversary of the Charter, and to have media at the announcement.

While some advocacy organizations have pressed for more women to be appointed to the SCC, other organizations have pushed against this, although not always publicly. Resistance was stronger during the first appointments during the 1980s. Within this context, "A senior political advisor recalled that the 'establishment' in the Ontario legal community had been "shameless in making the case that [Wilson] wasn't 'ready' and that there were other (male) candidates who were better 'qualified'" (Backhouse 2019: 149). And after the second woman, L'Heureux-Dube, was appointed, a fellow SCC justice expressed disappointment and both she and Wilson faced hostility from the other justices. Importantly, the Canadian Bar Association opposed the appointments of both Wilson and L'Heureux-Dube (Backhouse 2019: 236).

The Canadian chapter of the IAWJ has played an important role in calling for more women at all levels of the judiciary. L'Heureux-Dube presided over the chapter's inaugural meeting in 1994 in Toronto (records of the Canadian Chapter of IAWJ). Even before the Canadian Chapter was officially formed, records indicate that 76 judges had already joined the IAWJ as individual members of the transnational organization. The Constitution and Bylaws of the Canadian Chapter of the IAWJ indicate that part of the objectives is to "increase the number of women judges appointed" (1995: 2).

With Canada's ratification of CEDAW in 1981, and the adoption of the Canadian Charter of Rights and Freedoms in the same year, women's rights and gender equality have become front and center in the Canadian political and legal arenas. After ratifying CEDAW, Canada took seriously its reporting duties to the UN Committee on CEDAW. We were not able to obtain Canada's first report, but in response to the 1985 report, the CEDAW Committee raised questions to Canada about the "low representation of women in elected bodies, public office, the judiciary system and industrial management" (CEDAW Committee 1985: 9). By the time Canada's second report was filed in 1990, Canada was able to claim recognition for three of the nine sitting justices on the Supreme Court being women. In 2007, Canada reported that four of the nine judges on the Supreme Court were women, claiming to have, in the report's words, "the most gender-balanced high court in the world" (CEDAW Committee 2007: 31). In response, the Committee praised the number of women on the highest court (CEDAW Committee 2008). Again in 2016, Canada reported that four of the nine judges on the Supreme Court were women, which the Committee commended (CEDAW Committee 2016).

In addition to advocacy organizations and CEDAW commitments, regional influences have contributed to growing norms of gender equality on the highest court. After O'Connor was appointed to the United States Supreme Court in 1981, a member of parliament from the Canadian Conservative Party, Flora MacDonald, stood up in the House of Commons, calling upon Minister of Justice Jean Chrétien to follow the lead of the United States and appoint a woman to the SCC. Chrétien replied to MacDonald by explaining that his government had wanted to add a woman to the shortlist previously, but was unable find a sufficiently qualified woman for the position (Anderson 2001: 124–125). Chrétien's reply stirred outrage among the public, and women's advocacy organizations mobilized. In this way, when the norm of exclusively men high courts broke in the United States, it triggered a response among Canadian political elites and among the public, ramping up expectations for Canada to appoint a woman.

6.5.3 Ireland

In Ireland, domestic advocacy organizations have played a smaller role in co-creating and advancing norms of gender equity in the judiciary as compared to CEDAW commitments and regional norms. There are a number of domestic women's advocacy organizations in Ireland, but overall, few pressing for women's appointment to the Supreme Court. This is not to say that Irish society is unreceptive to increasing diversity and inclusion broadly. In the 1970s, the independent state agency, the Commission on the Status of Women, raised the issue of women's exclusion from government and the Supreme Court as a public problem. The Commission's Third Action Programme in 1991 called attention to women's underrepresentation in Ireland's decision-making bodies (Anasagasti and Wuiame 1999). In 1993, the Report of the Second Commission on the Status of Women rendered 211 recommendations, including to improve women's presence in politics and on state bodies (Galligan 2000). Founded in 1973 (the same year Ireland joined the EU), the National Women's Council of Ireland (NWCI), formerly the Council for the Status of Women, monitors the work of the Commission, and acts as an umbrella organization for more than 150 NGOs in Ireland. Over the years, the NWCI has directed its attention to a variety of issues but the selection of women judges less so.

The IAWJ lists an Irish chapter of its organization, but there is little mention of the organization in accounts of women's appointments to the Supreme Court. The Irish Women Lawyers Association supports the careers of women in the legal profession, promotes networking and education, but less is public about its role in specifically advocating for the appointment of women justices to the Supreme Court.

One advocacy organization focusing on women's appointments to courts is the Law Society of Ireland. This organization has pushed the government to open up judicial positions for solicitors. One domestic government initiative, the National Women's Strategy, which involves civil servants, NWCI, trade unions, and business groups, has tried to bring attention to the lack of women in the judiciary and propose concrete changes. For instance, the National Women's Strategy published a report (2013) recommending that the High Court create a job shadowing program for women solicitors, barristers, and senior counsel to help tackle the lack of women judges on that Court, and that the Judicial Appointments Advisory Board's mandate include the promotion of diversity in the judiciary.

Through interviews conducted by one of this book's authors with academics, judges, the Bar Association, women's advocacy groups, and a former official of the Ministry of Justice, it became clear that diversifying the judiciary was not a top priority for advocacy organizations. Instead, the bulk of advocacy organization efforts are focused more on getting women into elected positions, especially in parliament where the numbers have been relatively low, particularly in rural areas. In addition, women's organizations were also focused on repealing Ireland's abortion laws and addressing ongoing discrimination against Roma women and Irish Travellers (an Irish indigenous ethnic group) and access to education and work.

Periodic reporting to the CEDAW Committee has created a dialogue in which Ireland has increasingly focused on women's representation in governance, including the judiciary. While we were not able to locate Ireland's first report, the Committee's concluding observations on that study do not raise the issue of women's underrepresentation in the judiciary. In Ireland's combined second and third periodic reports, Ireland shared that one out of eight judges on the Supreme Court in 1996 were women, and that the percentage of barristers who are women increased between 1986 and 1993 (CEDAW Committee 1997b: 58). The CEDAW Committee replied to assert its "concern that women continue to be under-represented in public and political life" and specifically mentioned gender training in law school curriculum and continuing legal education, and ensuring adequate numbers of women to be appointed to specialized courts (CEDAW Committee 1999: paragraphs 189, 199).

Reinforcing the global and domestic expectation that women be included in governance, in the combined fourth and fifth periodic reports (2003 and 2005), Ireland reported extensively on the first woman elected as president in Ireland in 1990 and the representation of women in parliament, as cabinet ministers, in the civil service, and within each political party. One table was devoted to the number of women in the judiciary, with a line denoting the 25 percent women on the Irish Supreme Court (CEDAW Committee 2005b). Since then, Ireland has reported to CEDAW on the number of women on the Supreme Court and received praise from the treaty body for its inclusiveness. Interestingly, in a 2016 meeting organized by the Ministry of Justice on Ireland's draft response to the CEDAW Committee's List of Issues, a participant argued that Ireland should highlight that half of the Supreme Court justices are women, noting that, "The first CEDAW meeting was chaired by Justice Annie Ruth Jiagge, the first woman High Court judge in Ghana" (Department of Justice of Ireland 2016: 2).

Reporting in 2002 to the UN on Ireland's National Plan for Women, the government committed to both address the low representation of women at all decision-making levels, and to taking positive actions to catalyze change. As part of Ireland's National Development Plan (2000–2006), achieving these goals would be assisted by National Development Plan (2000–2006) Monitoring Committees.

In the report to the UN, Ireland promises to "disseminate the values and practices underlying gender equality" and "improve the understanding of issues related to direct and indirect gender discrimination" and to "develop the capacity of key players (independent bodies responsible for the promotion of gender equality, Social Partners and nongovernmental organizations especially at national, regional and local levels) to promote gender equality effectively" ("Report to the United Nations on the National Plan for Women 2002 on the Implementation of the Beijing Platform for Action" 2002: 35–6).

Regional norms exert considerable influence on Ireland to address gender equality more broadly, and to increase the number of women on the Supreme Court more specifically. As a member of the European Union, Ireland is connected to a complex and rich set of efforts to improve gender equity. Significant gender equality legislation was adopted in the 1970s after Ireland became a member of the EU in 1973, which at that time was the European Economic Community (EEC). Upon joining the EEC, Ireland had to reform its explicitly discriminatory laws. Ireland passed the Employment Equality Act of 1977 on gender discrimination. The government adopted the Civil Service (Employment of Married Women) Act of 1973, undoing a law that had prevented women from holding jobs in the civil service, including in the judiciary, upon marriage. In a further effort to comply with EU law, Ireland adopted the Employment Equality Act in 1998, which outlaws discrimination in employment, including on the basis of gender. And in 2000, the Equal Status Act was adopted to combat discrimination in non-workplace arenas.

European Union-led reports and initiatives have raised the issue of gender equality in the judiciary, among other arenas of governance. For instance, the European Commission published a report in 1999 entitled, "Women and decision-making in the judiciary in the European Union" (Anasagasti and Wuiame 1999). Calling for gender equality in decision-making structures, women's underrepresentation on courts across Europe was highlighted, and in particular the lower percentage of women on the Supreme Court of Ireland relative to other higher achieving member state peers. The recommendations for improvement included monitoring the percentage of women, greater transparency, and assessing the barriers created by the discretionary criteria in selection.

In a similar fashion, the Council of Europe has worked to disseminate norms of gender equality in governance. In 2009, the Council of Europe (CoE) produced a report entitled "Parity Democracy – A Far Cry from Reality." A comparative study of the results of the first and second rounds of monitoring, the report recommends gender equity in political and public decision-making. And a similar 2014 CoE survey on judicial systems ranked Ireland near the bottom among 47 European countries in judicial diversity (European Commission for the Efficiency of Justice 2014). Similarly, a 2016 report comparing European countries showed Ireland remained on the low end, grouping Ireland with Bosnia and Herzegovina, Greece,

Hungary, Serbia, Slovak Republic, and Turkey, and advocated for reaching the 40 to 60 percent range for women's share of the bench.

In short, regular monitoring of women in the judiciary by the European Commission and the CoE has heightened pressure to appoint more women to the Supreme Court of Ireland. Further, these regional pressures are nested within the broader international pressures stemming from regular reporting to the CEDAW Committee. Yet, at the domestic level, advocacy organizations have devoted less of their attention to women in the judiciary, relative to other governmental arenas.

6.5.4 Colombia

Advocacy groups and the CEDAW treaty body have also pressured for the appointment of women to high courts in Colombia. One of those advocacy groups leading the charge was Dejusticia. In August 2015, Director of the NGO Dejusticia and Universidad Nacional Professor Rodrigo Uprimny published an editorial calling on President Juan Manuel Santos to guarantee the advancement of women on the courts by delivering an all-women *terna* for the replacement of Constitutional Court magistrate Mauricio González. Uprimny (2015) argued an all-women list was needed to ensure highly qualified women gained access across the judiciary and especially on the high courts. The editorial provided a list of qualified women including those who had served as acting magistrates (*encargada),* long-time *magistradas auxiliares*, and distinguished scholars and professors of law. The women represented different universities, regions, and ideologies, underscoring the abundance of qualified women. Central to Uprimny's argument was that an all-women list was needed because of patriarchal bias in the Senate; only an all-woman list would guarantee a woman would be picked.

About a month after Uprimny's editorial, in September, a group of opinion leaders wrote an open letter publicly also calling on President Santos to appoint a woman to this vacancy. The 30 signatories included well-known columnists, leaders of NGOs, well-known political-legal scholars such as Cecilia Lopez (a former Minister and former senator), and Alfonso Gómez Méndez (former Minister of Justice and Attorney General). The letter identified 24 qualified women who had submitted their applications, stressing this was the ideal moment for the president to submit a *terna* of exclusively women.[2] Ultimately, a list was announced that included two women, Catalina Botero Marino and Magdalena Correa Henao. Yet, as discussed in chapter 5, observers commented that both

[2] As discussed in chapter 5, the selection process in Colombia involves a step where a call for applications is published and then individuals interested in being considered must submit documents such as a CV as part of an application.

were *rellena* with the election of the only man on the list, Alejandro Linares, who had been legal vice-president for Ecopetrol and had held other public sector posts, all but guaranteed.

While Uprimny and DeJusticia were advocating for the appointment of a woman to the Constitutional Court in 2015, other groups focused on increasing transparency in the selection of judges. The NGO Corporación Excelencia en la Justicia called on the Senate to conduct their plenary interviews with the short-listed candidates in public and to allow for the participation of civil society to pose questions and provide input so as to minimize the "clandestine lobby." In response, beginning in 2015, the plenary interviews were televised on the Congress's TV channel and live-streamed on the web. Additionally, representatives of academia and civil society were invited to the session and given the chance to question the candidates. The Senate also picked three questions from those submitted via Twitter for the candidates (Senate press release. "Con transparencia, candidatos a Magistrado harán su presentación en la Plenaria este Miércoles"). Additionally, calls for an increase in transparency have led Elección Visible (a group formed in 2008 as an academic-civil society partnership) to make publicly available not only information about candidates seeking elected office, but also nominees for the high courts and executive positions. While not a complete listing, this has produced increased public attention to, and information about, the courts.

Finally, while the efforts by Uprimny and DeJusticia to get an all-women *terna* in 2015 were not successful, the attention they garnered raised considerations of gender balance. In early 2017, the terms of four of the nine justices on the Constitutional Court expired with the president having the responsibility to fill two of the vacancies. Of the six names he put forward four were women, and one list was entirely women. The lists put forward by the Council of State and the Supreme Court also contained one woman each, and from the Supreme Court list the woman was selected. This produced a rapid gender shift in the court. With the appointment of two women in 2017, the Constitutional Court became one-third women for the first time.

Domestic advocacy organizations in Colombia have not traditionally lobbied for the inclusion of women on the court, so much as they have lobbied for an inclusion of feminist perspectives or feminist decisions. In reflecting on a Constitutional Court with a historic number of women, Alexandra Sandoval (director of the NGO Women's Link Worldwide) noted, "it is not sufficient that there are women. They have to be women judges committed to the protection of the human rights of women and girls" (Medellín Cano 2017). Some have resisted lobbying for the appointment of a particular judge so that they would not have a conflict of interest when appearing before her in the future. That said, some organizations realized that women may need encouragement to put their names forward for consideration. One aspirant interviewed for this project noted that one NGO was encouraging women to submit their names, even going so far as doing the leg work in assembling the application packet and taking it to be registered, thus removing one possible barrier.

CEDAW has played a role in raising norms of gender equity for Colombia. Colombia has regularly submitted reports to the CEDAW treaty body. While these reports have at times mentioned the judiciary, greater emphasis has been placed upon women's participation in other parts of government. When the judiciary does receive prominent attention, it is focused primarily on the decisions it has taken rather than its composition. This theme is consistent across all the different state reports. In its first report, submitted in 1986, Colombia mentioned that the Supreme Court of Justice and the Council of State each had a woman judge.

In 1993, in a combined report for the second and third reporting periods, Colombia noted that there were no women on the Constitutional Court or on the Supreme Court of Justice; one woman on the Supreme Council of the Judicature; and four women on the Council of State. (CEDAW Committee 1993: 34). In its 1997 report, Colombia similarly detailed women's representation across a variety of levels of its judiciary. In reply, the treaty body's concluding observations notes that "there is clearly resistance" to the adoption of temporary affirmative active measures, but does not specifically call for greater women's representation in the judiciary (CEDAW Committee 1999: paragraph 369).

In contrast to previous reports, Colombia's 2007 combined report for the fifth and sixth periods makes no mention of the number of women in the judiciary. In an important change, the committee replies by expressing concern: "The Committee calls upon the State party to expand its efforts towards achieving women's full and equal participation in all areas, and in particular in elected bodies and in the Judiciary" (CEDAW Committee 2005a: para 267, page 6). In 2013 (combined seventh and eighth periods), the state report mentions numbers, but sidesteps the question of recruitment, highlighting the newly formed Gender Commission in the Judiciary which has a focus on infusing gender sensitivity into judicial outcomes, not women's representation on courts. The summary report, however, criticized the Gender Commission as having little effect.

One of the most interesting elements about the 2013 combined report echoes the concerns of domestic advocacy organizations about the content of decisions rather than the composition of the bench. The shadow reports specifically mention the need for women to have access to justice, but despite criticizing numbers of women in executive and legislative bodies does not mention the judicial numbers. Moreover, of the 14 NGO reports submitted for this period *none* mentions the number of women or the gender composition of the courts. Yet over a third specifically mention lack of access to justice as a problem and even more cited specific Constitutional Court decisions as affecting the lives of women in important ways.

Colombia's 2017 report for the ninth period cites the recent appointments of women to the Constitutional Court. The report notes that the judiciary has incorporated gender equality as a principle and part of the selection criteria for candidate lists for higher courts. The Committee's concluding report writes that Colombia is moving in the right direction with capacity building programs on gender-related issues for the judiciary.

Although regional organizations have played a central role in diffusing norms of gender equality and women's rights in Latin America (Alvarez 2000; Friedman 2009), it was not until 2015 that domestic advocacy organization started to press for not only feminist decisions, but also women on the courts. And despite Colombia's participation in the CEDAW reporting process, in interviews conducted for this project, no mention was made of international influences driving or pressuring the appointment of women.

6.5.5 South Africa

Domestic advocacy organizations have played a key role in demanding the inclusion of women in decision-making posts in the executive and legislative branches in South Africa, and this activism has extended to the judiciary. Calls by legal advocacy groups and women's organizations for the gender transformation of the judiciary have brought attention to women's representation, or the lack thereof, on high courts.

In the 1980s and early 1990s, women's advocacy organizations challenged conventional ideas about who can participate in decision-making, argued for the inclusion of women in governance, and made women's rights central to the new constitution (Hassim 2006). Of the concerns raised by the Women's National Coalition, a movement body that brought together a wide range of women's organizations, the inclusion of women in the judiciary was one of them. In their Women's Charter for Effective Equality, released in February 1994, Article 2 specifically states that, "Women shall be equally represented on, and participate in the selection of, the constitutional court, the judiciary, the magistracy, all tribunals and commissions, including the Human Rights Commission, and in the Department of Justice" (quoted from Hassim 2006: 271). Thus, at a critical turning point in South Africa's history, women's groups reimagined the judiciary as one where women have equal representation.

The idea that women ought to be represented in the judiciary was recognized in the 1993 Interim Constitution and enshrined in the 1996 Constitution under the watch of women law experts such as Christina Murray and legal advocacy organizations (Albertyn 2014: 259). Their vigilance helped inform the writing of Section 174 (2) of the Constitution, which stipulates, "The need for the judiciary to reflect broadly the racial and gender composition of South Africa must be considered when judicial officers are appointed." As discussed in chapter 5, this clause shapes the way appointers and the informed public talk about judicial appointments, and the 1993 version of it encouraged the appointment of women to the Constitutional Court at its outset.

After the democratic transition, however, the appointment of women judges to the Constitutional Court considerably slowed. Of the 12 new justices elevated to the Court between 1998 and 2012, only two were women (16.7 percent). President Jacob Zuma, who took office in May 2009, appointed men either as new justices or as Chief Justice seven times in a row.

Frustrated with women's underrepresentation on the Constitutional Court, some advocacy groups began to more vociferously call for change. In 2012, the Democratic Governance and Rights Unit (DGRU) at the University of Cape Town and Sonke Gender Justice filed a complaint about the lack of gender inclusivity in the judiciary with South Africa's Commission for Gender Equality (CGE). The CGE is a state entity created by the constitution to monitor the country's compliance with treaties and laws concerning gender equality. In their complaint, the DGRU and Sonke Gender Justice referenced Section 174 (2) of the constitution and called upon the CGE to assess "South Africa's compliance with the Convention on the Elimination of All Forms of Discrimination Against Women (CEDAW) and all other legal International obligations that South Africa has ratified and that are relevant to this complaint. This includes the African Protocol on Women's Rights and the SADC Gender Protocol" (Commission for Gender Equality 2012: 3). In this way, advocacy groups in South Africa used domestic and international law to demand improvements in women's judicial representation.

When the Commission for Gender Equality did not reply to the DGRU and Sonke Gender Justice, Sonke Gender Justice and other organizations co-wrote press releases and spoke to the national media about the CGE's lack of response in 2013. In 2015, the CGE began an investigation into the lack of gender transformation in the judiciary. In 2016, the Commission submitted a report on "The Lack of Gender Transformation in the Judiciary" to President Zuma, the minister of justice, the Judicial Service Commission (JSC), and the chief justice of the Constitutional Court calling for more extensive measures to improve women's judicial representation at all levels.

In May 2014, Justice Thembile Skweyiya retired from the Constitutional Court. During his farewell speech to Skweyiya, Chief Justice Mogoeng said that he preferred that a woman be appointed. The seat was left vacant for more than a year, ostensibly to allow possible women candidates to serve as an acting judge. As discussed in chapter 5, the JSC that makes the shortlist informally preferred candidates who had held an acting stint on the court. When the application process officially opened, however, few knew about it. In April 2015, Judges Matter—a group that monitors the judiciary and promotes transparency in the selection of judges—sent a letter to Mogoeng, asking him to extend the deadline to allow for a broader pool of candidates (i.e., women) to apply. The letter argued that the JSC had not given enough time for organizations to identify and encourage women to submit their dossiers. Eleven additional organizations such as the Centre for Applied Legal Studies, Centre for Environmental Rights, Rape Crisis Cape Town Trust, Social and Economic Rights Institute, Section 27, and Sonke Gender Justice signed the letter.

In response, the JSC extended the deadline to May 11, and in June, the Commission announced it would interview four candidates for the position—all women: Nonkonsi Zoliswa Mhlantla, Leona Theron, Dhaya Pillay, and Zukisa Tshiqui. The Commission for Gender Equality (2015) issued a press release applauding the JSC for compiling an all-woman shortlist, noting that 50 percent women's representation falls in line with the SADC's Protocol on Gender and Development. In July, the JSC interviewed the candidates and recommended all four women to President Zuma, who selected Justice Mhlantla. JSC spokesperson Dumisa Ntsebeza said that the shortlist, "was a response to a cry that arose when it was felt that the numbers of females, especially at the highest court in the land, were depleting" (Eyewitness News 2015). And in 2017, President Zuma appointed Theron to fill the vacancy created by Johann van der Westhuizen's departure from the Constitutional Court.

Some advocacy groups have used state institutions and the media to draw national attention to women's underrepresentation in the judiciary in South Africa. A wider range of groups have worked behind the scenes to recruit individual women to submit dossiers for vacancies and submitted letters of nomination for women. This work can be important in encouraging individuals (both men and women) who might initially be reluctant to apply. As former Constitutional Court Justice Yvonne Mokgoro once said, she had not initially thought of herself as a judge, "And then, I think there were about four or five nominations, and then I thought maybe I can do that" (Constitutional Court Trust Oral History Project 2011: 4). Organizations that have nominated women for Constitutional Court vacancies include the Black Sash, Centre for Applied Legal Studies, Gender Health and Justice Unit, National Association of Democratic Lawyers (NADEL), Sonke Gender Justice, South Africa Women Lawyers Association, and Women's Legal Centre.

According to a study of lower-court appointments, the South African Chapter of the IAWJ was one of the most active organizations in writing letters of nomination for candidates—especially women—behind only the Black Lawyers Association and NADEL (Oxtoby and Masengu 2017). Founded in 2004, the South African Chapter has also submitted letters of support for women for vacancies in the Constitutional Court and the Supreme Court of Appeal. In 2017, the South African Chapter had 342 members (International Association of Women Judges 2018). Founding members of the chapter include Mandisa Maya, who became President of the Supreme Court of Appeal in 2017, and Constitutional Court Justice Theron.

Domestic advocacy groups in South Africa have sometimes invoked international agreements to demand better women's representation in the judiciary, and one of them was CEDAW. South Africa ratified the convention in 1995 amid its transition away from Apartheid rule. Since then, the government has participated in the CEDAW reporting process, co-creating the norm of gender equity in governance broadly and the judiciary specifically. We are careful to not argue that the reporting process in and of itself causes selectors to appoint women justices. Rather, we contend that this back-and-forth between countries and the UN helps construct shared ideas about women's representation in the judiciary.

In 1998, South Africa submitted its first CEDAW report, which noted that none of the 18 judges in the appellate division of the Supreme Court were women, and that two women were appointed to the Constitutional Court (CEDAW Committee 1998a). In response, the CEDAW Committee expressed concern that, "women have problems gaining access to high judicial office" and recommended that the country adopt temporary measures to increase the number of women in the judiciary (CEDAW Committee 1998b: points 129–130). South Africa's next report claimed that the country has made "remarkable progress" in the gender transformation of the judiciary and that, "South Africa can boast the appointment of one of its women judges to the International Criminal Court, Judge Navi Pillay" (CEDAW Committee 2010: point 7). A civil society shadow report, however, argued that, "the judiciary remains male-dominated" and that the country still lacks a law "compelling the appointment of women" (Center for the Study of Violence and Reconciliation 2011: 68). In turn, the treaty body asked South Africa to "accelerate women's full and equal participation in public and political life, in particular within the judiciary" (CEDAW Committee 2011b: point 29).

While advocacy organizations and legal commitments have been sources of pressure for the appointment of women to high courts, the influence of regional norms in South Africa is less clear. According to interviews with women's activists, members of the judicial selection committee, and observers of judicial politics, neither advocacy organizations nor government officials compare South Africa to the rest of Africa in discussions about gender equity in the judiciary. This may be because South Africa is often framed as a progressive model in promoting women's rights. Indeed, other countries on the continent have taken South Africa's constitutional clause on gender in the judiciary as a model. For instance, emulating South Africa, the Constitution of Zimbabwe states that, "appointments to the judiciary must reflect broadly the diversity and gender composition of Zimbabwe" (Government of Zimbabwe 2013: Section 184). Thus, African regional norms do not seem to raise expectations about the appointment of women in South Africa. In fact, being a role model in the region may have encouraged South Africa's selectors to rest on its laurels for a time, until domestic groups made women's underrepresentation a national and public issue.

6.6 Conclusion

As shown in this chapter, new ideas circulating at domestic, regional, and international levels promoted the inclusion of women in the judiciary and on high courts. For example, as norms surrounding women's presence on the high court changed internationally and within Canada, by the late 1990s, the appointment of women to the Supreme Court became a widely shared expectation. This expectation is highlighted in a 1997 news article in the *Globe & Mail* speculating about the replacement for Justice John Sopinka that mused, "Among the chief factors the government must consider this time are gender—a new woman judge is seen in many quarters as overdue" (Makin 1997). Thus, with every appointment to the Supreme Court from the 1990s onward, the gender composition of the court loomed as a salient factor among the public.

We theorized three mechanisms linking new ideas about gender equality in governance to the appointment of women: domestic advocacy organizations, CEDAW commitments, and regional norms. Each of these mechanisms played a differently salient role in our case studies. Among these mechanisms, domestic advocacy organizations are the one that played an active and strong role. Advocacy groups raised the salience of women's exclusion from high courts, building demand for women on the highest court. They helped make the lack of women judges and attention to women's issues on the courts a visible and salient public problem. To think of the counterfactual, if no organizations had cared whether women were appointed, selectors may have continued the tradition of appointing only men to the country's highest bench.

Advocacy organizations are often part of a broader, international women's movement. Canada, South Africa, and the United States have national chapters of the International Association of Women Judges, and these groups have played a role both domestically in calling for women on the high court, and in connecting with women judges around the world to share ideas and practices. Domestic advocacy organizations in the United States clearly played a role in creating demand for the advancement of women in the judiciary and Supreme Court. The Canadian feminist movement that galvanized around putting women's equality into the country's Charter extended its demands to call for more women on the Supreme Court. In Colombia, in addition to calling for more women, domestic advocacy organizations have also worked to advance the status of women on the courts by helping women gain consideration. In South Africa, advocacy organizations put women's equality on the national agenda during the democratic transition and called for more women on the high courts. In Ireland, there are many vibrant women's domestic advocacy organizations, but there appears to be less demand from them for the diversification of the judiciary.

In some instances, there was a clear connection between women's advocacy organizations and CEDAW. In South Africa, domestic advocacy groups invoked

CEDAW and other global, regional, and subregional women's rights treaties in their complaint to a state oversight agency about the exclusion of women from the judiciary. Not all women's groups seeking to improve women's representation on high courts utilize CEDAW in this way, and not all attempts to leverage it are successful.

Ideas about gender equity in the judiciary can develop and spread through countries' commitments to international women's rights law. We find that, over time, the CEDAW Committee and member states co-created the expectation of gender equity in the judiciary and on high courts. In the 1980s, discussion of women's inclusion on the bench was relatively rare in CEDAW reports. By the mid-1990s, reporting on women's representation in the judiciary was more consistent; all four of our member states reported on the number or percentage of women in the judiciary at least once. In the case of Colombia, the dearth of women on the high court became evident. Again, in the 2000s and 2010s, the four countries reported on women's representation in the judiciary to the CEDAW Committee. All four countries seek to claim credit in some way or another in addressing gender equalities in the judiciary.

In the 1990s, Colombia and South Africa, but not Canada and Ireland, were admonished by the CEDAW Committee. In the 2000s and 2010s, Colombia and South Africa were again criticized by the Committee, whereas the Committee praised Canada and Ireland for appointing women to the peak bench. Given that the United States has not ratified CEDAW, there is no reporting process and so this linkage mechanism is absent.

Our case studies illustrate how regional norms can matter for women's appointments to some high courts. The dynamic between the United States and Canada, illustrated through a Canadian MP citing on the floor of the House of Commons the appointment of the first woman to the Supreme Court of the United States, does support demonstration effects as Canada followed the United States in appointing the first woman in the 1980s. The role of the European Union in collecting and monitoring data on women in the judiciary across Europe, and pointing out the relatively low ranking of Ireland, certainly ratcheted up pressure on Ireland to improve gender equality on the highest court. In Colombia, South Africa, and the United States, regional peer pressure does not seem to be influential.

New ideas about what is to be valued transcend national borders. Changing perceptions of what is in the realm of possibility can disrupt conventional thinking. Old habits die hard, but when confronted with changing expectations of gender equity, selectors may see the high court in new ways and appoint women, when in previous decades, continuing all-men benches was unquestioned.

PART III

CONCLUSION

Conclusion

Reimagining High Courts

UN Secretary General António Guterres has said that "gender equality and women's rights are fundamental to global progress on peace and security, human rights, and sustainable development" (United Nations Secretary-General 2019). Indeed, laws and institutions that improve gender justice and equality promote sustainable and equitable futures. Domestic judicial institutions are pivotal for advancing and protecting human rights (Cross 1999; Powell and Staton 2009).

The constitutions of most countries around the world include some form of protection of gender equality (Scribner and Lambert 2010; World Policy Analysis Center 2014; Bettinger-Lopez and Cleaveland 2020). These constitutional protections can be extended through case law, and individuals and organizations can strategically leverage both constitutional provisions and case law to expand rights. Important strides have been made in recent decades in every region of the world. For example, legislation addressing domestic violence has been adopted in 125 countries, equal pay, and anti-sexual harassment policies have been adopted in 117 countries, and inheritance rights have been extended to women in 93 countries (Bachelet 2011).

Despite the Beijing Declaration and Platform for Action declaring "women's rights are human rights" in 1995, even in 2020, discriminatory laws persist worldwide. Women average only three-fourths of the legal rights granted to men (Women, Business, and the Law 2020: 1). The scope of these legal rights encompasses the workplace, pay, mobility, marriage, parenthood, entrepreneurship, assets, and pensions. Among the 190 countries in the Women, Business, and the Law Index in 2020, 90 still prohibit women from holding certain kinds of jobs (Women, Business, and the Law 2020: 9).

Implementation gaps dampen the effects of constitutional provisions, laws, and policies for women's everyday lives. Importantly, "for most of the world's women the laws that exist on paper do not always translate into equality and justice" (Turquet et al. 2012: 8). Through judicial review and interpretation, the judiciary plays a vital role in fulfilling women's rights. Realizing an end to discrimination, pay inequities, sexual harassment, and violence against women often requires more than new laws. The role of the highest courts in adjudicating these laws is integral to their efficacy.

Reimagining the Judiciary: Women's Representation on High Courts Worldwide. Maria C. Escobar-Lemmon, Valerie J. Hoekstra, Alice J. Kang, and Miki Caul Kittilson, Oxford University Press. DOI: 10.1093/oso/9780198861577.003.0007

Women are not just passive subjects of laws, but pivotal agents in the process of justice and the rule of law. In 2015, UN Sustainable Development Goal 5 (SDG 5) called for gender equality, the empowerment of women, and "ensuring women's full and effective participation and equal opportunity for leadership at all levels of decision making in politics, economy and public life." In this way, women's representation on high courts establishes women's agency in reviewing and interpreting laws that affect them and all of society on a day-to-day basis.

In addition to women's equal opportunity in interpreting laws and participating in government, women's representation on high courts benefits judicial processes and societal outcomes. Gender equality on the bench can enhance representation, public confidence in the judiciary, and access to the judicial process.

7.1 Reimagine. Challenge. Change.

The focus of this book has been on women's representation among judges on high courts. Women were traditionally excluded from sitting on high courts in a number of countries around the world, and in recent decades that exclusion has been reversed. As we examine the factors that often filter out women, we simultaneously consider promoters of women's advancement, offering insights for how high courts can be re-built to heighten the representation of women. While it is important to identify barriers to women's appointments, we are ultimately concerned with what works to bring improvement.

Taken together, our findings suggest a chain of favorable promoters: new norms of gender equality encourage **reimagining** the composition of courts; advocacy organizations **challenge** the status quo; and windows of opportunity enable **change**. As new ideas about gender equality are increasingly salient around the world, and as countries make international commitments to advance women, it is more common to envision women as potential appointees to the highest bench. Often, these ideas are bolstered by action. Domestic advocacy groups have challenged selectors in many countries, and in many cases their efforts are connected across borders. New ideas and advocacy group demands are more likely to result in women's appointment when there is a window of opportunity. More opportunities to appoint facilitated by a larger court enable growing norms of gender equality among judges to become a reality.

We have examined pipelines and pathways to high courts, and gender balance along the way is vital. The pipeline analogy suggests a passive process in which women and other underrepresented groups somehow drop out of the progression. Instead, we find that institutions can act as filters, excluding or marginalizing women from consideration in processes of high court appointments. Sticky institutions, such as reliance on the entrenched networks of men, can actively work against women's advancement to the group of those considered for selection.

At the same time, our findings suggest that when it comes to driving change, ideas matter. Shared ideas about who can and should wield power in the legal process are key to imagining diverse and inclusive high courts. Both international commitments and regional norms challenge existing expectations about who can and should sit on the bench. Not only are international agreements important to shaping ideas, but so is the behavior of regional cohorts, and the historical composition of the court itself. Having women on the high court within a country or a regional peer normalizes women's presence and sets an expectation for the future. We find that countries that appoint the first woman frequently continue to include at least one woman.

Domestic advocacy organizations build pressure for gender equality in decision-making, and in some countries, organizations focus on women's representation among judges. Commitment to international treaties such as the Convention on Elimination of All Forms of Discrimination Against Women (CEDAW) can act as a platform upon which women's organizations stake their claims. In institutional contexts where selectors are electorally accountable, advocacy organizations may leverage these incentives to point out the benefits of selecting a woman for targeting women in the electorate.

That group action and new ideas are so central to breaking the status quo reveals that agency is critical to women's advancement in the judiciary. Selectors can choose women when they see fit to do so. Further, the weak explanatory power of democracy and GDP reveal that the ability to have a gender inclusive judiciary is not limited to only wealthy democracies. Women can advance anywhere that the choice is made to select women for seats on the bench.

Our findings speak to the gender and politics literature. The comparative focus on the legislative and executive branches has overlooked the importance of the judiciary for women's representation in governance. With our comparable, cross-national, longitudinal data on high courts, we now have a benchmark to gauge the dynamics of women's representation on high courts from a global perspective.

Importantly, our findings also speak to the field of comparative judicial politics. The composition of high courts matters and is a worthy topic of study in and of itself, not only because of the effect it might have upon the decisions made by a court. The institutions, practices, and ideas that shape appointments were built excluding women. Our work also sheds light on the importance of informal institutions in gatekeeping who sits on high courts. We have emphasized how they exclude women, but they also likely lead to the exclusion of others from the bench. Through their adjudication on anti-discrimination laws, domestic high courts play an indispensable role in advancing women's rights and women's economic empowerment. The lived experiences, legacy of exclusion, and perspectives of who sits on supreme and constitutional courts matters for adjudication, especially for cases related to equality and non-discrimination.

7.2 A Global and Longitudinal Lens

By 2017, relatively few high courts remained all men. Thus, most high courts have had at least one woman appointed. Once a country has appointed its first woman to a high court, it is unusual for a court to revert to an all-men bench for an extended period of time. The first trailblazing woman on the court usually sets a precedent for at least one seat for a woman.

Chapter 2 asked, why did women start appearing on high courts when they did? No single explanation suffices. Our cross-national and longitudinal perspective reveals several important influences on the appointment of women on high courts. Taken together, pipelines and international norms of gender equality in governance matter for women's appointments. Pipeline explanations matter for the timing of the first woman: when there is greater gender equality in education, the first woman is appointed sooner. International factors also matter for the appointment of the first woman. The prevalence of women's nongovernmental organizations that are internationally networked catalyzes the appointment of the first woman. Further, within a region, the more courts that had the first woman, the sooner the men-only high court disappears.

After the novelty of the first woman, subsequent appointments of women are shaped by multiple factors, few of which overlap with explaining the timing of the first woman. Chapter 3 examined why women's representation advanced where it did. The domestic institution with the most explanatory power for overall composition is the size of the court. Because there are more opportunities to appoint newcomers, larger courts enable the appointment of more women.

Importantly, our cross-national analyses reveal that international and regional norms erode traditional expectations about who can and ought to serve. The only factor that emerges as a statistically significant indicator of the timing of the first woman and for subsequent appointments is regional effects. Regional peer effects are robust for both first women and number of women on the court. And when it comes to the composition of the high court, commitment to international law, as evidenced by the length of time since ratification of CEDAW, is an important factor. Long-term commitment to CEDAW signifies greater exposure and connection to norms of gender equality in governance.

Equally as interesting as what does matter are the factors that exert little influence on either the appointment of the first woman or subsequent appointments. Neither democracies nor countries with larger economies are more likely to appoint women. Thus, women's appointments to high courts can potentially happen anywhere, without socioeconomic or political prerequisites. In contrast to suggestions in previous scholarship, the method of selection plays little role. Although Valdini and Shortell (2016) find exposed selectors are more likely to appoint women, their analyses are limited to a set of wealthy democracies. For our cross-national analysis, electorally accountable selectors are no more likely to select women, all else being equal.

7.3 Lessons from the Country Case Studies

To gain a better picture of how women's representation on high courts comes about, we have taken a deeper look at women's appointments to high courts in Canada, Colombia, Ireland, South Africa, and the United States. Our country case studies provide more nuanced information about the appointment processes, and for some countries interviews with former office holders who were part of the selection process gave us a glimpse of the decision calculus of those charged with appointing justices. Above all, our case studies emphasize the importance of the broader context in each country and yield constellations of factors that work together in indivisible ways. For theoretical clarity, we discuss categories of explanation in the chapters in part II. Yet every influence operates within the broader constellation, and to fully understand change over time, we must consider these forces in a holistic manner.

In each case, despite relatively rich supply in pipelines, gendered selection mechanisms have limited women's advancement at one point or another. For a few countries, filters in the pipelines are lifted earlier than in others. Striking differences emerge across cases in the lapse of time from when women were formally allowed to become lawyers and judges and when the first woman was appointed to a high court. We traced some typical paths in terms of professions that act as the usual springboards to high courts, which vary across countries. Women's share of the eligible pool roughly foreshadows women's representation on the high courts of Colombia and Ireland over time. In contrast, in Canada and South Africa, the percentage of women on the high court accelerates earlier than one may plausibly expect, if only basing those expectations on the traditional pipeline. Yet change is not well depicted by a simple linear trajectory. Instead, there are periods of lagging and periods of catching up. Ireland and Colombia's appointments of women were sluggish at a few points, and then increased rapidly to reach the one-third benchmark in recent years.

As Annesley, Beckwith, and Franceschet (2018) did for cabinet selection, we have considered both the formal and informal institutions that structure the selection process for the highest courts. We find that both formal and informal aspects of the selection process can constrain and/or enable the choices of selectors.

A commonly heard quotation among engineers reminds us that "Every system is perfectly designed to get the results it gets" (Batalden and Conway 2015). This refrain resonates with our analysis of gender equality on high courts. The supply of women with the requisite career credentials has grown tremendously in the post-WWII era, and yet systems of appointment continue to exclude and hinder women's participation on high courts. The systemic discrimination takes different forms and is often found in gendered professional networks and persistent exclusionary ideas about who should be appointed. Informal norms and structural inequalities still dampen women's ascendence to the highest courts.

The case studies suggest that context matters greatly for how electoral accountability works. As detailed in the cases of the United States and Canada, when selectors perceive electoral benefit from selecting a woman, and can be held accountable by their electorate, they are more likely to do so. Even when formal barriers to women's appointment are removed, informal norms in the selection process can still act as exclusionary influences. In South Africa and Ireland, both sides of the split bar are formally eligible for selection to the high court, but in practice it is the barristers in Ireland and the advocates in South Africa who have had the edge in the career ladder. Who is "qualified" for high courts is socially constructed by those who already wield power. Taken together, the cases reveal that gender segregated networks and gender biased ideas about qualifications often act as filters to hinder the appointment of women. When selectors or their key advisors decide to do so, they can disrupt reliance on these traditional networks by looking beyond the usual suspects as they draw up their shortlists.

Theoretically, a new court can provide opportunities for appointing women. In South Africa, when the Constitutional Court was created, multiple women were included on the inaugural bench. However, in the case of Colombia, the first woman was not appointed to the new Constitutional Court until ten years after its creation. Clearly, the introduction of a new court does not operate independent of the broader context and thus is not by itself sufficient to improve women's representation.

Ideology, as a set of ideas, can be considered an institution. Our findings are mixed on the role of ideology in the appointment of women. Ideas about gender equality can coincide with political party affiliation in some instances, but in many others they do not. The role of judicial nominating committees is similarly mixed. In combination with affirmative legal language and pressure from domestic advocacy organizations, the judicial nominating commission in South Africa has promoted greater gender equality on the high court at certain points in time. However, in our other case where a nominating commission is used (Ireland) the commission has not yielded a record number of women on the shortlists.

The case studies draw out some of the ways that international factors can catalyze change and encourage the appointment of women to high courts. We have focused on three factors: advocacy organizations, commitment to CEDAW, and regional norms. Advocacy organizations have heightened attention to women's exclusion from and underrepresentation on high courts, albeit to varying degrees across case countries. In some instances, these organizations are part of a broader movement. The Canadian, South African, and United States national chapters of the International Association of Women Judges (IAWJ) provide examples of this connectedness. Regional norms of gender equity in governance, including in the judiciary, are evident within the regions that contain our case study countries—Africa, North America, Europe, and Latin America. The role of the EU stood out for the collection and monitoring of data on women in government and the accountability this created for Ireland. By the mid-1990s, all four of our case countries that ratified CEDAW were reporting on the inclusion of women in the judiciary in their CEDAW reports. In short, the ascendance of new ideas about gender equality—at the domestic, regional, and global levels—has cast a shadow on traditional images of men as the only occupiers of high court seats.

7.4 What Kind of Diversity for Justice?

Women have a human right to participate in making decisions that affect them. Justice cannot be rendered if those making the final calls about women's bodies and women's lives are all men. Appointing more women to the bench—and in so doing, diversifying the judiciary—can have a positive impact not just for women, but for promoting a more just and equitable society. For the judiciary, reaching decisions that render justice means including a variety of voices and perspectives in the deliberation process. Many readers here might picture an individual judge issuing a decision and ask themselves whether a woman judge decides differently than a judge who is a man. Like Kenney (2012), we do not assume that women and men are inherently different. In cases of individual decision-making, men judges can issue feminist judgments, and women can make antifeminist decisions. Our focus is not on the individual judge per se, but on the bench as a panel.

But does a diverse and inclusive bench necessarily produce justice for all? Not all diversely composed courts will promote equality in unequal societies. Even with a panel of all women judges, there is no guarantee that it will decide in favor of the rights of women. In line with previous legal thinkers, we propose that decision-making panels can best promote justice through feminist judging processes (Hunter 2008; Hunter, McGlynn, and Rackley 2010; Kenney 2012). Hunter (2015) explains that there are many ways of doing feminist judging, "including noticing the gender implications of apparently neutral rules and practices, challenging gender bias in legal doctrine and judicial reasoning, or promoting substantive equality" (131). As an approach to decision-making, feminist judging considers stakeholders who have been excluded or marginalized in the past and contextualizes the facts of the case. A justice-minded panel that has a broader range of understanding of the facts is more likely to render justice than one whose collective knowledge is limited in scope.

True justice and equity, then, requires an intersectional approach that considers multiple and overlapping sources of inequality and privilege (Crenshaw 1989;

Hancock 2016; Dawuni 2018). A diverse set of women's voices shape how problems are perceived, understood, and discussed, and the range of proposed solutions. Focusing only on the categories of men and women, therefore, obscures racial, class, and other sources of advantage and disadvantage within groups that have significance for devising appropriate courses of social action. Yet, in many countries, the gains made by women on high courts have been largely among privileged racial, ethnic, religious, and socioeconomic groups. Where judiciaries have been dominated by White judges such as in Europe, there is an especially urgent need for Black high court justices including Black women justices (Solanke 2009; Solanke 2019).

Lazos Vargas (2004: 139) argues for the appointment of judges with "outsider" perspectives to achieve an inclusive rule of law. In her "pluralistic process-based model of judging," decision-makers seek to promote substantive rights. In contexts such as the United States where racism is a structural impediment to justice, pluralistic decision making must incorporate the realities of racial majorities and racial minorities. This is more likely to occur if a panel collectively encompasses a wide range of experiences and kinds of knowledge. This is not to argue that adding one Black man justice or one Muslim woman justice is sufficient. In a speech to law students at UC Berkeley, United States Supreme Court Justice Sonia Sotomayor (2002) said, "No one person, judge or nominee will speak in a female or people of color voice" (91). She further stated:

> However, to understand takes time and effort, something that not all people are willing to give. For others, their experiences limit their ability to understand the experiences of others. Other simply do not care. Hence, one must accept the proposition that a difference there will be by the presence of women and people of color on the bench (2002: 92).

If judging is "a series of choices that we must make," then a bench whose justices together comprise multiple viewpoints is more inclusive than one with a homogenous set of perspectives (93).

In the context of legislative representation, Celis and Childs (2020) argue intersectional representation is an active and dynamic process that requires redesigning democratic institutions to better capture a multitude of perspectives. Like Lazos Vargas, they call for a process-based approach, rather than focusing on the outcome or policy positions. A representational process is feminist in so far as it is inclusive, egalitarian, and responsive. Prioritizing these principles allows for including heterogeneous conceptions of what is in "women's interests." Women are, after all, differently situated and heterogeneous in multiple ways, including race, ethnicity, socioeconomic status, religion, and sexuality. Significant power differentials among women must be recognized when thinking about diversity on high courts. We have focused on the inclusion of women in this book. Future research should consider multiple forms of marginalization or exclusion based on race, ethnicity, sexuality, class, and religion, for instance (Kang et al. 2020).

Just adding a woman to the bench, or even the presence of multiple women from only the dominant group, falls short of meaningful inclusion. To bring an end to women's exclusion from the judicial decision-making process, deeply held norms must be altered to reimagine who can and should be a judge, accompanied by new ideas about how to best deliver justice for all—not just for the most powerful groups.

7.5 What Works for Advancing Diversity on High Courts?

The OECD Development Assistance Committee has spent billions of dollars on justice programs, and of that, hundreds of millions have been dedicated to gender equality in the judicial system (Bachelet 2011). Clearly, powerful international organizations see the need for gender equality in the judicial system to promote good governance and the rule of law. The key is to invest in what works. Thus, policymakers and practitioners need to know what sorts of interventions promote women's agency in the judicial and legal systems. Women's presence on high courts plays a vital role in that agentic process.

Despite progress toward women's equal representation on high courts, the participation of women still falls short of parity nearly everywhere. What works for advancing and keeping more women on high courts? Given the systemic nature of the problem, a systemic approach is needed. There are several interventions to consider in tandem. First, disaggregating data on high court appointments by gender is an important step. What has been lacking to this point are systematic data, and this book helps fills that gap. Benchmarking and ranking countries on women's representation allows for tracking progress (or stagnation) over time and can be used to incentivize countries to make changes or adopt new strategies. With such data, domestic actors such as women's advocacy groups, policy agencies, and the media can hold selectors accountable for their progress in the years to come. By considering women's exclusion and underrepresentation, discourse about who judges is altered. This process of benchmarking and highlighting women's representation has been quite common for parliaments around the world and is just as necessary for high courts. For future progress, comparable data at lower levels of judicial systems must also be collected and made accessible. Any systematic and comprehensive data collection requires resources for and a means of publicizing the rankings. Simply put, international organizations should fund long-term and global data collection.

At the same time, we recognize the limitations of data collection and numbers for actualizing meaningful change. As Merry (2019) cogently points out, an overabundance of attention on measurement can overlook fundamental structural problems. While benchmarking the number of women on high courts can be a useful tool for highlighting inequalities, measurement is not a substitute for a holistic consideration of context and history to capture complex power inequities in the judiciary. A critical eye is particularly important given that anti-democratic leaders can strategically select women and members of other marginalized groups to take on visible roles while at the same time take measures that undermine equality for all.

Pipelines certainly matter for women's appointments to high courts. Therefore, supporting women's careers in law and at lower rungs of the judiciary are both necessary and important supply-side factors. Gender equality in education and in law programs are integral to sustaining the rich supply of women for judicial appointments. Domestic professional organizations that play a gatekeeping role and international organizations ought to advocate to sustain and expand these hard won gains.

All too often, explanations for women's underrepresentation in the judiciary have overvalued individual-level accounts. The do-it-yourself approach deflects blame from the institutions that reproduce the inequities. Individual-level factors are part of the story, and so too are the structures of the existing system. Most fundamentally, our findings call for a shift in mindset from placing the onus on women to thinking about *institutional transformation*. The inclusion of women in decision-making is not simply about having women in the pipeline (although our findings show this is important) or solely about providing more training for women. We must also redesign established practices of selection and reimagine who can and should serve on the bench.

How can high courts be redesigned to enable broader representation? Because established norms and practices reproduce old patterns of exclusion, countries should look to reform their selection processes for the judiciary. In some cases, much of the process relies on informal norms and identifying potential candidates from small circles of networked judges. To build more diverse shortlists, there must be less reliance on inner circles dominated by existing power holders and explicit attention to nominating a diverse array of judges. Selection for top positions is often done behind closed doors. Instead, open and inclusive discussion about what "merit" really means can reveal biases. Often, the qualifications are met by a large number of aspirants, and only a few are selected for the top positions.

Overall, there is a need for more transparency and less bias in processes of selection. Public discussion of what qualifications mean can unpack some of the biases that have long favored men. Opening up and standardizing selection processes may involve a broader range of stakeholders, including civil society organizations. Advocates for diversity and inclusion should identify windows of opportunity to push for reforms to selection processes.

Expanding the size of small courts may be necessary to transform homogenously-composed high courts into rich, intersectionally diverse high courts. As mentioned above, a pluralistic process of judicial panel decision making is better able to capture a range of lived experiences when it has more members and when there are more opportunities for newcomers. Yet, more than half of the high courts in our study have 11 or fewer seats, which limits both opportunities to appoint newcomers and restricts the ability to appoint differently situated women and men. Writing about the United States Supreme Court, Onwuachi-Willig (2005) calls for increasing the size of the United States Supreme Court from 9 to 15, to "increase the representation of various demographic groups and ensure proper representation of all voices" (1258). Our cross-national findings from chapter 3 support this idea, as the size of court is a statistically significant predictor of the number of women justices on the bench, all else being equal. In an era of stronger norms of gender equality on the judiciary, the likelihood that some newcomers to an expanded bench would be women or members of other under-represented groups is higher. Further, high courts must include women (and men) whose experience and knowledge broadens the court's range of understanding of the facts—women (and men) whose perspectives enable the bench to contextualize how people are differently affected by the law and the legal process. One token woman on the court is not sufficient.

Democratic design should be underpinned by democratic principles such as inclusiveness and egalitarianism and aims to reform structures, practices, and rules to actualize those goals (Celis and Childs 2020). Targets and quotas have worked to increase women's representation in parliaments around the world (Murray 2004; Dahlerup and Freidenvall 2005; Tripp and Kang 2008; Krook 2006; Paxton et al. 2010; Paxton and Hughes 2015). By extension, adopting quotas or targets that aim to enhance the representation of women in their full diversity could be effective. Some argue that aspirational targets or quotas violate the principle of equal treatment or lead to the selection of less qualified judges. Yet these arguments are rarely invoked with courts that adhere to balanced representation based on geographical region (Malleson 2009; Malleson 2014). Selectors from around the world already adhere to either formal rules or informal norms designed to intentionally include a variety of perspectives, backgrounds, and experiences on their high courts. Some courts are deliberately balanced so that the justices reflect a variety of regions across the country, expertise in different areas of the law, languages, religions, or ethnicities.

Why stop these practices of diversifying high courts when it comes to women and other underrepresented groups? While the adoption of gender quotas in the judiciary has not been widespread, there are a number of formalized quotas in place. For example, Burundi requires that at least three members of the Constitutional Court be women. The Venice Report (1997) lists informal targets for women on the Constitutional Courts of Italy, Belgium, Austria, France, Armenia, Latvia, Lithuania, Slovakia, Germany, and Finland. When considering targets or quotas, attention should be paid, however, to whether the use of gender and ethnic quotas in tandem would marginalize women in underrepresented groups.

International entities such as UN Women provide a forum for domestic actors to share best practices and toolkits for bringing about change. The IAWJ in particular brings together women judges from around the world to share ideas and experiences. As Kenney (2013) points out, "Women will not inevitably nor steadily increase their representation in the judiciary without a concerted and intentional effort" (475). Empowering and resourcing women's NGOs that focus on gender justice and women in the judiciary is necessary for keeping the issue on the agenda and continuing pressure on selectors to transform the judiciary.

International forums enable both bottom up mobilization and top down pressure to enact change. Yet it has been 25 years since the last UN World Conference on Women convened (in Beijing). Since 1995, new issues of importance for advocates of justice and equality have come to the fore such as the rights of transgender women, and many other preexisting challenges affecting women such as climate change and economic inequality remain salient. A new global conference on women would provide a forum for advocacy organizations, scholars, and governmental leaders to come together to discuss goals and strategy for transforming the judiciary. While previous UN conferences sought to address women's rights and gender equity in governance, the proceedings often defaulted to a focus on legislatures and on women as a single axis of identity. A renewed global conversation on the judiciary can spark new ideas, new solutions, and new approaches to seeking justice for women in all their heterogeneity.

Importantly, gains in the representation of historically excluded groups—in this book, women—on the bench are not automatic, nor are they guaranteed. Therefore, women's inclusion should not be taken for granted, and requires long-term commitment. Institutional change—including reforming the selection process, enlarging the size of the court, and enacting quotas—can be a positive force for changing the calculus of selectors. Our case studies suggest the changing calculus may also come from having more women as selectors or among the selector's inner circle and from growing domestic and international expectations about gender equality. Those expectations are enriched when they transcend the idea of having just one woman, or just one kind of woman—to represent women in their full diversity. Achieving this goal requires us all to reimagine the judiciary and envision a bench where marginalized voices gain the power to adjudicate over matters that affect them and society.

APPENDIX 1

Data Coverage

This book draws on our original Women on High Courts Database, which contains cross-national and over-time data on women's representation on high courts. We began searching out and compiling this information in 2012. There are two main global datasets in the Database and employed in the book, one that looks at the timing of the appointment of the first woman used in chapter 2 and a second examining the composition of courts used in chapter 3. While we sought to obtain complete information for all high courts in the world, despite our best efforts there were countries or country courts for which we were unable to obtain any data and courts for which we were only able to obtain partial data (i.e., some years). In this Appendix, we assess the completeness of our coverage for both datasets separately.

Before we discuss the first woman dataset, it is important to clarify how we determine whether a country court ought to be included in the universe of sought-after courts. First, we decided to focus on independent countries that had a population greater than 200,000 in 2010. Second, we drew on several sources to compile a primary list of high courts in these countries. These include the New York University School of Law's GlobaLex and country or region-specific secondary articles.

It is also worth noting that a country court may be missing from one dataset, but not the other. For instance, we might be able to confirm the appointment of the first woman that happened early, but then not be able to confirm the composition of the court again until a later point in time. In this case, the country court would be missing for some years in the compositional dataset. In other cases, where we cannot confirm the appointment of the first woman, but we have recent years of compositional data, which include that in the compositional dataset.

A1.1 Data Coverage on the First Woman

Out of the 265 country courts that we know existed by the end of 2013 we have data on the year the first woman was appointed for 210 of them. Not all 210 enter into the statistical analysis in chapter 2 for two main reasons. First are high courts where the first woman was appointed prior to 1970 (see Table 2.1 for the list of country courts). Even though these cases are excluded from the analysis for reasons discussed in that chapter, they are not missing. Second, for some country courts we are missing information on independent variables, and these missing data cause them to be excluded from the analysis. Together this explains why the number of courts reported in Table 2.3 is 133.

One question that might be asked is whether we are missing data at random or whether there is bias introduced by the nature of our missing data. Of the 55 courts where we are missing data on the timing of the appointment of the first woman, roughly half (30 courts) are high appellate courts. This is a function of the difficulty in obtaining data on some of these courts. While in many countries constitutional courts and supreme courts enjoy a high degree of prestige and concomitant visibility in the news media, peak appellate bodies often operate out of the limelight. In many of these cases we were able to confirm the initial

Table A1.1 Year First Woman was Appointed, by Country and Court Type

	Appellate	Constitutional	Supreme
Afghanistan			2020
Albania	missing	1992	
Algeria	missing	1999	
Angola	1980	2008	
Argentina			1970
Armenia	1991	1996	
Australia			1987
Austria	1988	1994	
Azerbaijan	1991	1998	
Bahamas			1996
Bahrain	none as of 2020	2007	
Bangladesh	2011	2000	
Barbados			1995
Belarus	missing	1994	
Belgium	1978	1984	
Belize			2006
Benin	1973	1993	
Bhutan			2012
Bolivia	2012	1999	
Bosnia and Herzegovina	2004	1998	
Botswana	none as of 2020	1998	
Brazil			2000
Brunei			2001
Bulgaria	1957	1991	
Burkina Faso	1983	2002	
Burundi	missing	1992	
Cambodia	missing	2004	
Cameroon	1988	-a-	
Canada			1982
Cape Verde	1990	-a-	
Central African Republic	missing	1996	
Chad	missing	missing	
Chile	2002	1989	
China			1963
Colombia	1983	2001	
Comoros	missing	none as of 2020	
Congo, Dem. Rep.	missing	-a-	
Congo, Rep.	1982	2003	
Costa Rica	1984	1993	
Cote d'Ivoire	1994	1995	
Croatia	1995	1999	
Cuba			missing
Cyprus			2004
Czech Republic	1993	1993	
Denmark			1953
Djibouti	1997	2005	
Dominican Republic	1996	missing	
Ecuador	2007	missing	
Egypt	none as of 2020	2003	
El Salvador			1994

Equatorial Guinea	missing	missing	
Eritrea			missing
Estonia			missing
Eswatini	none as of 2020	missing	
Ethiopia			1983
Fiji			none as of 2020
Finland			1970
France	1946	1992	
Gabon	1983	1991	
Gambia, The			none as of 2020
Georgia	missing	1996	
Germany	1951	1951	
Ghana			1961
Greece			2005
Guatemala	1982	1995	
Guinea	1986	-a-	
Guinea-Bissau			1996
Guyana			missing
Haiti			1986
Honduras			1996
Hungary	1956	1999	
Iceland			1982
India			1989
Indonesia	1968	2008	
Iran, Islamic Rep.			none as of 2020
Iraq			none as of 2020
Ireland			1992
Israel			1976
Italy	1988	1996	
Jamaica	2006	missing	
Japan			1994
Jordan	2017	2020	
Kazakhstan	missing	2002	
Kenya			1998
Korea, Dem. Rep. (North)			missing
Korea, Rep. (South)	2004	2003	
Kosovo	missing	2009	
Kuwait	none as of 2020	none as of 2020	
Kyrgyz Republic	missing	missing	
Laos			missing
Latvia	1991	1996	
Lebanon	missing	none as of 2020	
Lesotho	2004	2002	
Liberia			1977
Libya			2010
Lithuania	missing	1993	
Luxembourg	missing	1998	
Macedonia	1991	1991	
Madagascar	missing	1991	
Malawi			2007
Malaysia			2001
Maldives			none as of 2020

Continued

Table A1.1 *Continued*

	Appellate	Constitutional	Supreme
Mali	2000	1994	
Malta	missing	missing	
Mauritania	none as of 2020	none as of 2020	
Mauritius			1993
Mexico			1961
Moldova	1991	2001	
Mongolia	missing	missing	
Montenegro	missing	missing	
Morocco	1978	1999	
Mozambique	missing	2003	
Myanmar			none as of 2020
Namibia			none as of 2020
Nepal			2001
Netherlands			1967
New Zealand			1993
Nicaragua			1979
Niger	1996	2003	
Nigeria			2005
Norway			1968
Oman			none as of 2020
Pakistan			none as of 2020
Panama			1983
Papua New Guinea			2001
Paraguay			2004
Peru	1993	1996	
Philippines			1973
Poland	1948	1985	
Portugal	2004	1989	
Qatar	none as of 2020	none as of 2020	
Romania	1965	2004	
Russia	1991	1991	
Rwanda			1994
Saudi Arabia			none as of 2020
Senegal	missing	1993	
Serbia	missing	1992	
Sierra Leone			1976
Singapore			1994
Slovakia	1993	1993	
Slovenia	1991	1998	
Solomon Islands	none as of 2020	missing	
Somalia			missing
South Africa	1991	1994	
South Sudan			missing
Spain	2002	1980	
Sri Lanka			1996
Sudan	1967	missing	
Suriname	2001	-a-	
Sweden			1968
Switzerland			1975

Syrian Arab Republic	missing	none as of 2020	
Taiwan	1956	1967	
Tajikistan	missing	2009	
Tanzania			2002
Thailand	1995	missing	
Timor-Leste			2003
Togo	missing	2007	
Trinidad and Tobago			1972
Tunisia	missing	missing	
Turkey	1954	1995	
Turkmenistan			missing
Uganda			1997
Ukraine	1991	1996	
United Arab Emirates			none as of 2020
United Kingdom			2004
United States			1981
Uruguay			1981
Uzbekistan	missing	2011	
Vanuatu			none as of 2020
Venezuela	missing	missing	
Vietnam			missing
Yemen, Rep.			2006
Zambia	1982	-a-	
Zimbabwe	2001	2013	

Notes: -a- indicates that the court was either created and filled after 2013 when we stopped collecting data or had been created on paper, but not filled by 2013.

Source: The Women on High Courts Database.

inclusion of women on the bench, in some cases going back to the 1970s, but in others, we were not able to definitively confirm who was the first woman justice on the highest appellate court. While data are more likely to be missing from appellate courts than either constitutional or supreme courts, there are no other obvious differences between the courts for which we obtained data and those for which we are missing data.

In Table A1.1 we list country courts in the world indicating either the year in which the first woman was appointed or whether this is a country court on which we are missing data. Missing information for courts known to exist are denoted with the word "missing." For countries where the first woman was appointed after 2013, we have filled in these dates even though in the models estimated in chapter 2 these observations are treated as censored. For those countries which as of December 31, 2020 had not appointed the first woman we indicate "none as of 2020." If the cell appears blank the court does not exist. This occurs because given the way in which we have constructed the coding of the court type variable, a country can have either a peak appellate court and constitutional court or a supreme court; it cannot have all three.

A1.2 Data Coverage on the Composition of High Courts

As in the first woman dataset, we set out to collect compositional data for all high courts in independent countries with a population greater than 200,000 in 2010. These data proved

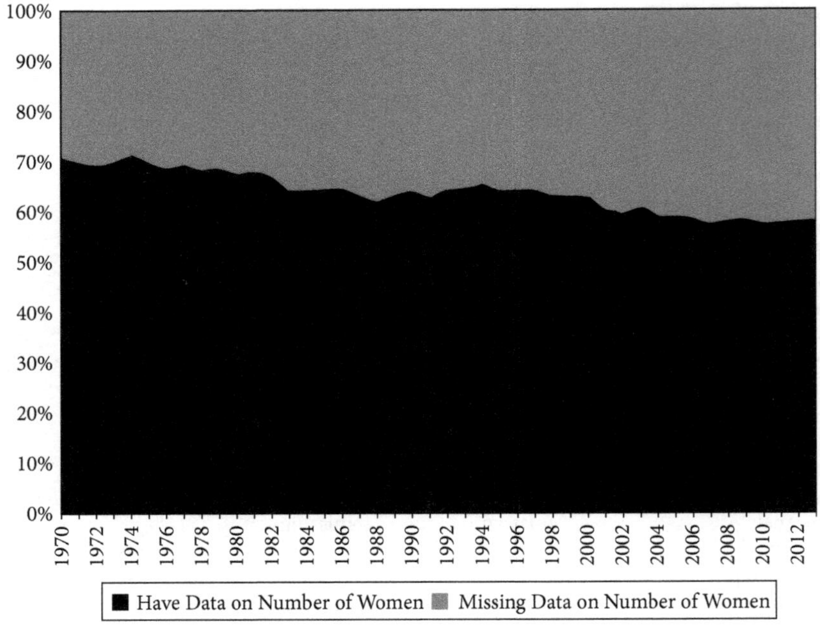

Figure A1.1 Data Coverage on the Number of Women on High Courts, 1970–2013
Source: The Women on High Courts Database.

to be more challenging to collect than we had initially anticipated, and despite our best attempts we were not always able to complete a full time series for courts we believe existed. In assessing whether a high court is missing from the compositional analysis conducted in chapter 3, it is necessary not only to ask if the court is missing, but also for what years. Because both the number of courts on which we could have collected data and the number on which we were actually able to collect data varies over time, Figure A1.1 illustrates our coverage by year.

While we do not show the number of courts in the figure itself, we note that the number of high courts in the universe is not static, but has changed over time. This reflects a confluence of various trends: the creation of separate constitutional courts and the creation of new sovereign countries. As discussed in chapter 2 during the 1990 in particular, multiple countries adopted new institutional structures that included the creation of stand-alone constitutional courts. This phenomenon, common across Africa, Latin America, and post-Soviet Asia following the end of communism, dramatically expanded the number of courts. Additionally, we observe the creation of new countries in Eastern Europe and Soviet Asia in particular, as well as across the African continent. This means that the number of courts upon which we could have collected data (the denominator in assessing percent coverage) increases over time.

Our best estimate of the universe of observations—that is, the total number of country court-years between 1970 and 2013—for which we should have data is 8,980. To present the most difficult test possible we erred on the side of overestimating the number of country court years for which we might have needed to collect data by counting courts in countries that were temporarily suspended (e.g., Guatemala's constitutional and appellate courts from 1983–1985 during the military dictatorship, Argentina's supreme court from

1971–1973). We have also included country court-years where we were unsure if the court existed (e.g., North Korea's highest court, Somalia's highest court). A court cannot be missing if the country did not exist at that time or if it was before the court's creation.

The numerator for the percentage of country courts covered is based on whether we had data on the number of women on the court. A couple of common-sense rules govern our determination of whether a country court is deemed to be missing in the compositional dataset for a given year. A court is deemed to be missing if we believe the court existed, but we were not able to obtain information. For courts created after 1970, the court is not considered missing until after the first justices are actually seated. A court where we do not know the names or number of the men holding seats, but can confirm there were no women (e.g., prior to the confirmed appointment of the first woman) is not deemed to be missing and is recorded as having zero women. For some courts we were able to obtain some data, especially for more recent years, but were not able to complete the time series.

In the most recent version of our compositional dataset, we have 5,675 observations for the number of women on high courts (63.2 percent coverage) and 5,655 observations on the percentage of women on high courts (63.0 percent). The number of observations on women's representation slightly differ because in specific instances we found information on the number of women justices, but not the size of the court. In other cases, we found credible sources reporting the percentage of women, but lacking information on the size of the court we were unable to retrieve the number of women judges.

Comparing the courts that we believe to exist with courts for which we were able to obtain information on the number of women holding seats reveals that we were able to obtain information for between 58 and 71 percent by year of all courts. A principal concern is not whether we were able to obtain data on the universe of high courts, but whether there is systematic bias in the data we were not able to obtain. If so, this would limit the generalizability of the conclusions we draw in chapter 3. As might be expected based on the previous discussion, we are missing more data on appellate courts than constitutional or supreme courts. Across the 1970 to 2013 time period, for data on the number of women, we obtained information on 47 percent of appellate courts compared with 72 percent of constitutional courts and 75 percent of supreme courts. Thus, one caution to be kept in mind is that our findings are more likely to be generalizable to constitutional courts and supreme courts, which receive more attention than peak appellate benches.

APPENDIX 2

Descriptive Statistics

Table A2.1 Descriptive Statistics for Chapter 2

Variable	Obs	Mean	Std. Dev.	Min	Max
First woman	2299	0.05	0.22	0	1
Log women to men tertiary completion, 20-year lag	2299	−1.24	0.80	−4.05	1.99
Electorally accountable	2299	0.65	0.48	0	1
Religious law	2299	0.30	0.46	0	1
Newer court	2299	0.01	0.12	0	1
Log years since CEDAW	2299	−2.95	4.44	−6.91	3.47
Log WINGOs	2299	2.99	0.93	−6.91	4.91
Regional peer effects	2299	35.08	24.81	0	100
Appellate court	2299	0.41	0.49	0	1
Civil law	2299	0.37	0.48	0	1
Level of democracy	2299	0.52	7.50	−10	10
Log GDP per capita	2299	8.18	1.43	5.31	11.78

Note: Descriptive statistics are based on the sample of 133 country courts in Table 2.3.

Table A2.2 Descriptive Statistics for Chapter 3

Variable	Obs	Mean	Std. Dev.	Min	Max
Number of women	746	2.72	2.96	0	28
Log women to men tertiary completion, 20-year lag	746	−0.78	0.66	−3.11	1.66
Electorally accountable	746	.84	.37	0	1
Religious law	746	.08	.27	0	1
Newer court	746	.28	.45	0	1
Court size	746	13.92	8.50	4	51
Log years since CEDAW	746	1.46	3.15	−6.91	3.48
Log WINGOs	746	3.86	.65	0	5.02
Regional peer effects	746	14.16	9.06	0	34.91
Appellate court	746	.17	.37	0	1
Civil law	746	.64	.48	0	1
Level of democracy	746	6.48	4.84	−9	10
Log GDP per capita	746	8.86	1.47	4.79	11.42
Period	746	1999.57	10.13	1970	2012

Note: Descriptive statistics are based on the sample of 101 country courts in Table 3.3.

References

Abdelkader, Engy. 2013–2014. To Judge or Not to Judge: A Comparative Analysis of Islamic Jurisprudential Approaches to Female Judges in the Muslim World. *Fordham International Law Journal* 37: 309.

Abel, Richard L., Ole Hammerslev, Hilary Sommerlad, and Ulrike Schultz. 2020. *Lawyers in 21st-Century Societies. Vol. 1: National Reports*. London: Bloomsbury.

Abraham, Henry. 2008. *Justices, Presidents, and Senators: A History of the U.S. Supreme Court Appointments from Washington to Clinton*. Lanham, MD: Rowman & Littlefield.

Adams, Melinda, and Kang, Alice. 2007. Regional Advocacy Networks and the Protocol on the Rights of Women in Africa. *Politics & Gender* 3 (3): 451–474.

African Union. 2009. Gender Policy. Addis Ababa: African Union. Accessed January 13, 2021: https://www.un.org/en/africa/osaa/pdf/au/gender_policy_2009.pdf.

Albertyn, Catherine. 2014. Judicial Diversity. In *The Judiciary in South Africa*, eds. Cora Hoexter and Morné Olivier, 245–287. Cape Town: Juta and Co.

Alozie, Nicholas. 1990. The Distribution of Women and Minority Judges: The Effects of Judicial Selection Methods. *Social Science Quarterly* 71 (2): 315–325.

Alozie, Nicholas. 1996. Selection Methods and the Recruitment of Women to State Courts of Last Resort. *Social Science Quarterly* 77 (1): 110–126.

Alvarez, Sonia E. 2000. Translating the Global: Effects of Transnational Organizing on Local Feminist Discourses and Practices in Latin America. *Meridians* 1 (1): 29–67.

American Bar Association. 2001. Women in the Profession Statistics. Accessed December 20, 2020: https://www.americanbar.org/groups/diversity/women/resources/statistics/.

American Bar Association. 2009. A Current Glance at Women in the Law 2009 (November 13, 2009). Commission on Women in the Profession. Accessed September 14, 2020: https://www.americanbar.org/content/dam/aba/administrative/women/CurrentGlaceStatistics2009.pdf.

American Bar Association. 2015. Standard 509 Information Report. Enrollment Data Archives. Accessed January 12, 2021: https://www.americanbar.org/groups/legal_education/resources/statistics/statistics-archives/.

Anasagasti, Miriam, and Nathalie Wuiame. 1999. *Women and Decision-making in the Judiciary in the European Union*. Directorate-General for Employment and Social Affairs. European Commission.

Anderson, Ellen. 2001. *Judging Bertha Wilson: Law as Large as Life*. Toronto: University of Toronto Press.

Andrews, Penelope E. 2006. The South African Judicial Appointments Process. *Osgoode Hall Law Journal* 44 (3): 555–572.

Annesley, Claire, Karen Beckwith, and Susan Franceschet. 2019. *Cabinets, Ministers, and Gender*. Oxford: Oxford University Press.

Apreza Salgado, Socorro. 2014. *Libro homenaje a la jurista María Cristina Salmorán Tamayo*. Mexico City: Universidad Nacional Autónoma de Mexico.

Arabeyre, Patrick, Jean-Louis Halpérin, and Jacques Krynen, eds. 2007. *Dictionnaire historique des juristes français (XIIe-XXe siècle)*. Paris: Presses Universitaires de France.

Arana Araya, Ignacio, Melanie M. Hughes, and Aníbal Pérez-Liñán. 2021. Judicial Reshuffles and Women Justices in Latin America. *American Journal of Political Science* 65 (2): 373–388.

Arrington, Nancy B. 2018. Gender and Judicial Replacement: The Case of US State Supreme Courts. *Journal of Law and Courts* 6 (1): 127–154.

Arrington, Nancy B. N.d. Judicial Merit Selection: Beliefs About Fairness and Undermining Gender Diversity on the Bench. *Political Research Quarterly*. https://doi.org/10.1177/1065912920971712.

Arrington, Nancy B. 2020. Group Selection and Opportunities for Gender Diversity in the Judiciary. *Representation* 56 (2): 149–171.

Arriola, Leonardo R., and Martha C. Johnson. 2014. Ethnic Politics and Women's Empowerment in Africa: Ministerial Appointments to Executive Cabinets. *American Journal of Political Science* 58 (2): 495–510.

Atchison, Amy. 2015. The Impact of Female Cabinet Ministers on a Female-Friendly Labor Environment. *Journal of Women, Politics & Policy* 36 (4): 388–414.

Atchison, Amy, and Ian Down. 2009. Women Cabinet Ministers and Female-Friendly Social Policy. *Poverty & Public Policy* 1 (2): 1–23.

Bachelet, Michelle. 2011. Foreword. *Progress of the World's Women: In Pursuit of Justice.* NY: United Nations Women.

Bacik, Ivana, Cathryn Costello, and Eileen Drew. 2003. *Gender InJustice: Feminising the Legal Profession?* Dublin: Trinity College.

Backhouse, Constance. 2019. *Two Firsts: Bertha Wilson and Claire L'Heureux-Dube at the Supreme Court of Canada*. Toronto: Second Story Press.

Balanced Participation of Women and Men in Decision-making. 2016. Analytical Report. Gender Equality Commission, Council of Europe.

Baldez, Lisa. 2014. *Defying Convention: US Resistance to the UN Treaty on Women's Rights.* Cambridge: Cambridge University Press.

Barmes, Lizzie, and Kate Malleson. 2011. The Legal Profession as Gatekeeper to the Judiciary: Design Faults in Measures to Enhance Diversity. *The Modern Law Review* 74 (2): 245–271.

Barnes, Tiffany, and Diana Z. O'Brien. 2018. Defending the Realm: The Appointment of Female Defense Ministers Worldwide. *American Journal of Political Science* 62 (2): 355–368.

Bartholomew, Paul C. 1971. *The Irish Judiciary*. Dublin: Institute of Public Administration.

Barro, Robert, and Jong Wha Lee. 2013. A New Data Set of Educational Attainment in the World, 1950–2010. *Journal of Development Economics* 104 (September): 184–198.

Batalden, Paul, and Earl Conway. 2015. Like Magic? ("Every System is Perfectly Designed…"). Institute for Healthcare Improvement. August 21. Accessed June 8, 2021: http://www.ihi.org/communities/blogs/origin-of-every-system-is-perfectly-designed-quote.

Bauer, Gretchen, and Josephine Dawuni, eds. 2016. *Gender and the Judiciary in Africa: From Obscurity to Parity?* New York: Routledge.

Bauer, Gretchen, and Rachel Ellett. 2016. Botswana: Delayed Indigenization and Feminization of the Judiciary. In *Gender and the Judiciary in Africa: From Obscurity to Parity?*, eds. Gretchen Bauer and Josephine Dawuni, 49–64. New York: Routledge.

Beckwith, Karen. 1992. Comparative Research and Electoral Systems: Lessons from France and Italy. *Women & Politics* 12 (1): 1–33.

Berkovitch, Nitza. 1999. *From Motherhood to Citizenship: Women's Rights and International Organizations.* Baltimore, MD: Johns Hopkins University Press.

Bettinger-Lopez, Caroline, and Delphi Cleaveland. 2020. Constitutionalizing Equality. Council on Foreign Relations. Accessed January 28, 2021: https://www.cfr.org/blog/constitutionalizing-equality-equal-rights-amendment-catalyst-change.

Biskupic, Joan. 2000. Politics Snares Court, Hopes of Minorities, and Women. *USA Today*, August 22, 2000.

Blum, Karen. 1990. Portia Today: No Need for 'Drag'. *Advocate* 3 (1): 12–18.

Boigeol, Anne. 2003. Male Strategies in the Face of the Feminisation of a Profession: The Case of the French Judiciary. In *Women in the World's Legal Professions*, eds. Ulrike Schultz and Gisela Shaw, 401–418. Oxford: Hart Publishing.

Boigeol, Anne. 2013. Feminization of the French Magistrature: Gender and Judging in a Feminised Context. In *Gender and Judging*, eds. Ulrike Schultz and Gisela Shaw, 125–143. Oxford: Hart Publishing.

Boli, John, and George M. Thomas. 1997. World Culture in the World Polity: A Century of International Non-Governmental Organization. *American Sociological Review* 62 (2): 171–190.

Bolívar Galindo, Cielito. 2019. Camino que recorrió María Cristina Salmorán de Tamayo para ser la primera ministra de la Suprema Corte de Justicia de la Nación *Quíd Jurís* 43 (enero-marzo). Accessed December 23, 2020: https://revistas-colaboracion.juridicas.unam.mx/index.php/quid-iuris/article/view/37379/34287.

Bonelli, Maria da Gloria. 2015. Brazilian Judges In-Between Professionalism, Gender and Difference. *International Journal of the Legal Profession* 22 (2): 134–150.

Bonilla-Silva, Eduardo. 2017. *Racism Without Racists*. NY: Rowman & Littlefield.

Bonthuys, Elsje. 2013. Gender and the Chief Justice: Principle or Pretext? *Journal of Southern African Studies* 39 (1): 59–76.

Boyd, Christina L. 2016. Representation on the Courts? The Effects of Trial Judges' Sex and Race. *Political Research Quarterly* 69 (4): 788–799.

Boyd, Christina L., Lee Epstein, and Andrew D. Martin. 2010. Untangling the Causal Effects of Sex on Judging. *American Journal of Political Science* 54 (2): 389–411.

Box-Steffensmeier, Janet, and Brad Jones. 2004. *Event History Analysis: A Guide for Social Scientists*. Cambridge: Cambridge University Press.

Bratton, Kathleen, and Rorie Spill. 2002. Existing Diversity and Judicial Selection: The Role of the Appointment Method in Establishing Gender Diversity in State Supreme Courts. *Social Science Quarterly* 83 (2): 504–518.

Brenner, Hannah, and Renee Newman Knake, 2011. Rethinking Gender Equality in the Legal Profession's Pipeline to Power: A Study on Media Coverage of Supreme Court Nominees (Phase I, the Introduction Week). *Temple Law Review* 84: 325.

Brown, Nathan J. 2016. Egypt's Judiciary in a Postrevolutionary Era. In *Egypt's Revolutions: Politics, Religion, and Social Movements*, eds. Bernard Rougier and Stephane Lacroix, 108. New York: Palgrave Macmillan.

Bush, Sarah Sunn. 2011. International Politics and the Spread of Quotas for Women in Legislatures. *International Organization* 65 (1): 103–137.

Cajas Sarria, Mario Alberto. 2015. *La Historia de la Corte Suprema de Justicia de Colombia, 1886–1991 Tomo II: Del Frente Nacional a la Asamblea Constituyente, 1958–1991*. Bogotá, Colombia: Universidad de los Andes.

Cammack, Mark. 1989. Islamic Law in Indonesia's New Order. *International & Comparative Law Quarterly* 38 (1): 53–73.

Cardinal, Monique. 2008. Women and the Judiciary in Syria: Appointments Process, Training, and Career Paths. *International Journal of the Legal Profession* 15 (1–2): 123–139.

Carroll, Jennifer. 2005. You Be the Judge Part II: The Politics and Processes of Judicial Appointments in Ireland. *Bar Review* 10: 182–188.

Carroll, Susan J. 2001. *The Impact of Women in Public Office*. Bloomington, IN: Indiana University Press.

Castagnola, Andrea. 2018. *Manipulating Courts in New Democracies: Forcing Judges off the Bench in Argentina*. New York: Taylor & Francis.

CEDAW Committee. 1985. Report of the Committee on the Elimination of Discrimination against Women (Fourth Session), 19 April. Supplement No. 45 A/40/45. New York: United Nations.

CEDAW Committee. 1993. Consideration of Reports Submitted by States Parties under Article 18 of the Convention: Combined Second and Third Periodic Reports of States Parties: Colombia. CEDAW/C/COL/2–3. New York: United Nations.

CEDAW Committee. 1997a. Consideration of Reports Submitted by States Parties under Article 18 of the Convention on the Elimination of All Forms of Discrimination against Women: Fourth Periodic Reports of State Parties: Colombia. CEDAW/C/COL/4. New York: United Nations.

CEDAW Committee. 1997b. Consideration of Reports Submitted by States Parties under Article 18 of the Convention on the Elimination of All Forms of Discrimination against Women: Second and Third Periodic Reports of States Parties: Ireland. CEDAW/C/IRL/2–3. New York: United Nations.

CEDAW Committee. 1997c. CEDAW General Recommendation No. 23: Political and Public Life. A/52/38. New York: United Nations.

CEDAW Committee. 1998a. Consideration of Reports Submitted by States Parties under Article 18 of the Convention on the Elimination of All Forms of Discrimination against Women: Initial Report of States Parties: South Africa. CEDAW/C/ZAF/1. New York: United Nations.

CEDAW Committee. 1998b. Report of the Committee on the Elimination of Discrimination against Women (Eighteen and Nineteenth Sessions). Consideration of Reports of State Parties: South Africa. General Assembly Official Records Fifty-Third Session Supplement No. 38 (A/53/38/Rev.1). New York: United Nations.

CEDAW Committee. 1999. Report of the Committee on the Elimination of Discrimination against Women (Twentieth and Twenty-First Sessions). General Assembly Official Records Fifty-Fourth Session Supplement No. 38 (A/54/38/Rev.1). New York: United Nations.

CEDAW Committee. 2005a. Consideration of Reports Submitted by States Parties under Article 18 of the Convention on the Elimination of All Forms of Discrimination against Women: Combined Sixth and Seventh Periodic Reports of States Parties: Colombia. CEDAW/C/COL/5–6. New York: United Nations.

CEDAW Committee. 2005b. Consideration of Reports Submitted by States Parties under Article 18 of the Convention on the Elimination of All Forms of Discrimination against Women: Combined Fourth and Fifth Periodic Reports of States Parties: Ireland. CEDAW/C/IRL/4–5. New York: United Nations.

CEDAW Committee. 2007. Consideration of Reports Submitted by States Parties under Article 18 of the Convention on the Elimination of All Forms of Discrimination against Women: Combined Sixth and Seventh Periodic Reports of States Parties: Canada. CEDAW/C/CAN/7. New York: United Nations.

CEDAW Committee. 2008. Concluding Observations of the Committee on the Elimination of Discrimination against Women: Canada. Forty-Second Session, 28 October-7 November. CEDAW/C/CAN/CO/7. New York: United Nations.

CEDAW Committee. 2009. Consideration of Reports Submitted by States Parties under Article 18 of the Convention on the Elimination of All Forms of Discrimination against Women: Sixth Periodic Reports of States Parties due in 2009: Sierra Leone. CEDAW/C/SLE/6. New York: United Nations.

CEDAW Committee. 2010. Consideration of Reports Submitted by States Parties under Article 18 of the Convention on the Elimination of All Forms of Discrimination against Women: Combined Second, Third, and Fourth Periodic Report of States Parties: South Africa. CEDAW/C/ZAF/2–4. New York: United Nations.

CEDAW Committee. 2011a. Combined Initial and Second Periodic Reports of States Parties: Afghanistan. CEDAW/C/AFG/CO/1–2. New York: United Nations.

CEDAW Committee. 2011b. Concluding Observations of the Committee on the Elimination of Discrimination against Women: South Africa. Forty-Eighth Session, 17 January-4 February. CEDAW/C/ZAF/CO/4. New York: United Nations.

CEDAW Committee. 2013. Concluding Observations on the Combined Initial and Second Periodic Reports of Afghanistan. CEDAW/C/AFG/1–2. New York: United Nations.

CEDAW Committee. 2016. Concluding Observations on the Combined Eighth and Ninth Periodic Reports of Canada. CEDAW/C/CAN/CO/8–9. New York: United Nations.

Celis, Karen, and Sarah Childs. 2020. *Feminist Democratic Representation*. Oxford: Oxford University Press.

Celis, Karen, and Sylvia Erzeel. 2017. Third Round of Monitoring on the Implementation of Balanced Participation of Men and Women in Political and Public Life. Strasbourg: Council of Europe.

Center for the Study of Violence and Reconciliation, People Opposing Women Abuse, Western Cape Network on Violence against Women. 2011. South African Shadow Report on the Implementation of the Convention on the Elimination of All Forms of Discrimination against Women Submitted to the CEDAW Committee's 48th Session, 17 January – 4 February 2011.

Centre for Applied Legal Studies. 2014. Transformation of the Legal Profession. August. Johannesburg: University of Witwatersrand.

Cepeda Espinosa, Manuel Jose, and David Landau. 2017. *Colombian Constitutional Law: Leading Cases*. New York: Oxford University Press.

Chappell, Louise. 2015. *The Politics of Gender Justice at the International Criminal Court: Legacies and Legitimacy*. Oxford: Oxford University Press.

Childs, Sarah. 2008. *Women and British Party Politics: Descriptive, Substantive and Symbolic Representation*. New York: Routledge.

Childs, Sarah, and Paul Webb. 2012. *Sex, Gender and the Conservative Party: From Iron Lady to Kitten Heels*. Basingstoke: Palgrave.

Clark, Mary L. 2002. Changing the Face of the Law: How Women's Advocacy Groups Put Women on the Federal Judicial Appointments Agenda. *Yale Journal of Law and Feminism* 14: 243.

Clark, Tom S., and Drew A. Linzer. 2015. Should I Use Fixed or Random Effects. *Political Science Research and Methods* 3 (2): 399–408.

Clayton, Amanda, Diana Z. O'Brien, and Jennifer M. Piscopo. 2019. All Male Panels? Representation and Democratic Legitimacy. *American Journal of Political Science* 63 (1): 113–129.

Clayton, Amanda, and Pär Zetterberg. 2018. Quota Shocks: Electoral Gender Quotas and Government Spending Priorities Worldwide. *The Journal of Politics* 80 (3): 916–932.

Cole, Wade M. 2013. Government Respect for Gendered Rights: The Effect of the Convention on the Elimination of Discrimination against Women on Women's Rights Outcomes, 1981–2004. *International Studies Quarterly* 57 (2): 233–249.

Commission for Gender Equality. 2012. Complaint Form Received on October 12, 2012. Braamfontein: South Africa.

Commission for Gender Equality. 2015. Commission for Gender Equality on Redressing Judicial Gender Injustice. Accessed December 22, 2020: http://allafrica.com/stories/201507091091.html.

Constitutional Court of Burundi. N.d. Les membres de la cour constitutionnelle de 1992 à nos jours. Bujumbura: Constitutional Court.

Constitutional Court Trust Oral History Project. 1993. Bizos, George (x2), 27 pages, 13:18:17. University of the Witwatersrand: Historical Papers Research Archive: AG3368, Item Number B6.

Constitutional Court Trust Oral History Project. 2011. Mokgoro, Yvonne, 29 pages, 14:28:57. University of the Witwatersrand: Historical Papers Research Archive: AG3368, Item Number M60.

Cook, Beverly B. 1982. Women as Supreme Court Candidates. *Judicature* 65 (6): 314–326.

Cook, Beverly B. 1984. Women Judges: A Preface to Their History. *Golden Gate University Law Review* 14 (3): 573–610.

Cook, Beverly B. 2018. Will Women Judges Make a Difference in Women's Legal Rights? In *Women, Power, and Political Systems*, ed. Margherita Rendel, 216–239. New York: Routledge.

Copelon, Rhonda. 2000. Gender Crimes as War Crimes: Integrating Crimes Against Women into International Law. *McGill Law Journal* 46: 217.

Corder, Hugh. 2011. Appointment, Discipline, and Removal of Judges in South Africa. In *Judiciaries in Comparative Perspective*, ed. H.P. Lee, 96–116. Cambridge: Cambridge University Press.

Corporación Simsa Mujer. 2007. *Informe Colombia: Diagnóstico de la Situación de las Mujeres en la Administración de Justicia en Colombia.* Bogotá, Colombia: Corporación Simsa Mujer.

Correa Henao, Néstor Raúl. 2013. Gráficas de Participación de la Mujer en la Rama Judicial in Género y Justicia Transicional. Comisión Nacional de Genero de la Rama Judicial, Republica de Colombia.

Corte Interamericana de Derechos Humanos. 2019. *Composiciones: Corte Interamericana de Derechos Humanos 1979–2019.* San José, Costa Rica: Corte IDH.

Corte Suprema de Justicia de la Nacion (Supreme Court of Mexico). N.d. Medalla María Cristina Salmorán de Tamayo. Accessed December 23, 2020: https://www.scjn.gob.mx/igualdad-de-genero/medalla-maria-cristina-salmoran-de-tamayo.

Courts and Court Officers Act. 2002. Section 5. Office of the Attorney General, Ireland. http://www.irishstatutebook.ie/eli/2002/act/15/enacted/en/print#sec4.

Cowan, Ruth B. 2006. Women's Representation on the Courts in the Republic of South Africa. *University of Maryland Law Journal of Race, Religion, Gender, and Class* 6: 291.

Crenshaw, Kimberlé. 1989. Demarginalizing the Intersection of Race and Sex: A Black Feminist Critique of Antidiscrimination Doctrine, Feminist Theory, and Antiracist Politics. *University of Chicago Legal Forum* 1: 139.

Cross, Frank B. 1999. The Relevance of Law in Human Rights Protection. *International Review of Law and Economics* 19 (1): 87–98.

Dahlerup, Drude, and Lenita Freidenvall. 2005. Quotas as a 'Fast Track' to Equal Representation for Women. *International Feminist Journal of Politics* 7 (1): 26–48.

Davis, Mattie Belle. 1982. National Association of Women Judges—Third Annual Conference. *Women Lawyers Journal* 68 (1): 18–20.

Davis, Rebecca Howard. 1997. *Women and Power in Parliamentary Democracies: Cabinet Appointments in Western Europe, 1968–1992.* Vol. 2. Lincoln, NE: University of Nebraska Press.

Davis, Richard. 2005. *Electing Justice: Fixing the Supreme Court Nomination Process.* Oxford: Oxford University Press.

Davis, Richard. 2017. *Supreme Democracy: The End of Elitism in Supreme Court Nominations.* Oxford: Oxford University Press.

Dawuni, Josephine Jarpa. 2011. Justice Annie Jiagge. In *Dictionary of African Biography*, eds. Emmanuel Kwaku Akyeampong and Henry Louis Gates, 207–208. London: Oxford University Press.

Dawuni, Josephine Jarpa. 2016. To 'Mother' or Not to 'Mother': The Representative Roles of Women Judges in Ghana. *Journal of African Law* 60 (3): 419–440.

Dawuni, Josephine Jarpa. 2017. Akua Kuenyehia: Leaving a Mark Along the Journey for Human Rights. In *International Courts and the African Woman Judge: Unveiled Narratives*, eds. Josephine Jarpa Dawuni and Akua Kuenyehia, 58–76. New York: Routledge.

Dawuni, J. Jarpa. 2018. African Woman Judges on International Courts: Symbolic or Substantive Gains? *University of Baltimore Law Review* 47 (2): 199–245.

Dawuni, J. Jarpa. 2020. Vive la Diversité or Aluta Continua? Achieving Gender Equity on the African Court on Human and Peoples' Rights. *Connecticut Journal of International Law.* 34 (3): 380–402.

Dawuni, Josephine Jarpa, and Alice J. Kang. 2015. Her Ladyship Chief Justice: The Rise of Female Leaders in the Judiciary in Africa. *Africa Today* 62 (2): 45–69.

Dawuni, Josephine Jarpa, and Akua Kuenyehia, eds. 2018. *International Courts and the African Woman Judge: Unveiled Narratives.* New York: Routledge.

Department of Justice of Ireland. 2016. Report of Issues Raised at CEDAW Consultation. Atrium, Department of Justice and Equality, 51 St. Stephen's Green, July 19, 2016.

De Lauri, Antonio. 2020. Women Judges in Afghanistan: An Interview with Anisa Rasooli. *CMI Insight* 4: 1–5.

Diascro, Jennifer Segal, and Rorie Spill Solberg. 2009. George W. Bush's Legacy on the Federal Bench: Policy in the Face of Diversity. *Judicature* 92: 289.

Dixon, Rosalind, and Theunis Roux, eds. 2018. *Constitutional Triumphs, Constitutional Disappointments: A Critical Assessment of the 1996 South African Constitution's Local and International Influence.* Cambridge: Cambridge University Press.

Dovi, Suzanne, and Francy Luna. 2020. Women "Doing" the Judiciary: Rethinking the Justice Argument for Descriptive Representation. *Politics, Groups, and Identities* 8 (4): 790–802.

Drachman, Virginia. 2001. *Sisters in Law: Women Lawyers in Modern American History.* Cambridge, MA: Harvard University Press.

Driscoll, Amanda, and Michael J. Nelson. 2012. The Political Origins of Judicial Elections: Evidence from the United States and Bolivia. *Judicature* 96 (4): 151–160.

Driscoll, Amanda, and Michael J. Nelson. 2015. Judicial Selection and the Democratization of Justice. *Journal of Law and Courts* 3 (1): 115–148.

Duverger, Maurice. 1955. *The Political Role of Women.* NY: UNESCO.

Ellett, Rachel, and Tererai R. Mafukidze. 2013. Importing Justice? The Politics of Expatriate Judicial Appointments in Southern Africa. International Political Science Association RC 09 (Comparative Judicial Studies), Dublin, Ireland, July 22–24, 2013.

El Espectador. “La importancia de que en la Corte Constitucional haya tres magistradas” by María José Medellín Cano, 19 July 2017.

El Tiempo. 2007. Mauricio González, secretario jurídico del Presidente, es nuevo magistrado de Corte Constitucional. *El Tiempo*, August 28, 2007.

El Tiempo. 2014a. Denuncian falta de transparencia en elección de magistrado. *El Tiempo*, April 24, 2014.

El Tiempo. 2014b. Lista la terna para reemplazaral magistrado Nilson Pinilla. *El Tiempo*, April 24, 2014.

El Tiempo. 2015. Quienes son los ternados para la Corte Constitucional. *El Tiempo*, October 7, 2015. http://www.eltiempo.com/politica/justicia/ternadosparacorteconstitucional/16397916.

Epstein, Lee, Jack Knight, and Andrew D. Martin. 2003. The Norm of Prior Judicial Experience and its Consequences for Career Diversity on the U.S. Supreme Court. *California Law Review* 91 (4): 903–966.

Epstein, Lee, Jeffrey A. Segal, Harold J. Spaeth, and Thomas G. Walker. 2015. *The Supreme Court Compendium: Data, Decisions, and Developments*. Washington, DC: CQ Press.

Epstein, Lee, Thomas G. Walker, Nancy Staudt, Scott Hendrickson, and Jason Roberts. 2019. The U.S. Supreme Court Justices Database. July 30. Accessed December 20, 2020: http://epstein.wustl.edu/research/justicesdata.html.

Escobar-Lemmon, Maria C., and Michelle M. Taylor-Robinson. 2005. Women Ministers in Latin American Government: When, Where, and Why? *American Journal of Political Science* 49 (4): 822–844.

Escobar-Lemmon, Maria C., and Michelle M. Taylor-Robinson, eds. 2014. *Representation: The Case of Women*. New York: Oxford University Press.

Escobar-Lemmon, Maria C., and Michelle M. Taylor-Robinson. 2016. *Women in Presidential Cabinets: Power Players or Abundant Tokens*. New York: Oxford University Press.

Escobar-Lemmon, Maria C., Valerie Hoekstra, Alice J. Kang, and Miki Caul Kittilson. 2016. Just the Facts? Media Coverage of Female and Male High Court Appointees in Five Democracies. *Politics & Gender* 12 (2): 254–274.

Escobar-Lemmon, Maria C., Valerie Hoekstra, Alice J. Kang, and Miki Caul Kittilson. 2021. Breaking the Judicial Glass Ceiling: The Appointment of Women to High Court Worldwide. *The Journal of Politics* 83 (2): 662–674.

European Commission for the Efficiency of Justice (CEPEJ). 2014. European Judicial Systems: Efficiency and Quality of Justice. Council of Europe.

Eyewitness News. 2015. Zuma Appoints Judge Zoliswa Mhlantla to ConCourt. *Eyewitness News*, November 9. Accessed December 27, 2020: https://ewn.co.za/2015/11/09/Zuma-appoints-Judge-Zoliswa-Mhlantla-to-ConCourt.

Fair Trade Commission. 1990. Report of Study into Restrictive Practices in the Legal Profession. Dublin: National Library of Ireland.

Fallon, Kathleen M., Liam Swiss, and Jocelyn Viterna. 2012. Democracy Paradox: Democratization and Women's Legislative Representation in Developing Nations, 1975–2009. *American Sociological Review* 77 (3): 380–408.

Farhang, Sean, and Gregory Wawro. 2004. Institutional Dynamics on the US Court of Appeals: Minority Representation under Panel Decision Making. *Journal of Law, Economics, and Organization* 20 (2): 299–330.

Ferejohn, John, and Pasquale Pasquino. 2002. Constitutional Courts as Deliberative Institutions: Towards an Institutional Theory of Constitutional Justice. In *Constitutional Justice, East and West: Democratic Legitimacy and Constitutional Courts in Post-Communist Europe in a Comparative Perspective*, ed. Wojciech Sadurski, 21–36. Dordrecht: Springer.

Finnemore, Martha. 1993. International Organizations as Teachers of Norms: The United Nations Educational, Scientific, and Cultural Organization and Science Policy. *International Organization* 47 (4): 565–597.

Franceschet, Susan, Mona Lena Krook, and Jennifer M. Piscopo, eds. 2012. *The Impact of Gender Quotas*. New York: Oxford University Press.

Friedman, Elisabeth Jay. 2009. Re(gion)alizing Women's Human Rights in Latin America. *Politics & Gender* 5 (3): 349–375.

Fundación Justicia y Género. 2021. Encuentro Magistradas Iberoamericanas. Accessed January 20, 2021: https://fundacionjyg.org/encuentro-magistradas-iberoamericanas/.

Galligan, Yvonne. 2000. The Development of Mechanisms to Monitor Progress in Achieving Gender Equality in Ireland. Report Commissioned by the Department of Justice, Equality and Law Reform.

García Goldar, Mónica. 2020.The Glass Ceiling at the Highest Levels of the Spanish Judiciary. *International Journal of the Legal Profession* 27 (2): 189–202.

García Villegas, Mauricio, and María Adelaida Ceballos Bedoya. 2019. *La Profesión Jurídica en Colombia: Falta de Reglas y Exceso de Mercado*. Bogotá, Colombia: Editorial Dejusticia.

Gibson, James L, Gregory A. Caldeira, and Vanessa Baird. 1998. On the Legitimacy of High Courts. *American Political Science Review* 92 (2): 343–358.

Gill, Rebecca D., Sylvia R. Lazos, and Mallory M. Waters. 2011. Are Judicial Performance Evaluations Fair to Women and Minorities? A Cautionary Tale from Clark County, Nevada. *Law & Society Review* 45 (3): 731–759.

Ginsburg, Ruth Bader, and Laura W. Brill. 1995. Women in the Federal Judiciary: Three Way Pavers and the Exhilarating Charge President Carter Wrought. *Fordham Law Review* 64: 281.

Ginsburg, Tom. 2003. *Judicial Review in New Democracies: Constitutional Courts in Asian Cases*. Cambridge: Cambridge University Press.

Ginsburg, Tom, and Tamir Moustafa. 2008. *Rule by Law: The Politics of Courts in Authoritarian Regimes*. Cambridge: Cambridge University Press.

Goelzhauser, Greg. 2011. Diversifying State Supreme Courts. *Law and Society Review* 45 (3): 761–781.

Goelzhauser, Greg. 2016. *Choosing State Supreme Court Justices: Merit Selection and the Conse-quences of Institutional Reform*. Philadelphia: Temple University Press.

Goelzhauser, Greg. 2018. Does Merit Selection Work? Evidence from Commission and Gubernatorial Choices. *Journal of Law and Courts* 6 (1): 155–187.

Goldman, Sheldon. 1999. *Picking Federal Judges: Lower Court Selection from Roosevelt through Reagan*. New Haven: Yale University Press.

Goodman, Ryan, and Derek Jinks. 2004. How to Influence States: Socialization and International Human Rights Law. *Duke Law Journal* 54 (3): 621–703.

Government of South Africa. 1993. Interim Constitution of the Republic of South Africa.

Government of South Africa. 1996. Constitution of the Republic of South Africa.

Government of Zimbabwe. 2013. Constitution of the Republic of Zimbabwe.

Graham, Benjamin, and Jacob Tucker. 2017. The International Political Economy Data Resource. *Review of International Organizations* 14 (1): 149–161.

Gramlich, John. 2018. Trump has Appointed a Larger Share of Female Judges than Other GOP Presidents. Pew Research. October 2. Accessed January 28, 2021: https://www.pewresearch.org/fact-tank/2018/10/02/trump-has-appointed-a-larger-share-of-female-judges-than-other-gop-presidents-but-lags-obama/.

Gray, Mark M., Miki Caul Kittilson, and Wayne Sandholtz. 2006. Women and Globalization: A Study of 180 countries, 1975–2000. *International Organization* 60 (2): 293–333.

Grossman, Nienke. 2016. Achieving Sex-Representative International Court Benches. *American Journal of International Law* 110: 82–95.

Gryski, Gerard S., Eleanor C. Main, and William J. Dixon. 1986. Models of State High Court Decision Making in Sex Discrimination Cases. *The Journal of Politics* 48 (1): 143–155.

Haire, Susan B., Laura P. Moyer, and Shawn Treier. 2013. Diversity, Deliberation and Judicial Opinion Writing. *Journal of Law and Courts* 1 (2): 303–30.

Haire, Susan B. 2001. Rating the Ratings of the American Bar Association Standing Committee on Federal Judiciary. *The Justice System Journal* 22 (1): 1–17.

Haire, Susan B., and Laura P. Moyer. 2015. *Diversity Matters: Judicial Policymaking in the U.S. Courts of Appeals.* Charlottesville: University of Virginia Press.

Hancock, Ange-Marie. 2016. *Intersectionality: An Intellectual History.* Oxford: Oxford University Press.

Harris, Allison P., and Maya Sen. 2019. Bias and Judging. *Annual Review of Political Science* 21: 241–259.

Hassim, Shireen. 2006. *Women's Organizations and Democracy in South Africa: Contesting Authority.* Madison: University of Wisconsin Press.

Helmke, Gretchen, and Steven Levitsky, eds. 2006. *Informal Institutions and Democracy: Lessons from Latin America.* Baltimore: John Hopkins University Press.

Hill Jr., Daniel W. 2010. Estimating the Effects of Human Rights Treaties on State Behavior. *The Journal of Politics* 72 (4): 1161–1174.

Hoekstra, Valerie. 2010. Increasing the Gender Diversity of High Courts: A Comparative View. *Politics & Gender* 6 (3): 474–484.

Hoekstra, Valerie, Miki Kittilson, and Elizabeth Andrews Bond. 2014. Gender, High Courts and Ideas about Representation in Western Europe. In *Representation: The Case of Women*, eds. Maria C. Escobar-Lemmon and Michelle M. Taylor-Robinson, 103–117. Oxford: Oxford University Press.

Holmes, Lisa M., and Jolly A. Emrey. 2006. Court Diversification: Staffing the State Courts of Last Resort through Interim Appointments. *Justice System Journal* 27 (1): 1–13.

Htun, Mala. 2005. Women, Political Parties and Electoral Systems in Latin America. In *Women in Parliament. Beyond Numbers. A New Edition*, eds. Julie Ballington and Azza Karam. Stockholm: International IDEA.

Htun, Mala, and S. Laurel Weldon. 2012. The Civic Origins of Progressive Policy Change: Combatting Violence Against Women in Global Perspective, 1975–2005. *American Political Science Review* 106 (3): 548–569.

Htun, Mala, and S. Laurel Weldon. 2015. Religious Power, the State, Women's Rights, and Family Law. *Politics & Gender* 11 (3): 451–477.

Htun, Mala, and S. Laurel Weldon. 2018. *The Logics of Gender Justice: State Action on Women's Rights around the World.* New York: Cambridge University Press.

Hudson, Valerie, Donna Lee Bowen, and Perpetua Lynne Nielsen. 2020. *The First Political Order: How Sex Shapes Governance and National Security Worldwide.* New York: Columbia University Press.

Hughes, Melanie M. 2009. Armed Conflict, International Linkages, and Women's Parliamentary Representation in Developing Nations. *Social Problems* 56 (1): 174–204.

Hughes, Melanie M., Mona Lena Krook, and Pamela Paxton. 2015. Transnational Women's Activism and the Global Diffusion of Gender Quotas. *International Studies Quarterly* 59 (2): 357–372.

Hughes, Melanie M., Pamela Paxton, Sharon Quinsaat, and Nicholas Reith. 2017. Women's International Nongovernmental Organizations, 1950–2013. [Computer file]. Ann Arbor, MI: Inter-university Consortium for Political and Social Research [distributor], http://doi.org/10.3886/E100514V1.

Hughes, Melanie M., and Aili Mari Tripp. 2015. Civil War and Trajectories of Change in Women's Political Representation in Africa, 1985–2010. *Social Forces* 93 (4): 1513–1540.

Human Rights Watch. 2004. Divorced from Justice: Women's Unequal Access to Divorce in Egypt. 16, 8 (E). https://www.hrw.org/reports/2004/egypt1204/egypt1204.pdf.

Hunter, Rosemary. 2008. Can Feminist Judges Make a Difference? *International Journal of the Legal Profession* 15 (1–2): 7–36.

Hunter, Rosemary, Clare McGlynn, and Erika Rackley, eds. 2010. *Feminist Judgments: From Theory to Practice*. Oxford: Hart Publishing.

Hunter, Rosemary. 2015. More than Just a Different Face? Judicial Diversity and Decisionmaking. *Current Legal Problems* 68: 119–141.

Hurwitz, Mark, and Drew Lanier. 2001. Women and Minorities on State and Federal Appellate Benches, 1985 and 1999. *Judicature* 85 (2): 84–91.

Hurwitz, Mark, and Drew Lanier. 2003. Explaining Judicial Diversity: The Differential Ability of Women and Minorities to Attain Seats on State Supreme and Appellate Courts. *State Politics and Policy Quarterly* 3 (4): 329–352.

Inglehart, Ronald, and Pippa Norris. 2003. *Rising Tide: Gender Equality and Cultural Change Around the World*. Cambridge: Cambridge University Press.

Institute for Democratic Alternatives in South Africa (IDASA). 2005. Debating the Transformation of the Judiciary: Rhetoric and Substance. *ePoliticsSA* 3. Accessed January 12, 2021: https://static.pmg.org.za/bills/050518pims.pdf.

International Association of Women Judges. 2018. IAWJ Africa Region Report: May 2016-May 2018. Accessed June 9, 2021: http://www.iawj.org/iawj-africa-region-country-reports-may-2016-2018/.

Inter-Parliamentary Union. 2020. Women in Politics: 2020. Accessed January 20, 2021: https://www.ipu.org/resources/publications/infographics/2020-03/women-in-politics-2020.

Ireland Bar Association. 2017. Accessed July 15, 2017: https://www.hg.org/bar-associations-ireland.asp.

Irving, Helen. 2009. *Gender and the Constitution: Equity and Agency in Comparative Constitutional Design*. Cambridge: Cambridge University Press.

Jacob, Suraj, John A. Scherpereel, and Melinda Adams. 2014. Gender Norms and Women's Political Representation: A Global Analysis of Cabinets, 1979–2009. *Governance: An International Journal of Policy, Administration, and Institutions* 27 (2): 321–345.

Jalalzai, Farida. 2013. *Shattered, Cracked, or Firmly Intact?: Women and the Executive Glass Ceiling Worldwide*. New York: Oxford University Press.

Jaramillo, Isabel Cristina. 2000. Legal Reform, Feminism, and Patriarchy in Colombia: The Case of the Law of Quotas for Women in High-Decision Making Positions Within the Executive Branch. Doctoral Dissertation, Harvard Law School.

Judiciary of Rwanda. 2012. The Supreme Court: Judges. Archive.org capture on September 2, 2012. Accessed December 20, 2020: https://web.archive.org/web/20120902121423/http://www.judiciary.gov.rw/sc/judgessc.aspx.

JuriGlobe. 2015. Legal Systems Classification. University of Ottawa Faculty of Law World Legal Systems Research Group. Accessed October 13, 2015: http://www.juriglobe.ca/eng/sys-juri/index.php.

Kahn, Ellison. 1989. The Wits Faculty of Law: 1922–1989. *Consultus* 2 (2): 103–112.

Kalem, Seda. 2020. Being a Woman Judge in Turkish Judicial Culture. *International Journal of the Legal Profession* 27 (2): 119–144.

Kamau, Winifred. 2013. Women Judges and Magistrates in Kenya: Challenges, Opportunities, and Contributions. In *Gender and Judging*, eds. Ulrike Schultz and Gisela Shaw, 167–190. Oxford: Hart Publishing.

Kang, Alice J., Miki Caul Kittilson, Valerie Hoekstra, and Maria C. Escobar-Lemmon. 2020. Diverse and Inclusive High Courts: A Global and Intersectional Perspective. *Politics, Groups, and Identities* 8 (4): 812–821.

Kang, Alice J., and Aili Mari Tripp. 2018. Coalitions Matter: Citizenship, Women, and Quota Adoption in Africa. *Perspectives on Politics* 16 (1): 73–91.

Kaufman, Natalie Hevener, and Stefanie A. Lindquist. 1995. Critiquing Gender-Neutral Treaty Language: The Convention on the Elimination of All Forms of Discrimination Against Women. In *Women's Rights, Human Rights: International Feminist Perspectives*, eds. Julie Peters and Andrea Wolper, 114–126. New York: Routledge.

Kay, Fiona, and Joan Brockman. 2000. Barriers to Gender Equality in the Canadian Legal Establishment. *Feminist Legal Studies* 8 (2): 169–198.

Keck, Margaret, and Kathryn Sikkink. 1998. *Activists Beyond Borders: Advocacy Networks in International Politics.* Ithaca, NY: Cornell University Press.

Kenney, Sally J. 2008. Gender on the Agenda: How the Paucity of Women Judges Became an Issue. *The Journal of Politics* 70 (3): 717–735.

Kenney, Sally J. 2013. *Gender and Justice: Why Women in the Judiciary Really Matter.* New York: Routledge.

Kenney, Sally J. 2012. Choosing Judges: A Bumpy Road to Women's Equality and a Long Way to Go. *Michigan State Law Review* 1499.

Kim, Haesook. 2009. The Avalanche Perspective: Women Jurists in Korea, 1952–2008. *Feminist Legal Studies* 17: 61–77.

Kimble, Sara L., and Marion Röwekamp, eds. 2017. *New Perspectives on European Women's Legal History.* New York: Routledge.

Kimble, Sara L., and Marion Röwekamp. 2018. Exclusion and Inclusion in the Legal Professions: Negotiating Gender in Central Europe, 1887–1945. *Acta Poloniae Historica* 117, special volume on Gender and Science in East-Central Europe: 51–93.

Kittilson, Miki Caul. 2006. *Challenging Parties, Changing Parliaments: Women and Elected Office in Contemporary Western Europe.* Columbus: Ohio State University Press.

Klibi, Salsabil. 2016. Tunisia: A New Constitution and More Women Judges. In *Gender and the Judiciary in Africa: From Obscurity to Parity?*, eds. Gretchen Bauer and Josephine Dawuni, 80–92. New York: Routledge.

Krook, Mona Lena. 2006. Reforming Representation: The Diffusion of Candidate Gender Quotas Worldwide. *Politics & Gender* 2 (3): 303–327.

Krook, Mona Lena, and Diana Z. O'Brien. 2012. All the President's Men? The Appointment of Female Cabinet Ministers Worldwide. *The Journal of Politics* 74 (3): 840–855.

Krook, Mona Lena, and Jacqui True. 2012. Rethinking the Life Cycles of International Norms: The United Nations and the Global Promotion of Gender Equality. *European Journal of International Relations* 18 (1): 103–127.

Latz, Isabel et al. 2014. Equal Rights for Women and Girls in the World's Constitutions. *World Policy Forum*, Los Angeles, CA: UCLA.

Law Society of Ireland. 2017. Accessed July 15, 2017: https://www.lawsociety.ie/.

Lazos Vargas, Sylvia R. 2004. Does a Diverse Judiciary Attain a Rule of Law that is Inclusive: What Grutter v. Bollinger Has to Say about Diversity on the Bench. *Michigan Journal Race and Law* 10: 101.

Liathain, Maeve. 2019. Women and the Law. Dublin: Oireachtas Library and Research Services, Houses of the Oireachtas Tithe an Oireachtais.

Lindbekk, Monika. 2017. Women Judges in Egypt: Discourse and Practice. In *Women Judges in the Muslim World: A Comparative Study of Discourse and Practice*, eds. Nadia Sonneveld and Monika Lindbekk, 284–316. Leiden: Brill.

Lovenduski, Joni, and Pippa Norris. 1993. *Gender and Party Politics*. London: Sage.

Luhiste, Maarja. 2015. Party Gatekeepers' Support for Viable Female Candidacy in PR-List Systems. *Politics & Gender* 11 (1): 89–116.

Lupu, Yonatan. 2013. The Informative Power of Treaty Commitment: Using the Spatial Model to Address Selection Effects. *American Journal of Political Science* 57 (4): 912–925.

Mac Cormaic, Ruadhan. 2013. The Supreme Court: Where Politics and the Law Meet. *Irish Times*. July 9. https://www.irishtimes.com/news/crime-and-law/the-supreme-court-where-politics-and-the-law-meet-1.1456895.

MacNeill, Jennifer. 2016. *The Politics of Judicial Selection in Ireland*. Dublin: Four Courts Press.

Makin, Kirk. 1997. Supreme Court Selection Not Easy Pickings Ontario Judges Arbour, Abella, Laskin and Doherty Considered Top Candidates by Legal Community. *Globe and Mail*. December 3.

Malleson, Kate. 2003. Prospects for Parity: The Position of Women in the Judiciary in England and Wales. In *Women in the World's Legal Professions*, eds. Gisela Shaw and Ulrike Schultz, 175–190. Oxford: Hart Publishing.

Malleson, Kate. 2006a. Rethinking the Merit Principle in Judicial Selection. *Journal of Law and Society* 33 (1): 126–140.

Malleson, Kate. 2006b. Introduction. In *Appointing Judges in an Age of Judicial Power: Critical Perspectives from around the World*, eds. Kate Malleson and Peter Russell, 3–10. Toronto: University of Toronto Press.

Malleson, Kate. 2009. Diversity in the Judiciary: The Case for Positive Action. *Journal of Law and Society* 36 (3): 376–402.

Malleson, Kate. 2014. The Case for Gender Quotas for Appointments to the Supreme Court. UK Supreme Court Blog. June 27. Accessed January 20, 2021: http://ukscblog.com/case-gender-quotas-appointments-supreme-court.

Malleson, Kate, and Peter H. Russell, eds. 2006. *Appointing Judges in an Age of Judicial Power: Critical Perspectives from Around the World*. Toronto: University of Toronto Press.

Mannix, Elizabeth, and Margaret A. Neale. 2005. What Differences Make a Difference? The Promise and Reality of Diverse Teams in Organizations. *Psychological Science in the Public Interest* 6 (2): 31–55.

Mansbridge, Jane. 1999. Should Blacks Represent Blacks and Women Represent Women? A Contingent 'Yes'. *The Journal of Politics* 61 (3): 628–657.

Marshall, Monty G., Ted Robert Gurr, and Keith Jaggers. 2015. Polity IV Project: Political Regime Characteristics and Transitions, 1800–2015. http://www.systemicpeace.org/inscrdata.html.

Martin, Elaine. 1993. The Representative Role of Women Judges. *Judicature* 77: 166.

Martin, Elaine. 1987. Gender and Judicial Selection: A Comparison of the Reagan and Carter Administration. *Judicature* 71: 136.

Martin, Susan Ehrlich, and Nancy C. Jurik. 2006. *Doing Justice, Doing Gender: Women in Legal and Criminal Justice Occupations*. Thousand Oaks: Sage Publications.

Masengu, Tabeth. 2015. A Perspective on Women and Leadership in the South African Judiciary. *South African Journal of Human Rights* 3: 655.

Masengu, Tabeth. 2016. It's a Man's World: Barriers to Gender Transformation in the South African Judiciary: Perspectives from Women Advocates and Attorney. *International Journal of the Legal Profession* 23 (3): 305–319.

Masengu, Tabeth. 2020. The Judicial Service Commission and the Appointment of Women: More to It than Meets the Eye. *International Journal of the Legal Profession* 27 (2): 161–174.

Matland, Richard. 1998. Women's Representation in National Legislatures: Developed and Developing Countries. *Legislative Studies Quarterly* 23 (1): 109–125.

Matland, Richard E., and Donley T. Studlar. 1996. The Contagion of Women Candidates in Single-Member District and Proportional Representation Electoral Systems: Canada and Norway. *The Journal of Politics* 58 (3): 707–733.

Medellín Cano, María José. 2017. La importancia de que en la Corte Constitucional haya tres magistradas. *El Espectador*, June 19, 2017.

McAuley, Adam. 2012. Judicial Appointment Process: Is Ireland a Conformist or Outlier? Paper Presented at the International Political Science Association, Madrid.

McCormick, Peter, and Ian Greene. 1990. *Judges and Judging: Inside the Canadian Judicial System*. Toronto: James Lorimer and Co.

McElroy, Gail. 2017. Party Competition in Ireland: The Emergence of a Left-Right Dimension? In *A Conservation Revolution? Electoral Change in Twenty-First Century Ireland*, eds, Michael Marsh, David M. Farrell, and Gail McElroy, 61–82. Oxford: Oxford University Press.

McKinsey Global Institute. 2015. "How Advancing Women's Equality Can Add $12 Trillion to Global Growth." *Institute Report*. Accessed December 18, 2020: https://www.mckinsey.com/featured-insights/employment-and-growth/how-advancing-womens-equality-can-add-12-trillion-to-global-growth#.

Means, Taneisha N. 2018. Race, Gender, and the Battle to Seat Constance Baker Motley, the First Black Woman Appointed to the Federal Bench. In *Race, Gender, Sexuality, and the Politics of the American Judiciary*, eds. Samantha Hernandez and Sharon Navarro, 98–122. Cambridge: Cambridge University Press.

Means, Taneisha N., Andrew Eslich, and Kaitlin Prado. 2019. Judicial Diversity in the United States Federal Judiciary. In *Research Handbook on Law and Courts*, eds. Susan Sterett and Lee Walker, 231–245. Northampton, MA: Edward Elgar Publishing.

Merry, Sally Engle. 2006. *Human Rights and Gender Violence: Translating International Law into Local Justice*. Chicago: University of Chicago Press.

Merry, Sally Engle. 2011. Measuring the World: Indicators, Human Rights, and Global Governance. *Cultural Anthropology* 52 (3): S83.

Merry, Sally Engle. 2019. The Sustainable Development Goals Confront the Infrastructure of Measurement. *Global Policy* 10 (1): 146–156.

Michelson, Ethan. 2013. Women in the Legal Profession, 1970–2010: A Study of the Global Supply of Lawyers. *Indiana Journal of Global Legal Studies* 20 (2): 1071–1137.

Mohd Zin, Najibah. 2018. Female Judges in Malaysian Shari'a Courts: A Problem of Gender or Legal Interpretation? In *Women Judges in the Muslim World: A Comparative Study of Discourse and Practice*, eds. Nadia Sonneveld and Monika Lindbekk, 153–177. Leiden: Brill.

Montoya, Ana María. 2013. 'Si No Vas al Senado, No Te Eligen Magistrado.' Instituciones Informales y Criterios de Selección de los Magistrados de la Corte Constitucional Colombiana en el Senado (1992–2009). *Colombia Internacional* 79 (Sept–Dec): 155–190.

Morrison, Linda C. 2002. The National Association of Women Judges: Agent of Change. *Wisconsin Women's Law Journal* 17 (2): 291–320.

Moseneke, Dikgang. 2016. *My Own Liberator: A Memoir.* Johannesburg: Picador Africa.

Moustafa, Tamir. 2007. *The Struggle for Constitutional Power: Law, Politics, and Economic Development in Egypt.* Cambridge: Cambridge University Press.

Moyer, Laura P. 2019. Gender on the International Bench. In *Research Handbook on Law and Courts,* eds. Susan M. Sterett and Lee Demetrius Walker, 187–199. Northampton, MA: Edward Elgar Publishing.

Moyer, Laura P., John Szmer, Susan Haire, and Robert K. Christensen. 2020. Diversity, Consensus and Decision Making: Evidence from the U.S. Courts of Appeal. *Politics, Groups and Identities* 8 (4): 822–833.

Moyer, Laura P., and Holley Tankersley. 2012. Judicial Innovation and Sexual Harassment Doctrine in the US Courts of Appeals. *Political Research Quarterly* 65 (4): 784–798.

Murray, Rainbow. 2004. Why Didn't Parity Work? A Closer Examination of the 2002 Election Results. *French Politics* 2 (3): 347–362.

National Women's Strategy. 2013. Towards Gender Parity in Decision Making in Ireland. Dublin: Department of Justice and Equality.

Nemacheck, Christine L. 2008. Strategic Selection: Presidential Nomination of Supreme Court Justices From Herbert Hoover through George W. Bush. Charlottesville: University of Virginia Press.

Ní Liatháin, Maeve. 2019. Women and the Law: 100 Years of Progress Since the Sex Disqualification (Removal) Act 1919. Houses of the Oireachtas/Oireachtas Library and Research Service. Retrieved at bit.y/35lsaem.

Ngcukaitobi, Tembeka. 2018. *The Land is Ours: South Africa's First Black Lawyers and the Birth of Constitutionalism.* Johannesburg: Penguin Random House South Africa.

Ngoepe, B. M. 2000. White Paper on the Judicial System. *Advocate* 13 (1): 27–32.

Norris, Pippa, and Joni Lovenduski. 1995. *Political Recruitment: Gender, Race and Class in the British Parliament.* Cambridge University Press.

Norris, Pippa, and Ronald Inglehart. 2001. Women and Democracy: Cultural Obstacles to Equal Representation. *Journal of Democracy* 12 (3): 126–140.

O'Brien, Diana. 2015. Rising to the Top: Gender, Political Performance, and Party Leadership in Parliamentary Democracies. *American Journal of Political Science* 59 (4): 1022–1039.

O'Brien, Diana Z., Matthew Mendez, Jordan Carr Peterson, and Jihyun Shin. 2015. Letting down the Ladder or Shutting the Door: Female Prime Ministers, Party Leaders, and Cabinet Ministers. *Politics & Gender* 11 (4): 689–717.

Onwuachi-Willig, Angela. 2005. Representative Government, Representative Court? The Supreme Court as a Representative Body. *Minnesota Law Review* 90: 1252.

Organization of American States. 2021. Inter-American Commission of Women. Accessed January 20, 2021: https://oas.org/en/cim/default.asp.

Oxtoby, Chris, and Tabeth Masengu. 2017. Who Nominates? Some Issues Underlying the Appointment of Judges in South Africa. *Stellenbosch Law Review* 3: 541–562.

Palmer, Barbara. 2001a. To Do Justly: The Integration of Women into the American Judiciary. *Political Science and Politics* 34 (2): 235–239.

Palmer, Barbara. 2001b. Women in the American Judiciary *Women & Politics* 23 (3): 91–101.

Participación de la Mujer en la Rama Judicial Año. 2014. Consejo Superior de la Juridicatura. Accessed August 6, 2017: https://www.ramajudicial.gov.co/documents/573203/1435206/ESTADISTICAS+G%C%A9nero_2014_mujer+V.2.pdf/8229193a-c887-43b4-8edd-99fe44740e4d.

Paxton, Pamela. 1997. Women in National Legislatures: A Cross-National Analysis. *Social Science Research* 26 (4): 442–464.

Paxton, Pamela, Melanie M. Hughes, and Jennifer L. Green. 2006. The International Women's Movement and Women's Political Representation, 1893–2003. *American Sociological Review* 71 (6): 898–920.

Paxton, Pamela, Melanie M. Hughes, and Matthew Painter. 2010. The Difference Time Makes: Latent Growth Curve Models of Women's Political Representation. *European Journal of Political Research* 49 (1): 25–52.

Paxton, Pamela, and Melanie M. Hughes. 2015. The Increasing Effectiveness of National Gender Quotas. *Legislative Studies Quarterly* 40 (3): 331–362.

Penrose, Meg. 2018. The Way Pavers: Eleven Supreme Court-worthy Women. *Harvard Journal of Law and Gender* 1: 1–32.

Peresie, Jennifer L. 2005. Female Judges Matter: Gender and Collegial Decisionmaking in the Federal Appellate Courts. *The Yale Law Journal* 114 (7): 1759–1790.

Peretti, Terri L. 2007. Where Have All the Politicians Gone? *Judicature* 91: 112–123.

Peters v. Kiff, 407 U.S. 493 (1972).

Phillips, Katherine. 2014. How Diversity Makes Us All Smarter. *Scientific American* 311 (4): 42–47.

Pitkin, Hannah Fenichel. 1967. *The Concept of Representation.* Berkeley and Los Angeles: University of California Press.

Powell Jr, G. Bingham, and Guy D. Whitten. 1993. A Cross-National Analysis of Economic Voting: Taking Account of the Political Context. *American Journal of Political Science* 37 (2): 391–414.

Powell, Emilia Justyna, and Jeffrey K. Staton. 2009. Domestic Judicial Institutions and Human Rights Treaty Violation. *International Studies Quarterly* 53 (1): 149–174.

Putnam, Robert. 1976. *The Comparative Study of Political Elites.* Englewood Cliffs, NJ: Prentice Hall.

Ramirez, Francisco O., Yasemin Soysal, and Suzanne Shanahan. 1997. The Changing Logic of Political Citizenship: Cross-National Acquisition of Women's Suffrage Rights, 1890–1990. *American Sociological Review* 62 (5): 735–745.

Reingold, Beth. 2003. *Representing Women: Sex, Gender, and Legislative Behavior in Arizona and California.* Chapel Hill: University of North Carolina Press.

Remiche, Adelaide. 2014. Belgian Parliament Introduces Sex Quota in Constitutional Court Oxford Human Rights Hub. April 21. Accessed January 21, 2021: http://ohrh.law.ox.ac.uk/belgian-parliament-introduces-sex-quota-in-constitutional-court/.

Report to the United Nations on the National Plan for Women 2002 on the Implementation of the Beijing Platform for Action. 2002. Dublin, Government Publications. Accessed December 22, 2020: http://www.justice.ie/en/JELR/UNReport Beijing.pdf/Files/UNReportBeijing.pdf.

Ríos-Figueroa, Julio. 2011. Institutions for Enforcing Constitutional Justice in Latin America. In *Courts in Latin America*, eds. Gretchen Helmke and Julio Ríos-Figueroa, 27–54. New York: Cambridge University Press.

Roche, Carme Luisa. 2003. Feminisation of the Legal Profession in Venezuela: Its Meaning for the Profession and for Women Lawyers. *International Journal of the Legal Profession* 10 (2): 209–226.

Rodríguez-Raga, Juan Carlos. 2011. Strategic Prudence in the Colombian Constitutional Court, 1992–2006. Doctoral Dissertation, University of Pittsburgh.

Rogowski, Jon C., and Andrew R. Stone. 2019. How Political Contestation Over Judicial Nominations Polarizes Americans' Attitudes Toward the Supreme Court. *British Journal of Political Science* 1–19.

Rossman, Lynn C. 1980. Women Judges Unite: A Report from the Founding Convention of the National Association of Women Judges *Golden Gate University Law Review* 10 (3): 1237–1266.

Rousselet, Marcel. 1957. *Histoire de la magistrature française: des origins à nos jours (Tome 1).* Paris: Librairie Plon.

Royzman, Irena, and Ann Hassett. 2018. Women Who Rule. *Landslide* 10 (4) Accessed June 2, 2021: https://www.americanbar.org/groups/intellectual_property_law/publications/landslide/2017-18/march-april/women-who-rule/.

Rule, Wilma. 1987. Electoral Systems, Contextual Factors and Women's Opportunity for Election to Parliament in Twenty-Three Democracies. *Western Political Quarterly* 40 (3): 477–498.

Ruth, Nancy. 2012. Speech on Organizing Around the Charter 1980–85. Dalhousie Law School, October 26.

Saad-Zoy, Souria, ed. 2010. *Femmes, droit de la famille et système judiciaire en Algérie, au Maroc et en Tunisie.* Rabat: UNESCO.

Sen, Maya. 2014. How Judicial Qualification Ratings May Disadvantage Minority and Female Candidates. *Journal of Law and Courts* 2 (1): 33–65.

Schandevyl, Eva, ed. 2014. *Women in Law and Lawmaking in the Nineteenth and Twentieth Century Europe.* Farnham: Ashgate.

Scherer, Nancy, and Brett Curry. 2010. Does Descriptive Race Representation Enhance Institutional Legitimacy? The Case of the US Courts. *The Journal of Politics* 72 (1): 90–104.

Scherpereel, John A., Melinda Adams, and Suraj Jacob. 2018. Ratchets and See-Saws: Divergent Institutional Patterns in Women's Political Representation. *Socius* 4: 1–13.

Schultz, Ulrike, and Tabeth Masengu. 2020. Women and Judicial Appointments. *International Journal of the Legal Profession* 27 (2): 113–17.

Schultz, Ulrike, and Gisela Shaw, eds. 2003. *Women in the World's Legal Professions.* Oxford: Hart Publishing.

Schultz, Ulrike, and Gisela Shaw, eds. 2013. *Gender and Judging.* Oxford: Hart Publishing.

Schumacher, Gijs, and Nathalie Giger. 2018. Do Leadership-Dominated Parties Change More? *Journal of Elections, Public Opinion, and Parties* 28 (3): 349–360.

Schwindt-Bayer, Leslie A. 2006. Still Supermadres? Gender and the Policy Priorities of Latin American Legislators. *American Journal of Political Science* 50 (3): 570–585.

Schwindt-Bayer, Leslie A. 2010. *Political Power and Women's Representation in Latin America.* New York: Oxford University Press.

Scribner, Druscilla, and Priscilla Lambert. 2010. Constitutionalizing Difference: A Case Study Analysis of Gender Provisions in Botswana and South Africa. *Politics & Gender* 6 (1): 37–61.

Segal, Jennifer A. 2000. Representative Decision Making on the Federal Bench: Clinton's District Court Appointees. *Political Research Quarterly* 53 (1): 137–150.

Segal, Jeffrey, and Harold Spaeth. 2002. *The Supreme Court and the Attitudinal Model Revisited.* Cambridge: Cambridge University Press.

Senate press release. Con transparencia, candidatos a Magistrado harán su presentación en la Plenaria este Miércoles.

Simmons, Beth A. 2009. *Mobilizing for Human Rights: International Law in Domestic Politics.* New York: Cambridge University Press.

Slaughter, Anne-Marie. 1994. A Typology of Transjudicial Communication. *University of Richmond Law Review* 29: 99–137.

Slotnick, Elliot. 1984. Judicial Selection Systems and Nomination Outcomes. *American Politics Quarterly* 12 (2): 225–240.

Slotnick, Elliot, Sheldon Goldman, and Sara Schiavoni. 2015. Writing the Book of Judges: Part 1: Obama's Judicial Appointments Record after Six Years. *Journal of Law and Courts* 3 (2): 331–367.

Slotnick, Elliott, Sara Schiavoni, and Sheldon Goldman. 2017. Obama's Judicial Legacy: The Final Chapter. *Journal of Law and Courts* 5 (2): 363–422.

Smelcer, Susan N., Amy Steigerwalt, and Richard L. Vining Jr. 2012. Bias and the Bar: Evaluating the ABA Ratings of Federal Judicial Nominees. *Political Research Quarterly* 65 (4): 827–840.

Solanke, Iyiola. 2009. Putting Race and Gender Together: A New Approach to Intersectionality. *Modern Law Review* 72 (5): 723–749.

Solanke, Iyiola. 2019. Where Are the Black Judges in Europe? *Connecticut Journal of International Law* 34 (3): 289–314.

Solberg, Rorie Spill, and Jennifer Segal Diascro. 2020. A Retrospective on Obama's Judges: Diversity, Intersectionality, and Symbolic Representation. *Politics, Groups, and Identities* 8 (3): 471–487.

Solberg, Rorie L. Spill, and Kathleen A. Bratton. 2005. Diversifying the Federal Bench: Presidential Patterns. *Justice System Journal* 26 (2): 119–133.

Sommerlad, Hilary. 1994. The Myth of Feminisation: Women and Cultural Change in the Legal Profession. *International Journal of the Legal Profession* 1 (1): 31–53.

Sommerlad, Hilary. 2015. The 'Social Magic' of Merit: Diversity, Equity, and Inclusion in the English and Welsh Legal Profession. *Fordham Law Review* 83: 2325–2347.

Songer, Donald R., and Kelley A. Crews-Meyer. 2000. Does Judge Gender Matter? Decision Making in State Supreme Courts. *Social Science Quarterly* 81 (3): 750–762.

Sonneveld, Nadia, and Monika Lindbekk, eds. 2017. *Women Judges in the Muslim World: A Comparative Study of Discourse and Practice.* Leiden: Brill.

Sotomayor, Sonia. 2002. A Latina Judge's Voice. *Berkeley La Raza* 13 (1): 87–94.

Southern African Development Community (SADC). 1997. Declaration on Gender and Development. Gaborone: SADC.

Southern African Development Community (SADC). 2008. Protocol on Gender and Development. Gaborone: SADC.

Spees, Pam, ed. 1999. The International Criminal Court: The Beijing Platform In Action. Accessed December 17, 2020: http://iccwomen.org/wigjdraft1/Archives/oldWCGJ/resources/bplus5/Introduction.html.

Spees, Pam. 2003. Women's Advocacy in the Creation of the International Criminal Court: Changing the Landscapes of Justice and Power. *Signs* 28 (4): 1233–1254.

Spill, Rorie L., and Kathleen A. Bratton. 2001. Clinton and Diversification of the Federal Bench. *Judicature* 84 (5): 256–261.

Statistics South Africa. 1980. Population Census 1980. DataFirst: University of Cape Town, Accessed June 26, 2017: https://www.datafirst.uct.ac.za/dataportal/index.php/catalog/252/get_microdata.

Stockemer, Daniel. 2014. Women's Descriptive Representation in Developed and Developing Countries. *International Political Science Review* 36 (4): 393–408.

Supreme Court of Ireland. 2017. Accessed July 15, 2017: http://www.supremecourt.ie/.

Swers, Michelle. 2002. *The Difference Women Make*. Chicago: University of Chicago Press.

Szto, Mary. 2008. Gender and the Chinese Legal Profession in Historical Perspective: From Heaven and Earth to Rule of Woman? *Hofstra University Legal Studies Research Paper* 18: 195.

Tate, C. Neal, and Torbjorn Vallinder, eds. 1995. *The Global Expansion of Judicial Power*. New York: New York University Press.

Thames, Frank, and Margaret Williams. 2013. *Contagious Representation: Women's Political Representation in Democracies around the World*. New York: New York University Press.

Thomas, Sue. 1991. The Impact of Women on State Legislative Policies. *The Journal of Politics* 53 (4): 958–976.

Thornton, Margaret. 2007. 'Otherness' on the Bench: How Merit is Gendered. *Sydney Law Review* 29: 391.

Towns, Ann E. 2012. Norms and Social Hierarchies: Understanding International Policy Diffusion from Below. *International Organization* 66 (2): 179–209.

Tripp, Aili Mari. 2015. *Women and Power in Postconflict Africa*. Cambridge: Cambridge University Press.

Tripp, Aili Mari. 2019. *Seeking Legitimacy: Why Arab Autocracies Adopt Women's Rights*. Cambridge: Cambridge University Press.

Tripp, Aili Mari, and Alice Kang. 2008. The Global Impact of Quotas: On the Fast Track to Increased Female Legislative Representation. *Comparative Political Studies* 41 (3): 338–361.

Tripp, Aili Mari, Isabel Casimiro, Joy Kwesiga, and Alice Mungwa. 2009. *African Women's Movements: Transforming Political Landscapes*. Cambridge: Cambridge University Press.

True, Jacqui, and Michael Mintrom. 2001.Transnational Networks and Policy Diffusion: The Case of Gender Mainstreaming. *International Studies Quarterly* 45 (1): 27–57.

Turquet, Laura, Papa Seck, Ginette Azcona, Roshni Menon, Caitlin Boyce, Nicole Pierron, and Emma Harbour. 2012. Progress of the World's Women: In Pursuit of Justice. New York: UN Women.

Una mujer para la Corte Constitucional. *Semana*, September 14, 2015.

United Nations. 1975. Report of the World Conference of the International Women's Year. E/CONF.66/34. NY: United Nations.

United Nations. 1979. Convention on the Elimination of All Forms of Discrimination Against Women. Accessed June 7, 2021: https://www.un.org/womenwatch/daw/cedaw/cedaw.htm.

United Nations. 1985. Nairobi Forward-looking Strategies for the Advancement of Women. A/CONF.116/28/Rev. NY: United Nations.

United Nations 1995. Fourth World Conference on Women: Beijing Declaration and Platform for Action. Accessed June 7, 2021: https://www.un.org/womenwatch/daw/beijing/platform/.

United Nations. 1998. Rome Statute of the International Criminal Court. A/CONF.183/9. NY: United Nations.

United Nations. [1980] 2017. Convention on the Elimination of All Forms of Discrimination against Women. *Treaty Series* 1249: 13. Accessed December 1, 2017: http://treaties.un.org/Pages/ViewDetails.aspx?src=TREATY&mtdsg_no=IV8&chapter=4&lang=en ().

United Nations Division for the Advancement of Women. 1996. Tribute by the United Nations Secretary-General, Dr. Boutros Boutros-Ghali, on the occasion of the memorial for Mrs. Justice Annie Ruth Jiagge, 3 August 1996. Accessed January 17, 2021: https://www.un.org/womenwatch/daw/news/jiagge.htm.

United Nations Office of the High Commissioner. 2020. UN Treaty Body Database. Accessed December 17, 2020: https://tbinternet.ohchr.org/_layouts/15/TreatyBodyExternal/Countries.aspx?.

United Nations Secretary-General. 2019. Remarks on International Women's Day 2019. March 8. Accessed June 11, 2021: https://www.un.org/sg/en/content/sg/speeches/2019-03-08/womens-day-2019-remarks.

United Nations Women. 2019. Equality in Law for Women and Girls by 2030. New York: United Nations.

Uprimny, Rodrigo. 2004. The Constitutional Court and Control of Presidential Extraordinary Powers in Colombia. In *Democratization and the Judiciary: The Accountability Function of Courts in New Democracies*, eds. Roberto Gargarella, Siri Gloppen, and Elin Skaar, 33–49. London: Frank Cass Publishers.

Uprimny, Rodrigo. 2015. Una Terna de Mujeres. *El Espectador*, August 15, 2015.

Uribe Restrepo, Fernando. 2006. El Viacrucis de la Justicia. *Apartes en Libro Blanco – 20 años del Palacio de Justicia* 30. Consejo Superior de la Judicatura, Bogotá.

Valdini, Melody Ellis. 2012. A Deterrent to Diversity: The Conditional Effect of Electoral Rules on the Nomination of Women Candidates. *Electoral Studies* 31 (4): 740–749.

Valdini, Melody Ellis, and Christopher Shortell. 2016. Women's Representation in the Highest Court: A Comparative Analysis of the Appointment of Female Justices. *Political Research Quarterly* 69 (4): 865–876.

Vauchez, Antoine. 2015. *Brokering Europe: Euro-lawyers and the Making of a Transnational Polity*. Cambridge: Cambridge University Press.

Venice Commission. 1997. The Composition of Constitutional Courts. European Commission for Democracy Through Law, Science and Technology of Democracy, No. 20.

Viterna, Jocelyn, Kathleen Fallon, and Jason Beckfield. 2008. How Development Matters: A Research Note on the Relationship between Development, Democracy, and Women's Political Representation. *International Journal of Comparative Sociology* 49 (6): 455–477.

Walker, Lee Demetrius. 2008. Gender and Attitudes toward Justice System Bias in Central America. *Latin American Research Review* 43 (2): 80–106.

Watson, Robert P., Alicia Jenick, and Judith A. Seltzer. 2005. Women World Leaders: Comparative Analysis and Gender Experiences. *Journal of International Women's Studies* 7 (2): 53–76.

Wiliarty, Sarah. 2010. *The CDU and the Politics of Gender in Germany: Bringing Women to the Party*. New York: Cambridge University Press.

Williams, Margaret S. 2007. Women's Representation on State Trial and Appellate Courts. *Social Science Quarterly* 88 (5): 1192–1204.

Williams, Margaret S., and Frank C. Thames. 2008. Women's Representation on High Courts in Advanced Industrialized Countries. *Politics & Gender* 4 (3): 451–471.

Women, Business, and the Law. 2020. Website. World Bank Group. Washington, DC.

World Bank. 2018. World Development Indicators. Accessed January 12, 2018: http://data.worldbank.org/datacatalog/world development-indicators.

World Bank. 2021. World Development Indicators. Accessed January 20, 2021: http://data.worldbank.org/datacatalog/world development-indicators.

Wotipka, Christina, and Francisco Ramirez. 2008. World Society and Human Rights: An Event History Analysis of the Convention on the Elimination of All Forms of Discrimination against Women. In *The Global Diffusion of Markets and Democracy*, eds. Beth Simmons, Frank Dobbin, and Geoffrey Garrett, 303–343. New York: Cambridge University Press.

Zippel, Kathrin S. 2006. *The Politics of Sexual Harassment: A Comparative Study of the United States, the European Union, and Germany*. Cambridge: Cambridge University Press.

Index

For the benefit of digital users, indexed terms that span two pages (e.g., 52–53) may, on occasion, appear on only one of those pages.